Beethoven's Skull

Beethoven's Skull

Dark, Strange, and Fascinating Tales from the World of Classical Music and Beyond

TIM RAYBORN

Skyhorse Publishing

Skyhorse Publishing books may be purchased in bulk at special discounts for sales promotion, corporate gifts, fund-raising, or educational purposes. Special editions can also be created to specifications. For details, contact the Special Sales Department, Skyhorse Publishing, 307 West 36th Street, 11th Floor, New York, NY 10018 or info@skyhorsepublishing.com.

Skyhorse® and Skyhorse Publishing® are registered trademarks of Skyhorse Publishing, Inc.®, a Delaware corporation.

Visit our website at www.skyhorsepublishing.com.
10 9 8 7 6 5 4 3 2 1

Library of Congress Cataloging-in-Publication Data is available on file.

Cover design by Rain Saukas

Print ISBN: 978-1-5107-1271-3
Ebook ISBN: 978-1-5107-1272-0

Printed in the United States of America

Contents

Introduction

The Grim and the Unusual in the History of Western Music

A dmit it, we all love a good gruesome story. The lure of the morbid and the grotesque, the forbidden and the terrifying fuels an endless number of horror movies, video games, novels, tabloid news outlets, conspiracy websites, reality TV shows, and boy bands. In this book, you will read about a hidden history, a behind-the-scenes look at some of the most unusual and frequently awful moments in music over the last two thousand years and even earlier.

When you ask people what their favorite subject in school was, History rarely seems to be at the top of the list. This is unfortunate and rather sad, because it's a wonderful and thrilling topic, one that is increasingly important in our very complex world. Far too many folks seem to associate the whole thing with endless boring names, dates, lists, battles, and goings-on in countries that no longer exist, involving dead people with unpronounceable names.

When you ask people what their favorite genre of music is, so-called classical music is also rarely at the top of the list, at least in the United States. Many in Europe and Asia love it, and to be fair, it has a devoted, if not huge, following in the USA. But many people wrongly associate it with snobbery, pretentiousness, and a general incomprehensibility: long, boring works written by dead composers with even less pronounceable names. It seems that the Euro-American culture that gave birth to this music has somewhat abandoned it for newer and cooler genres. The rise in popularity of music downloading (legal and otherwise) has made the idea of the "classical record album" seem even more obsolete. Then again, vinyl records have made a big comeback recently, and very few people saw that coming.

So in an effort to either completely obliterate the last remaining chances of making either genre interesting, or in the hope that two negatives will add up to a positive, this book combines both subjects to give the reader a sort-of introductory history to classical music, but with a significant, morbid twist. One thing to note: a few stories here go beyond the "classical" label, because they were simply too good and grim to pass up! There is a bit of jazz, some rock and pop, a smattering of folk, and some other music that defies categorization. Seriously, what genre is "fairy music" exactly? Pseudo-Celtic? Mythical crossover? Music of the Rich and "Fey-mous"? (*Note*: this may not be the last pun that you encounter in this book; there will be no apologies for this.)

No matter, the pages that follow will not bore you with mere dates and lists or expect you to pronounce a barrage of unfamiliar names on the first try—though maybe on the second or third. Instead, you will be treated to all manner of strange and surprising stories: tales of violence, revenge, blood and guts, death, disease, love won and lost, despair, decapitation and the removal of other specific body parts, ghosts, horrific nursery rhymes and fairy tales, magic, murder, war, and worst of all, cell phones.

Part I will introduce you to a good number of composers, from ancient Greece to the twentieth century. You will know some. Others will be new to you. Others you might want to forget. What they have in common is that they all led very odd lives and/or met with particularly unpleasant ends, and their fates were sometimes quite funny. These are the stories you don't often find in CD notes, or even in music history classes. You have been deprived, and now is the time to fix that!

People often believe that artists of any kind must suffer for their art for it truly to be "great." The romantic notion is of the painter, the poet, or the composer living in splendid squalor in a Parisian dive. Here he avoids creditors, sends away his pregnant mistress, knocks back hard liquor, and pounds out tortured masterpieces that will only be appreciated after his untimely death from liver disease, a self-inflicted gunshot wound, or a broken heart. Or perhaps it's the haunted Gothic writer or pianist. He creates after midnight (a dark and stormy one, of course) and lives a reclusive life in a lavish room lit only by a few candles (their light flickering in the empty eye sockets of a skull on the desk). He also knocks back hard liquor and pounds out tortured masterpieces that will only be appreciated after his untimely death from liver disease, a self-inflicted dagger wound, or a broken heart.

A surprising number of composers, if not exactly living the script to a Hammer Horror film, had to deal with some pretty violent, morbid, and completely strange events as a background to their creativity. It wasn't just their inner worlds that were in turmoil; many of them were also hit with hardships and tragedies from outside, often due to their inability to cope with life and all of its ups and downs. Alcohol, drugs, or retreats into delusions were frequently their only escapes from the stresses that "normal" society imposed on them, but out of these troubles could come great works of music that have endured through the years.

There were others who just seemed to have no luck, drew the short stick, and got dealt a bad hand in life. Some held very odd beliefs or did very strange things. Some engaged in criminal activities and/or behaviors that were frowned upon by either church or state, sometimes both. The ability to put pretty musical notes on paper was no guarantee of being an upstanding citizen, and there were those in our cast of musical stars (or rogues' gallery) who were reprobates of the very worst sort.

Here is an assortment of grotesque, bloody, tragic, macabre, or just plain odd facts, fancies, truths, and legends about some of the most famous (and most obscure) composers and musicians in Western music history. They appear in roughly chronological order, divided by the eras in which their music is usually classified: ancient, medieval, Renaissance, Baroque, Classical, Romantic, and modern—these eras coincide more or less with those also used in art history. Some of these tales are doubtful or even outright fabricated, more so the further back in time that one looks. The facts have never gotten in the way of a good story, then as now. There were no fact-checkers, social networks, blogs, or comment sections to keep them honest. Some stories, however, are very real and well documented. This mixture of fact and fiction should provide you with a good sense of just how strange and often twisted the history of Western music can be. So if you think you're having a bad day, try reading through a few of these and you might feel better.

In Part II, the search goes further afield and presents all kinds of surprises, a veritable bazaar of the bizarre. From strange truths to hoaxes and urban legends, you will discover a whole world of the unusual and the fascinating, the darkly amusing, and the downright horrible. As with Part I, many of these accounts are true. Some are speculation. Some were long believed to be true until proven otherwise. Some are lies that are so good, they're irresistible.

We will look at everything from the biological and mythological origins of music to some of the most gruesome examples of stories involving music and musicians. Did you know that Dracula really existed, and may have been even more horrible than his fictional counterpart? You might be surprised to learn that the Pied Piper may have been based on a real account, too. Why would a Renaissance queen insist that her musicians continually sing for her husband's corpse? And is there a cursed song that allegedly has driven any number of listeners to suicide? Would you have the courage to listen to it?

We'll look at why many believe that a composer must stop writing symphonies after the ninth, and various other superstitions associated with the art of music making. Those sweet little nursery rhymes you sang as a child? Some of them may have very gruesome origins, indeed! Is music a form of magic? Can it alter reality or drive ordinary people mad? Many ancient cultures believed so.

And of course, no discussion would be complete without looking at some of the ghostly phenomena associated with music over the centuries, a topic so vast that we can only glance at it here. Regardless of your beliefs on the subject, these accounts will certainly make you wonder, and maybe send a shiver down your spine. Those campfire ghost stories from your childhood have nothing on these tales of musicians and others who wouldn't stay dead.

Finally, we'll look at some of the odd after-life experiences of two of our greatest composers, Mozart and Beethoven (hint: these have to do with their skulls), and a few other tales from the musical grab bag.

Weirdness, it seems, is as ordinary a part of human experience as the ordinary itself. Wherever there are people, there will be strange stories about them and their activities. Unsolved mysteries and strange phenomena will always fascinate us. The sheer number of tales herein—and we've only scratched the surface—should be enough to give one pause about what exactly the "ordinary" is, anyway.

Some of these stories are funny, while others are poignant and tragic. Some are downright horrifying. There's certainly no intention to mock the pain and suffering of others, but rather to simply reflect on just how unexpected, for good or for ill, life can be. We shouldn't take things for granted, and these tales may actually be an inspiration to do our best in the face of adversity—a reminder of the shortness of our time here.

You do not need a special knowledge of classical music—or any music for that matter—to explore and enjoy these excursions. The book is not technical, and there won't be any quizzes at the end. It isn't a textbook or an academic tome filled with lots of boring footnotes. Consider it a fun chance to dip into a pool of the peculiar. You can read the whole thing in order if you'd like, which will give you some appreciation of how this music developed over time. You can also just open up anywhere and start reading. If it inspires you to seek out some of the music explored here, then so much the better.

You will be able to learn more by going to the section on further reading at the end of the book and delving into some of those suggestions. You may just discover a new love and fascination for music that you never even knew existed. Classical music is not boring, dated, or irrelevant. It's exciting, vibrant, meaningful, beautiful, moving, and it can be enjoyed by everyone. It just happens to be pretty grim sometimes.

So get some tea (or maybe something a little stronger), put on some music—preferably by one of the composers in Part I—and enjoy this excursion down some of the lesser-known paths of music history. You could wait for a dark and stormy night to read it for the maximum moody effect, but it's not absolutely necessary.

Part I

The Strange Lives, Stranger Deaths, and Odd Fates of Composers

1

Ancient Greece and Rome

Most everyone is familiar with the legacy of ancient civilizations such as Egypt, Greece, and Rome. Their impact is still felt on the modern Western world, in everything from laws to architecture. Museums showcase the art, students study the writings and history (and if they're really lucky, they get to delve into Latin or Greek!), and we're all at least a bit familiar with the mythologies and old stories. Schoolchildren everywhere have snickered at nude Greek Olympians, wondered if the Egyptians only had profiles, and marveled at how the Roman army conquered the Mediterranean world in short skirts.

Yet for all of our admiration and even worship of our ancient forebears, their music is unknown to everyone but a scholarly few. Obviously very little has survived, but amazingly, over fifty pieces of Greco-Roman music (many in fragments) have come down to us in notations that have been deciphered and can be read with relative ease. There are also a few pieces from Assyria that may or may not be readable, and various scholars have taken a shot at reproducing what they might sound like, with varying degrees of success. Still, even with this small amount of surviving work, the ancients loved to write *about* their music, and everyone from the philosopher Plato to various Roman emperors seems to have had something to say about it.

The names of individual composers from this time are sparse and often coincide with those of poets. A celebrated poet might well have written some music to a particular poem, but it hasn't survived, or people might not have considered a "poet" and a "composer" to be two separate things. Indeed, the idea of purely instrumental music was at times controversial—those crazy kids with their lyres and flutes. There were many wandering musicians who offered their skills for plays, religious festivals, celebrations, private parties, and any other function requiring singers and instrumentalists.

The history of this ancient music is vast and well worth exploring. We will look at just a handful of individuals whose musical pursuits led them into interesting fates, to say the least, from an arrogant young wind player who blew himself to death to an infamous Roman emperor who took his performances to a new level of mediocrity.

Terpander (seventh century BCE, *ca.* 675)

Choking on ill-gotten gains?

To the ancient Greeks, Terpander was *the* man, the father of Greek music and its lyric poetry. He was based in Sparta, and his own works were apparently rather simple for one so renowned, but he was credited with revamping and revitalizing the whole Greek musical system. He was said to have added more strings to the lyre, changing it from four to seven and so opening up new melodic possibilities. Or maybe he changed the structure of a certain type of ode from four sections to seven; the sources are a little vague on this one. He seems to have invented some new types of musical rhythms, and most importantly, composed a good number of drinking songs; maybe that was why he was so popular?

His birth and death dates are unknown, but according to one story, he died in a ridiculous way: during a successful performance in Sparta, an audience member tossed a fig to him, presumably in appreciation (apparently there were no roses on hand). Terpander had opened his mouth in preparation for singing, where said fruit landed and lodged, and he promptly choked on it. Similar stories were told about Sophocles (who choked on a grape) and Anacreon (who choked on a grape seed), so it's probably just an ancient urban legend. We have no record of what happened to the remorseful and mortified fan, but it probably wasn't pretty. At the very least, his fan-club membership must have been revoked.

Lamprus of Erythrae (early fifth century BCE)
Gull-able

Lamprus (or Lampros) seems to have been a player of the lyre and a dancer, who may have taught the great Greek playwright Sophocles, of choked-on-a-grape fame. Little is known about him, and he also may have been confused with another man of the same name from a few centuries later, maybe even deliberately. He seems to have lived a reserved life, refusing to drink wine—not exactly typical musician behavior. Athenaeus, a Greco-Egyptian writer from the third century CE, records an interesting bit of information in his work the *Deipnosophistae* (say that three times fast), a long series of discussions over dinner that give insight into life at the time. He writes that an earlier Greek commentator, Phrynichus, noted "that the gulls lamented, when Lamprus died among them, being a man who was a water-drinker, a subtle hypersophist, a dry skeleton of the Muses, a nightmare to nightingales, a hymn to hell."

That is one weird epitaph! We have no further information on how he died, but "the gulls" perhaps suggests on a beach, or maybe that he drowned, what with being a mere "water-drinker." The rest of it seems pretty insulting, too, so maybe Phrynichus had some kind of personal grudge. The implication is that his stick-in-the-mud lifestyle earned him the end he deserved. Let that be a lesson to all musicians who won't drink wine!

Harmonides (fourth century? BCE)
A breath of fresh air

Harmonides was a promising young student of Timotheus, an acclaimed musician during the time of Alexander the Great. Both were players of the aulos, an ancient wind instrument that sounds a bit like an oboe crossed with a kazoo. When Harmonides asked his teacher how to win acclaim for himself, Timotheus recommended that he start small and acquire a limited number of knowledgeable admirers; from there his reputation would grow. This is sound advice for any young musician. Young Harmonides was far too impatient to heed his master's counsel, of course, and so decided to start big.

He wanted to impress everyone at his first public performance, but according to the historian Lucian (*ca.* 125—after 180 CE), when he started his solo, he gave such a great blast of air into his instrument that he died on the spot. So he probably was remembered, just not in the way that he wanted.

Nero, Emperor of Rome (37–68 CE)

Fiddler on the roof

Nero is usually regarded as the cruel, tyrannical, and completely crazy Roman emperor who persecuted Christians and played a fiddle while Rome burned in 64 CE; many believed that he started the fire himself. Both fire-related accusations are false, as we'll see. It's fair to say that the man has certainly been on the receiving end of a lot of negative propaganda over the centuries. Most see him as one of the worst Roman rulers ever, along with Caligula and a few other deranged individuals. There are many well-attested accounts of his cruelty and megalomaniacal behavior, but what we want to explore are his strange and even comical excursions into music and public performance.

According to the historian Tacitus, Nero was passionate about music from a young age. Being the dilettante that all educated upper-class young men were expected to be, he made an extensive study of music and poetry, committing himself to the practice of performance. The problem, at least according to some of his contemporary historians, was he just wasn't that good. He wasn't horrible, he was just . . . okay.

As soon as he became emperor in the year 54, at the young age of seventeen, he embarked on a program of training that included special diets and enemas (!), and even weighed his chest down with lead plates, which he believed would strengthen his lung power and voice. He made his first public performances six years later, carefully observing all of the protocols. He also composed quite a bit of music, some of which continued to be performed after his death; unfortunately, none of it survives, so we can't judge its quality. He had a passion for music contests, but his family and high-ranking officials thought that it was outrageous for an emperor to share a stage with commoners.

Needless to say, his audience's responses were ecstatic; they really didn't have any other choice. Since he was the emperor, no one could leave the auditorium for any reason while he performed. The historian Suetonius notes with humor that women gave birth during his recitals, and some men either took the risk and snuck out by climbing over the high walls, or faked dying so that they could be carried out. Perhaps Nero actually was a decent singer, though Suetonius called his voice husky and lacking in fullness.

As for the whole fire-and-fiddling episode, it couldn't have been a fiddle, since bowed instruments did not make an appearance in Europe until the Middle Ages, coming from the Middle East. Might he have been playing his beloved kithara, a kind of large lyre? Tacitus, who was not overly fond of Nero, writes that as the fire raged, there was a rumor that Nero took to his personal stage and sang about the fall of Troy. He does stress that this was only rumor, though, and there are accounts that Nero was actually away from the city and rushed back when he heard the news, actively trying to contain the blaze and help its victims. He ordered certain public buildings to be opened to those made homeless, and later enacted new laws to help prevent such a tragedy from happening again.

Still, after the fire, he began construction of an enormous palace and pleasure garden on the site of some of the worst destruction, a palace that could not have been built without the flames conveniently having burned away the old buildings. Needless to say, this aroused suspicions. He also blamed the fire, with no real evidence, on a small religious group known as the Christians. He did rebuild various residential neighborhoods at his own expense, but maybe that was to deter such speculation.

Ultimately, relations with his advisors and senators deteriorated. A plot against him was uncovered, and there were many executions; some escaped by getting the chance to commit suicide. At the height of all of this tension, Nero trotted off to Greece to take part in the Olympic Games, where he naturally won prizes, since Greece was part of the Roman Empire at the time and had to honor him. He was enamored of all things Greek and would have been well suited to living there. His going off to the games was probably the last straw for his advisors, and soon there was an open revolt against him. Sections of the army, equally unhappy with his behavior, joined in the rebellion. Realizing that the end was near, Nero decided to stab himself. He couldn't go through with it, though, and forced his secretary, Epaphroditos, to assist him. Convinced to the end of his talent, he proclaimed: *qualis artifex pereo*— "What an artist dies in me!" Not everyone was inclined to agree.

St. Cecilia (later second century CE)

Head and shoulders above the rest

St. Cecilia is the patron saint of musicians, but her story is an odd one, because for well over one thousand years after her death, she had no association with music at all. Newly married to a Roman nobleman, Valerian, she informed him of her desire to remain a virgin because an angel had visited her and told her that Valerian would be punished for violating her, which made marital relations tricky at best. He was undoubtedly rather unhappy about this, but surprisingly ended up converting to Christianity, and then they were both promptly martyred, so the story goes, sometime between the years 176 and 180 CE (some accounts say later, about 230). It was said that Cecilia's neck was struck three times, but the executioner failed to sever her head. According to Roman law, he could not deliver another blow, so he let her be. She lived for another three days, long enough to ask that her house be made into a church.

All of this is quite grim and bloody, but there is an obvious absence of music in this tale. It appears that St. Cecilia was not associated with music until the fourteenth or (more likely) the fifteenth century, when music guilds began to adopt her as their patron. This may have been in part due to a mistranslation of the account of her wedding. Some scholars believe that guild masters misread a passage that described music playing and her singing to God in her heart as stating instead that she herself was playing the organ. For whatever reason, the association between this bloody martyr and music stuck, blossoming over the next few centuries. Indeed, composers such as Henry Purcell, George Frederic Handel, and Benjamin

Britten have all written music in her honor, and her feast day, November 22, is still celebrated by the Catholic Church.

To top it all off, she may not even have existed at all. Medieval legends of early saints and martyrs are notoriously difficult to document and are filled with fanciful additions, inconsistencies, and various other problems, so the martyrdom of Cecilia may be just another example.

Boethius (*ca.* 480–524/25 CE)

Musician, console thyself

Boethius was not a composer, but a philosopher. Born in Rome, he achieved a high status in his own time, and after his death, he became one of the most important of the early medieval philosophers, revered through the centuries for his many writings.

His contribution to the world of music comes from his work *De institutione musica,* a Latin translation of writings of the earlier Greek mathematicians Nichomacus and Ptolemy. It draws in the theories of Pythagoras (remember him from your high school Geometry class?), who also had a keen interest in music and its relation to mathematics. Pythagoras and his followers, conveniently named the Pythagoreans, believed that music derived its beauty from an ideal numerical realm. Indeed, Boethius stressed this in his own work, stating that essentially music was number made audible, demonstrating in sound the pure world of numbers. This view would be the cornerstone of European music theory for the next thousand years. Church music, in particular, would be composed based on numerical relations between notes, with some harmonies considered much stronger and more "pure" than others and therefore more favorable as the basis for composition.

Boethius listed three types of music:

- *Musica instrumentalis*: the "lowest" of the three, this was music that one could actually hear. Despite its name, it covered both vocal and instrumental music.

- *Musica humana*: the next level, this refers to the symmetry of the human body and the harmony between body and soul, this harmony being numerical and therefore a kind of music.

- *Musica mundana*: far from being "mundane," this was the highest form of music, most often known by its romanticized title, "the music of the spheres." This was the mathematics of the passage of time, the movement of the heavenly bodies, and the interaction of the four elements (earth, air, fire, and water).

In short, all aspects of creation were related to each other by numerical values and so they were all a kind of music, even if we could only hear the ones made by voices and instruments. The two lower levels of *musica* were just reflections of the perfect ratios that formed the structure of reality as created by God. All of this probably seems pretty obscure and esoteric to modern readers, but it was hugely important at the time, giving a kind of blueprint for reality and how music should be composed for centuries to come. It would appeal to philosophers and musicians through the Renaissance.

Boethius eventually ran afoul of his king, Theodoric the Great, and was imprisoned. He was sentenced to be executed on the false charge of plotting treason. While waiting for that unhappy fate, he wrote another book that many consider his greatest, *De consolatione philosophiae*, or "The Consolation of Philosophy"—an attempt to console himself about the nature of his misfortune.

Boethius died by the sword, or perhaps he was clubbed to death. Another account states that he was strangled until his eyes bulged and his skull broke. However it happened, it was a terrible and unjust end to one of the greatest minds of the age. Theodoric followed him to death not long after, opening up a renewed period of violence and war in the long era that was once known as the Dark Ages.

2

The Middle Ages

The "Middle Ages" is an odd term. Created by nineteenth-century academics and historians, it more or less means the "middle" period between the fall of Western Rome (in the fifth century) and the "rebirth" of classical learning that began in Italy in the fourteenth century and was in full swing by the fifteenth century. In other words, it was seen as the dark middle period between ancient Greco-Roman greatness and our own obvious modern greatness. Apparently nothing much existed in those thousand years except Viking raids, plagues, unwashed peasants, heretic burnings, knights slaughtering infidels, and monks—many monks.

People back then didn't think that they were living in the "middle" of anything. In fact, given that many lived in fear of the impending apocalypse, they would have been more likely to see themselves as living in the "End Ages."

If you've ever stood in a gothic cathedral, read an Arthurian romance, or viewed a stunning illuminated manuscript, you have seen that the people of the time weren't exactly uncivilized or uncultured; their music was pretty amazing, too. We need to be a little careful about proclaiming our superiority. Who knows? Maybe by the thirty-first century, they'll be classifying our era as the "late" Middle Ages—*remember when people used to believe that reality TV was entertaining, people invested money in Wall Street, and auto-tune sounded great? What a bunch of barbarians.*

As you can imagine, this vast period of time has quite a huge collection of odd and gruesome stories from all walks of life. So let's continue our historical tour with more bloody tales from the days of yore.

Deor (tenth century, or earlier)

Sour grapes

Deor may be the name of an Anglo-Saxon *scop* (pronounced "shop," a kind of early English minstrel or bard), or it may be a pseudonym. It literally means something like "wild animal" and may refer to the poet's low or "wild" station.

Whoever this was, he left behind a poem called (conveniently enough) "Deor," or sometimes "The Lament of Deor," though the surviving text doesn't have a title. It is found in a tenth-century manuscript known as the *Exeter Book*. It may have been meant to be proclaimed aloud, possibly in a mixture of singing and spoken word, accompanied by a lyre. Some scholars maintain that it was only a literary work, written in imitation of oral poems that no longer survive. In any case, the poem gives an account of some of the great tragedies and hardships of a number of folks from Anglo-Saxon and Germanic literature and legend, as can be seen in the opening lines:

> Wayland experienced torment from serpents [swords?]
> The strong-minded noble, he endured hardships,
> Sorrow and longing were his companions,
> In wintry exile, he often found misery . . .

Cheerful stuff. The full story that this particular verse refers to is told in the tongue-twisting *Völundarkviða* poem, from Old Norse (the language of the Vikings), and it is much worse than the brief excerpts related here. It was a story well known by the Germanic, Viking, and Anglo-Saxon peoples, who had many shared myths and cultural traditions.

Back to the "Deor" poem: it recounts various examples of suffering. Another verse reads:

> We have heard of Eormanric's wolfish mind;
> He ruled men in many places
> In the Goths' realm—that was a grim king.
> Many a man was surrounded by sorrows,
> Expecting misery, he often wished
> That the kingdom would be overcome.
> That went by, so may this.

Each verse always ends with the same line: "That went by [or passed away], so may this."

The stanzas revel in short stories of misery and death, telling us that the poet wishes "this" to pass away also, as these other sorrows did. So, what is the mysterious "this" that the poet alludes to? We find out in the last section, where he reveals that he was once an exalted poet to a lord who was dislodged from his position by someone else:

> I will say this of myself:
> For some time I was the Heodenings' poet,
> Dear to my lord, my name was "Deor."
> For many years I had a good position,
> And a loyal lord until now that Heorrenda,
> The man skilled in song, has received the estate
> That the warriors' guardian had given to me.
> That went by, so may this.

That's it. That's the great tragedy. He was fired, laid off, given the boot; that's the equivalent of all of these other heroic tragedies. Mass murder, imprisonment, torture, tyranny, unwanted pregnancy from a rape . . . all of that is easy, but losing his job? Now we're talking disaster. To be fair, when and if such a thing happened, the *scop* couldn't just go down to the local Anglo-Saxon unemployment office at the end of the village and collect a bagful of coins for a few weeks. Being cast out of a lord's service could be akin to banishment, along with the shame that accompanied such a fate, and there was no guarantee of being accepted elsewhere. So maybe he does have a right to whine after all.

Actually, the writer probably wasn't giving us his autobiography. The entire work is a fiction, with mythological content and probable ironic intent. Indeed, in this final verse, the poet speaks of being set out on his wretched path by the gods and serving mythical lords. He says Heorrenda, one of the names for the god Woden (Odin), has greater skill. Of course he does; Odin was the god of poets and verse-makers as well as war (the two often went hand in hand in that culture, with poetry existing to exalt the deeds of warriors). Really, Deor never had a chance; who can compete with a god, especially the god of the very same skill as the poet?

So, was "Deor" a real person giving some kind of odd autobiography laced with mythic imagery, perhaps to hide the real names of those whom he served and his replacement? Or is it all merely a clever literary device written in imitation of earlier oral poems and songs? We don't know for certain, but it makes for a fascinating glimpse into the possible world of Anglo-Saxon performance, and its stirring imagery is written in the words that are roots of our modern English language.

Adémar de Chabannes (998/99–1034)

Forging new alliances

Adémar was a monk, scribe, and writer of liturgical music (i.e., chant) at the abbey of St. Martial in the Limoges area of central France. He has the distinction of being the first medieval composer we know of who wrote surviving music in his own hand (quite rightly known as his "autograph"). But old Adémar has another, far more interesting distinction than this; he was also a forger of audacious proportions, who seemed not to care in the slightest about the possibility of getting caught or the consequences of his actions.

A pilgrims' legend had been circulating concerning a certain St. Martial, a third-century saint who had lived and preached in and around

Limoges. One legend claims that he had actually lived earlier and been one of Christ's original apostles. This strange tale found favor with Adémar for unknown reasons—perhaps because it built up the prestige of the region—and he set about doing everything he could to make it official. He forged a biography of Martial, and then wrote and borrowed mass music in support of the idea that Martial lived in the time of Christ. When a wandering monk, Benedict of Chiusa, learned of Adémar's actions in 1029, he immediately denounced them as fraudulent and heretical. The whole thing seemed on the verge of collapsing, but Adémar wasn't about to give up.

Instead he invented an entire church council, set in 1031, that supposedly confirmed St. Martial's status; he even forged a letter from then-Pope John XIX that did the same. You would think that making up such obvious lies would have landed him in very hot water, but this doesn't seem to have been the case. He continued with his forgeries and eventually went on a pilgrimage to Jerusalem in 1034, where he died of unknown causes.

Before he left, he had seen to it that his writings were deposited in the monastery library, where they continued contributing to the myth. Martial was venerated as an original apostle in the region through the nineteenth century. It was only in the 1920s that a historian by the name of Louis Saltet uncovered the web of lies and deceits woven by Adémar, and even then historians didn't fully acknowledge his crimes until a good while later. Somehow he got away with his crazy fictions and not only escaped the wrath of the Church authorities, but also contributed to a false history that endured for almost a thousand years. It makes those fake diaries allegedly by Hitler, Elvis, and others look even stupider for their quick rates of failure.

Taillefer (mid-eleventh century)

The world cannot be governed without juggling

Taillefer was said to be a Norman (i.e., northern French) musician and minstrel in the service of William the Conqueror. William had a claim to the throne of England and, as every student of history knows, invaded the south English coast in 1066, defeated the Anglo-Saxons at the Battle of Hastings in October of that year, and changed the course of English and world history.

His victory wasn't a foregone conclusion, however. The English had a better strategic position (up on a hill) and were pretty fired up. They'd just kicked some serious Viking butt up north a few days earlier, stopping an invasion by King Harald of Norway and killing him in the process. They weren't about to give up easily to a bunch of Frenchmen with outrageous accents (though the Normans were originally Vikings too, hence their name). William had his work cut out for him.

According to legend, as the battle was about to commence, Taillefer bravely rode out to confront and terrify the Anglo-Saxons . . . by juggling. Actually, it must have been an impressive sight. He juggled a sword and spear, to the opposition's great amusement, no doubt. They probably figured that if this was the best the Normans could do, the whole thing would be over quickly; they'd hand William's boys their Norman behinds and be home for mead and mutton (and maybe even a recital of "Deor") in no time. Their amusement ended abruptly when Taillefer unexpectedly flung the spear at a Saxon noble and killed him. The enraged English immediately charged and engulfed him; it was said that an Englishman named Leofwine killed him.

But Taillefer's brave sacrifice inspired the Norman troops. Another account says that he had recited the epic *Chanson de Roland* to the soldiers earlier in the day for morale building, though other evidence places the composition of this poem a few decades later. The Normans ultimately won the day and transformed England, and English history, forever. Did one musician contribute to all of that?

Whether the story is true or not (probably not), a lot of later medieval writers thought it was, and several mentioned him in the context of the Battle of Hastings as playing an important role. So a word to the wise . . . or at least to kings: beware of jugglers!

William IX (1071–1126)

Excommunication, eh, whatever

Also known as Guilhèm de Peitieus (say that three times fast), William was the Duke of Aquitaine and Gascony (both in modern-day south-western France) and the Count of Poitou (known there as William VII) from 1086 until his death. He is recognized today as the first identifiable troubadour, at least the first whose poems have survived.

And a brief clarification here: "troubadour" in its original definition is not a generic term for a minstrel going about in tights and pointy shoes, strumming lutes under windows and ducking various pieces of rotten fruits and vegetables thrown at him. It actually refers to a specific group of poet-musicians who were prominent in what is now southern France from the early twelfth to the mid-thirteenth centuries. They could even be nobles (as in William's case) and women (from whom a small but important number of poems survive). Their poetry is exquisite and quite sophisticated. Written in Occitan—a lovely Romance language related to modern Catalan in northeastern Spain—nearly 250 such poems survive with their music (there are many more poems preserved with their texts only). The song topics are varied, but often are about love (of course) and the pain it can bring (of course). But there are also satires, religious poems, and debates among the surviving works.

William was not the sensitive poetic type. He was basically a lustful, violent brute, a hothead who made bad decisions and whose actions got him in trouble on several occasions. He also happened to write good songs, not unlike a modern rock star.

As a military leader, on the other hand, he seems to have been fairly useless. Pushed into going on a crusade in 1101 (peer pressure was as effective then as it is now), he accomplished nothing and got most of his men killed when ambushed by the Turks not once, but several times. By the time he returned home, he obviously hadn't learned anything from his brushes with death and proceeded to flip off the Church establishment. He was excommunicated twice, a real accomplishment! The first time was in 1114, apparently for violating various Church tax laws and privileges. He didn't take too kindly to the idea. When Bishop Peter of Poitiers was due to read the bad news to him, he threatened said bishop at sword point with death, unless the bishop absolved him. William was nothing if not direct. The bishop pretended to comply, completed the excommunication once William's sword was withdrawn, and then calmly offered his neck to the enraged duke. William is said to have sheathed his sword and replied that he didn't love the bishop enough to send him to paradise.

He managed to get back into the good graces of the Church, but then blew it again when he "abducted" the Viscountess Dangereuse (what a great name; it sounds like a pin-up from the 1950s), the wife of none other than his vassal—a lesser lord who had vowed service to him. He took her to his castle in Poitiers; apparently the lady was not exactly an unwilling victim. William's wife, Philippa, was understandably furious. After unsuccessfully attempting to get him to dismiss his adulterous lover, she retired to a nunnery and died some time later.

William may have shown some remorse for his actions. In the song *Pos de chanter* he bemoans his predicament, which may well refer to one of his excommunications:

> Since I feel like singing,
> I will write a verse that I grieve over:
> I will never be a vassal anymore
> In Poitiers nor in Limoges
>
> For now I will be exiled:
> In a dreadful fright, in great peril

He was eventually absolved again by the Church in 1120, and turned his attention to the efforts to fight the Muslim Moors in Spain. However, during his time there, he acquired a taste for Moorish women and apparently tried to set up a Moorish-style harem for himself; so much for the Viscountess.

Although establishing a harem probably kept him busy, William also found the time to write creative and often amusing poems. Of the eleven that we have, only one fragment of a melody survives, and this might not even be his, since the attribution dates to several centuries later. One of the saucier examples describes how he satisfied two noble ladies; the poem is both a boast on his prowess and a tweak on the nose to the establishment to prove that he could do whatever he wanted:

Thereafter Dame Agnes told Dame Ermessen:
"He [William] is stupid, it is clear:
Sister, let's prepare for merriment and pleasure."
I lingered for forty-one days that way.

You shall hear how much I f***** them:
One hundred and eighty-eight times,
So much that they nearly broke my equipment and my tool;
And I cannot describe the aching, so much I was taken.

At least he had a sense of humor, if not humility.

Peter Abelard (1079–1142)

The most unkindest cut of all

Abelard was a brilliant French scholar, teacher, and lecturer. These days, he is more known to students of philosophy, at least those who didn't snooze through *Introduction to Medieval Philosophy* in their sophomore year. But Abelard was also a gifted composer of music, writing biblical laments and hymns for nuns as well as love songs for Héloïse (more on her in a minute). It was not exactly Top 40 stuff by our standards, but it was all the rage at the time. Unfortunately his Latin love songs do not survive, but six laments do. Written in the style called the *planctus*, they are based on biblical themes, and the melodies were popular enough to be borrowed and reused in a few later songs—a common practice at the time.

By 1115, he had established himself as one of the principal teachers of philosophy and theology in Paris. According to various accounts, he attracted thousands of enthusiastic students (remember, these were the days before frat parties, beer kegs, and spring break). Abelard eventually grew pretty cocky from the fame and adulation, believing that he could not be defeated in scholarly debates.

Sometime after his rise to prominence, he became the tutor to a beautiful young woman named Héloïse, the niece of a cathedral canon named Fulbert (not to be confused with the nut of a similar name). You can see where this is going; it was all rather like bad Internet fan fiction, but for real. Abelard declared that he was "utterly aflame with [his] passion for this maiden." Pretty soon the two of them were at it hot and heavy, and apparently everyone knew except poor Fulbert. When he eventually found out, he was naturally very upset and separated the two of them—well, maybe not literally, that would have been awkward.

Of course, like in any good forbidden romance, the two continued to meet in secret, and Héloïse eventually became pregnant, twelfth-century contraception being what it was. Abelard sent her packing off to Brittany for her own protection. Nine months later she gave birth to a son and named him Astrolabe, after the instrument designed for calculating latitude that had recently arrived in Europe from the Islamic world. Seriously. Can you imagine the teasing he must have endured in school?

Anyway, Abelard proposed a secret marriage with Fulbert's consent, after he had cooled down. It was secret so that Abelard's career in the Church could still advance; he was a shrewd thinker even here. She objected, desiring that they remain lovers only, but eventually agreed to the proposal. However, Fulbert did not keep the marriage secret, which forced Héloïse to publicly deny it so that Abelard could keep his position.

The stress of it all led her to seek refuge in the convent of Argenteuil, at Abelard's request. Fulbert was furious about this, thinking that the ever-crafty Peter had sent her away to become a nun to be rid of her. He plotted his revenge with the help of a few friends. Abelard himself told what happened, saying that in their anger they plotted against him. One night while he was asleep in his lodgings, they entered, having bribed one of his servants. They took their vengeance on him in a cruel and terrible way, shocking those who learned of it. Abelard lamented that they cut off those parts of him that had committed the offense, the parts that were the cause of their sorrow. Two of the perpetrators were later caught and had their eyes and genitals removed.

Thus, poor Abelard was a eunuch, left to seek refuge in a monastery. Héloïse likewise remained in the convent. His six musical laments date from this time, which is understandable, since he had a lot to lament about. The two former lovers continued to correspond for the rest of their lives, leaving behind a mixture of letters, philosophical discussions, and even a declaration from Abelard that he never really loved her, though the sincerity of this is certainly debatable. On the other hand, considering the loss of his most valued personal possessions, he may have been rather bitter.

Marcabru (*fl.* 1129–1150)

Rubbing everyone the wrong way

What little we know about Marcabru comes from two *vidas* about him. A mixture of fact and legend, *vidas* were short biographies of troubadours that appeared in much later manuscripts containing their works. Some are more accurate than others, but Marcabru's don't appear to be among the factual. We don't even know if that was his real name. Nevertheless, they variously record that his mother was named Marcabruna, or that he was an orphan abandoned at the door of a wealthy man, and that his original name was *Panperdut*, or "Lost Bread." What was with these medieval children's names?

Anyway, his songs were very critical of loose morals and poor behavior, and one of the *vidas* records that despite having generally poor musical skills, he became well-known enough to attract attention. He said harsh things about some of the lords in the Gascony area, and for this, they executed him (the manuscript does not record how). This may all be fanciful invention from a later time, but his words certainly were bristly and could have rubbed people the wrong way. In one song, addressed to a Sir Audric (*Seigner n'Audric*), he declares:

> Marcabru knows all of your habits and all of your ideal ways of life:
> Stuffing your face, and flouting and welcoming harlots.
> When you, alone, are well fed,
> Great bluster is certainly not far away from you

Sir Audric can't have been happy about being immortalized like this. In another song, *Lo vers comens* ("I start the verse"), Marcabru offers a more general condemnation of the lack of courtliness and virtue:

> Cowardice carries the key and casts prowess into exile.
> Hardly will you find that father and son are equals;
> I do not hear, except in Poitou, that one cultivates prowess.

> He prophesied right and wrong who said we will end up in reversal,
> The lord being a serf and the serf a lord: they already do that.
> The buzzards of Anjou have done so. What a fall!

He was an enthusiastic supporter of the Reconquista, the military efforts to retake southern Spain from Muslim control. He wrote a famous song (which survives with music) that begins with *Pax in nomine Domini* ("Peace in the name of the Lord") and contains the usual propaganda that such songs do when supporting military campaigns. However, he also managed to get in a dig at the French:

> The French are degenerates if they refuse to support God,
> For I have exhorted them.

So yes, he was rather talented at offending people, which may well have been enough to do him in.

Bertran de Born (1140s–*ca.* 1215)

With his head in his hands

Bertran was a minor noble but a very important troubadour who lived in the Limousin (not limousine) region of what is now south-central France. Like William IX before him, he was a titled man who did more than a bit of dabbling in music and poetry and produced some rather splendid results (though only one of his poems survives with music, an all-too-common fate for these early works). Also like William, he was a rather reprehensible fellow, though he did end his life as a monk, probably trying to atone for his ways.

Having developed quite a taste for battle and war as a young man, he actively supported the conflict that raged between members of the greatest family of the time—that of Henry II, King of England, and his wife Eleanor of Aquitaine. Indeed, he encouraged their oldest son, also named Henry, to revolt and fight against his father and younger brother Richard (the Lionhearted). When the young Henry was killed it created an awkward situation for Bertran, but he managed to get into Richard's good graces with some kissing up and pledges of support. In this promise, however, he was a little mixed. When Richard delayed in leaving for his crusade (known to history as the Third Crusade, 1189–1192), Bertran rebuked both Richard (now King of England) and Philip, King of France. He composed a song praising the courage of those in the Holy Land fighting their Muslim enemies, essentially saying "get on with it" while he himself bravely stayed at home, of course.

Bertran reveled in describing fighting and scenes of bloody carnage. One of the best examples of this is his song *Be.m plai lo gais temps de pascor*, or "The joyful springtime pleases me." Yes, that doesn't exactly sound like the opening to a war epic, and that's what makes it so strange. The first verse is given over to spring pleasantries like flowers, birds, and greenery, and it concludes with the joy of seeing pavilions and armored cavalry. Wait, what?

Bertran goes on to describe how cheerful spring is the perfect time to make peasants run for their lives, to besiege castles, beat down walls, and see lords leading the attack. It gets worse. The poet Ezra Pound provides a translation of the next part:

We shall see battle axes and swords, a-battering colored haumes and a-hacking through shields at entering melee; and many vassals smiting together, whence there run free the horses of the dead and wrecked. And when each man of prowess shall be come into the fray he thinks no more of (merely) breaking heads and arms, for a dead man is worth more than one taken alive.

I tell you that I find no such savor in eating butter and sleeping, as when I hear cried "On them!" and from both sides hear horses neighing through their head-guards, and hear shouted "To aid! To aid!" and see the dead with lance truncheons, the pennants still on them, piercing their sides.

After that he ends the work, complaining that there is too much peace about. One suspects that there is some tongue-in-cheek going on here, but this sort of war-mongering is also found in some of his other poems. Despite this approval of battle, he later became a peaceful monk. However, there was at least one writer who sought to punish him for his violent philosophy, not just with insults, but also with a literary eternal damnation of a rather nasty sort.

The great Italian poet Dante Alighieri (*ca.* 1265–1321) was repulsed by Bertran's war lust and his seeming delight in stirring up trouble between kings and families. For the sin of encouraging this strife, Dante placed him in the Eighth Circle of Hell in his *Inferno* (Canto XXVIII, the "Sowers of Discord"), saying that Bertran's soul walked about headless, holding his head by the hair like a lantern. In this sorry state, Bertran bemoans his condition and confesses his sins, saying his head is severed because he caused the ties between father and son, brother and brother to be severed, and that justice has been done. And there the narrator and his guide, Virgil, leave him, condemned to walk in that wretched state forever. Well, all right, then.

Richard I (1157–1199)

A lion undone by an ant

Richard the Lionhearted, the very essence of chivalry! The brave king of England went on crusade, fought his noble opponent Saladin to a draw in the Holy Land, and while he was away, managed to have his kingdom nearly stolen by his brother, the vile Prince John. Only Robin Hood and his Merry Men stood between John and his evil plans. Richard ultimately returned to claim his throne, pardon Robin and the outlaws of Sherwood Forest, and set things right in England.

It's the stuff of legends, then and now. The Robin Hood stories and Richard's place in them are a part of the collective myth of Western Civilization, popular for centuries. There is even a statue of Richard on horseback, with sword drawn as if leading an army, outside of the Houses of Parliament in London. Richard's deeds were spoken and sung of in his own time, so they must be true, right?

Well yes, somewhat, but with some very big qualifications. In addition to being King of England, Richard was the Duke of Normandy, Duke of Aquitaine, Duke of Gascony, Count of Anjou, Count of Nantes, Overlord of Brittany, and Lord of Ireland. That's a lot of titles! How would that all fit on a check? But the presence of all those non-English honors says something very important: being the great-grandson of that jerk, William IX, Richard's heart belonged to Aquitaine, and he really wasn't interested in England at all, except as his personal twelfth-century ATM. He used its considerable resources to finance his many war campaigns against various foes in France (a separate country from its modern western regions back then). Though he was born in Oxford, he spent only about ten months of his ten-year reign (1189–1199) in England, finding the place to be damp and dreary—some folks might say that not much has changed. He didn't even speak English. Actually, none of the monarchs in England spoke English as their native language, from William the Conqueror in 1066 until Henry IV, who usurped the throne in 1399, but that's a whole different story.

Richard had a bad temper and a reckless fearlessness in battle (hence his nickname); he loved a good fight and was a warrior king through and through—it was ultimately his undoing. So why is he listed here? Because he was also passionate about music and was a gifted songwriter himself. One of his pieces survives with music, and it's a real beauty.

He went on crusade in the year 1190 (having vowed to do so in 1187) and had a number of adventures along the way. His success in the Holy Land was limited. The goal was to retake Jerusalem, which had fallen to Saladin's forces in 1187, but Richard never achieved that. After a stalemate with Saladin he left the Middle East, vowing that he would never set foot in Jerusalem unless it was as its conqueror. However, he had made a number of enemies along the way back to his own continent. In order to get home safely, he had to sneak into Europe via the back door. Unfortunately for him, he was caught in Germany, imprisoned, and held for a huge ransom that his mother and family were obliged to pay to secure his release. This money was raised from, you guessed it, the taxpayers of England. Good King Richard wasn't so popular with the English in the 1190s.

It was during this time that he is said to have written the song *Je nuns hon pris* that survives with music. It has a beautiful melancholy quality, despite the less-than-humble content. The song begins:

> No prisoner will ever speak his mind fittingly
> Unless he speaks in grief
> But, for consolation, he can make a song.
> I have many friends, but their gifts are poor.
> It will be their shame if, for want of ransom,
> I stay a prisoner for these two winters.

A legend appeared in the thirteenth century (and has persisted into modern times) that Richard's trusty minstrel, Blondel, went in search of his master's place of imprisonment. He heard of one castle where an important man was held, but though Blondel stayed there for the whole winter, he could not learn this man's identity. At last he passed by Richard's dungeon (other stories place Richard in a tower), and Richard, seeing him through a window, sang a verse from a song they had co-written. Hearing this song, Blondel knew he had found Richard, so he sent news back to Eleanor.

It's a popular story with little basis in fact. There was a trouvère (the northern French equivalent of a troubadour) living at about that time named Blondel de Nesle, whom many would love to connect with this story, but the evidence is scant.

In any case, Eleanor paid the ransom and Richard did go back to England in 1194 for a short time to set in order some of John's screw-ups—and this is possibly one source for some of the Robin Hood legends. However, he happily returned to the continent soon after to begin waging wars again. He continued this life for another five years before meeting his end in a rather ridiculous way.

He was besieging a poorly defended castle called Chalûs-Chabrol. On the evening of March 25, 1199, Richard was walking the castle perimeter, without his armor, to see how preparations were going for the siege. He noticed a young man standing on one of the walls and holding a frying pan as a makeshift shield, which gives you a good idea of how well the place was being defended. Just then, a crossbow bolt struck him on the left shoulder. A surgeon was brought in to remove it, but he did a poor job and tore up Richard's wound badly. It quickly became gangrenous, and Richard knew he would die. There are different versions of what happened next. In one, Richard asked that the one who fired the shot be brought to him. He was a boy claiming that Richard had killed his father and brothers, and that he wanted revenge. Richard showed mercy, forgave him, and insisted that he be let go and given money for his suffering.

Richard died on April 6, 1199, in the arms of his mother, having willed his kingdom to John (and what a disaster that proved to be!). The boy he forgave didn't fare well, after all: a mercenary captain named Mercadier had the young man skinned alive and hanged as soon as Richard had died; so much for chivalry.

Richard's body parts were scattered into various resting places, a gross if not uncommon practice of the time, with his entrails buried where he died, his heart buried at Rouen in Normandy, and the rest of him buried at the feet of his father Henry II at Fontevraud Abbey in Anjou. Thus ended the life of the musician-king.

In the thirteenth century, the Bishop of Rochester claimed that Richard had spent thirty-three years in purgatory being cleansed of his sins and was admitted into heaven in March 1232. How the bishop arrived at these exact figures is unknown, but he was pretty confident about it.

The Monk of Montaudon (*fl.* 1193–1210/11)

Let me tell you what annoys me . . .

The Monk of Montaudon is a singularly curious figure in the history of medieval music. Possibly also known as Pèire de Vic, he was a noble who became a Benedictine monk around 1180, but who seems to have enjoyed deviating from monastic duties and activities. In fact, he suffered the fate that often befell younger male children of noble families who could not inherit their father's lands and titles: he was offered to a monastery. Such sons had no say in the matter and were understandably resentful.

Despite his enforced monastic vocation (or maybe even because of it), he showed a remarkable talent for vernacular poetry and music in the troubadour genre. Indeed, his work attracted the attention of the nobility and even led to patronage by some of his aristocratic admirers. The gifts they showered on him allowed him to benefit his monastery so much that he was released from his regular duties to serve King Alfonso II of Aragon (presumably to keep all that good money rolling in). This is what his biography relates, but the truth may be that he just left the order and re-entered the secular world. One of his poems mentions that he had "abandoned God for flesh."

While much of his writing is in the usual troubadour poetic forms of the time, his big claim to fame was his satirical songs and use of the form known as the *enueg*, or "annoyance," song. These gleefully sarcastic works are essentially long lists of things that he apparently got riled up about, in a seemingly random and nonsensical order. For example, he writes in *Be m'enueia* ("I find annoying, do you hear me?"):

> I can't stand a long wait,
> Or meat when it's badly cooked or tough,
> Or a priest who lies and perjures himself
> Or an old whore who is past it
> And—by Saint Delmas—I don't like
> A base man who enjoys too much comfort;
> And running when there's ice on the road,
> Or fleeing, armed on horseback
> Annoys me, as does hearing dicing maligned.

This goes on for nine verses; you get the idea. Among his other satirical works are two poems describing a debate in heaven between icons and painted ladies (i.e., practitioners of the world's oldest profession) over who has the right to use facial paint and for how long:

> Another time I was at a meeting in Heaven, by chance
> The statues were complaining about ladies who paint themselves
> I saw them complaining to God about women who improve their complexions
> And make their skin shine with paint that should be used on icons.

After much deliberation, God observes that such makeup attracts unwanted attention:

> Monk, this painting makes them endure many blows down below
> And do you think it pleases them when men make them bend over?

The Monk replies that he "cannot fill their holes" but asks that God spare one lady in particular, Elise of Montfort, who never used makeup or offended icons.

In the second song, St. Peter and St. Lawrence finally set the amount of time that each group (ladies and icons) is allowed to paint themselves, which is quite decent of them. However the ladies have no intention of going along with these new guidelines:

> Never were Saint Peter or Saint Lawrence
> Obeyed in this matter of the agreement which they caused to be made
> With these old women who have longer tusks than a wild boar.
> They've done worse—haven't you heard—
> They've sent up the price of saffron so much
> That as far away as Palestine the pilgrims have been talking about it:
> I must indeed lodge a complaint about this.

We often think of the Middle Ages as a stuffy, repressed time of heavy censorship and the silencing of ideas and joy, and to be sure, there were many instances of such things. But the mere fact that this kind of poetry could be written—by a monk who got away with it no less—shows that, at least in southern France, there was a more tolerant society willing to poke fun at things and be irreverent. It was a society that would soon meet a brutal and tragic end.

Folquet de Marselha (*fl.* 1179–1195, *d.* 1231)
Kill them all, let God sort them out

Folquet de Marselha, also known as Fulk, was a troubadour of some renown with a wealthy background as a merchant. He was well-known and admired for his songs, but sometime around 1195, he had a kind of religious conversion experience that caused him to renounce his life as a troubadour, enter the monastery of Thoronet in Provence, and drag his wife and sons into the monastic life along with him. They don't seem to have had any say in this; it was as bad as being offered up as a younger son! So deep was his devotion that he rapidly advanced in standing, and by 1205 he was elected Bishop of Toulouse.

One of his songs, *Vers Dieus*, showed his religious inclinations even in his song-writing days:

God, give me the knowledge and wisdom to learn your holy commandments,
To hear them, to understand them;
And may your pity save me and protect me from this world of earth
Let it not destroy me with itself.

Indeed, Fulk had no desire to maintain any connections with his previous secular life; demonstrating his commitment to his new-found faith, he became a committed enemy of the Cathars, a wildly popular religious movement in southern France that had been denounced as heretical by the Church and condemned. The Cathars denied the authority of the Roman Catholic Church and any validity to its sacraments, believing instead that the universe was ruled by the forces of light and darkness, forever in conflict. This is known as Dualism, and its long history goes back to at least ancient Persia. The good was pure spirit, so therefore, anything earthly, including the Church, was evil. I imagine that went over real well at the Papal Sunday brunch. Catharism was widely accepted (or at least tolerated) in the south, and many nobles professed it, possibly more to defy Church power than out of actual belief. These same nobles were often patrons to various troubadours, or were even troubadours themselves.

In 1215, Pope Innocent III declared a crusade against the Cathars, which opened up the floodgates for armies from northern France and farther afield to beat some sinners into submission and get a tan—but just as importantly, to get in on the land-grab and lootings that would inevitably follow the confiscation of the southerners' properties, castles, and estates. The famous phrase "Kill them all, God will know His own" was attributed to papal legate Abbot Arnold Amaury after the taking of one southern city and confusion over whom to spare and whom to kill.

An enthusiastic supporter of this crusade and such harsh sentiments, Fulk did what he could to assist, including helping to establish the Inquisition in southern France. The tragedy of this whole affair was that by the 1240s, the Cathars had indeed been all but wiped out, and with them the vibrant and rich troubadour culture that had flourished in a land of relative tolerance and openness. Various troubadours fled the dangers of the Languedoc and found new homes in Spain and Italy, but their time was ending and new musical tastes were fast supplanting them. Fulk, who died in 1231, had no remorse for helping to bring about the end of a culture he had once celebrated.

Châtelain de Coucy (*fl.* 1186–1203)

His heart just wasn't in it

This fellow with an exotic and romantic-sounding name was probably Guy de Couci ("Châtelain" is a title), who lived in a castle by the name of, well, Couci. He held this fancy position from 1186 until his death. The Châtelain was a trouvère who wrote poems in the Old French language. Incidentally, the trouvères did not suffer the same sad fate as their southern counterparts (troubadours), but rather continued to flourish right up until the beginning of the fourteenth century. The Châtelain has left behind an impressive collection of high-quality songs that are remarkably tuneful, even to the modern listener.

He rates a place here due to a curious legend that grew up around him after his death. It is said that he fell in love with a noble woman, the Lady of Fayel, who was—naturally—already married. Whether this story is true or not, his lyrics reflect the poetic ideal of love as a state of suffering, elevating self-pity to an art form:

Lady, I have no torment that is not my joy,
For without you, I could not live, and do not want to.
Without loving you, my life has no use
Unless I want to annoy everyone, or walk around dying.

At least he admitted to being annoying.

While the love conventions of the time encouraged, at least in theory, adulterous love, needless to say the Lady's husband, Sir Fayel, wasn't all that thrilled when he found out. In an attempt to trap them, or at least get Guy away from his wife, he suggested a joint pilgrimage to the Holy Land but then backed out, forcing Guy to go alone. He smugly thought he had gotten rid of the upstart. Sure enough, the poor Châtelain was mortally wounded. Knowing he would never see his beloved again, he instructed his faithful servant to remove his heart after his death, embalm it, and send it back to her as a token of his love, even beyond death.

Mean old Sir Fayel got wind of this plan as well (apparently he had spies everywhere) and devised a particularly cruel trick. After intercepting the heart, he had it prepared as a delicious-looking meal and served to his wife, who had no idea. After she finished eating it, he triumphantly told her the origins of her meal. Lady Fayel, upon hearing this, died. In some sources it is from grief, in others it is because, she says, she has eaten the most perfect food and so will never eat again.

This strange little story circulated widely and was known in other sources. It was popularized in a later thirteenth-century romance about the Châtelain's life. In fact, the same tale, which originally seems to have come from Brittany, was also told about a troubadour named Guilhem de Cabestaing and about a minnesinger (the German equivalent of the troubadours and trouvères) named Reinmar von Brennenberg. Hey, if you have a good story, why only use it once? This was pure tabloid fodder, and audiences were just as eager for it then as now.

Guilhem de la Tor (*fl.* 1216–1233)

She's just not that into you

Guilhem was a minor troubadour who left his home in Périgord, France, to work in Italy; it would have been a hellish commute otherwise. For a minor figure, he is lucky (?) to have a rather detailed and odd story recorded about him, though once again, it is likely just an embellished fiction. The source of this peculiar tale appears to be one of his own poems, *Uns amics et un'amia*, wherein he debates with another troubadour, Sordel, about whether one should follow their beloved to death or live on. Guilhem writes:

A lover and his beloved . . . are so entirely of one mind
That it seems to them one of them could not have joy without the
    other.
If then the woman died in circumstances where her lover . . . saw her
    death
What would be better for him to do: to live on after her or to die?

Sordel responds that he thinks the lover should also die, though Guilhem is not completely convinced, replying that the beloved does not benefit from this.

This song may have directly inspired his odd biography. According to the tale, Guilhem met and fell madly in love with a barber's wife in Milan and ran away with her to Como, near the border with modern Switzerland; actually, it seems that he may have abducted her. In any case, they married and he remained passionately in love with her. However, tragedy struck and she died, leaving poor Guilhem inconsolable and despairing to the point of madness.

He began to believe that she wasn't dead at all and was simply trying to find an excuse to leave him. That seems like a rather complicated plan; couldn't she have just run off with the stable boy? He spent ten days removing her from her tomb and holding her, asking her to tell him if she was alive or dead, and if she was in fact dead, to relate to him what she was experiencing in the afterlife, so that if necessary, he could have prayers and masses said for her. Needless to say, she wasn't particularly chatty.

City officials weren't overly pleased with his behavior. The poor man was expelled from the city and took to moving about looking for a wizard or sorcerer who could bring her back to life. He encountered a charlatan who was only too happy to give him detailed instructions. This was a complex and tortuous procedure involving saying 150 Lord's Prayers, reciting the entire Psalter (a medieval book of the psalms), and giving alms out to seven poor people each day before he himself could eat (basically turning his breakfast into a late lunch). He was told to do this for a year; his beloved would then come back from the dead but would be unable to speak, eat, or drink.

Gullible Guilhem enthusiastically undertook this laborious process, only to find, of course, that it had no effect whatsoever. He was said to have died of grief shortly after failing to bring about his lover's resurrection. It's doubtful that this story is true, though let's be honest, some medieval people *did* do very strange things.

Goliards (twelfth and thirteenth centuries)

Sex, booze, and rock 'n' roll

The goliards are sometimes seen as the medieval equivalent of frat boys, and probably also the first rock stars. William IX might have fit in well with them, had he lived in their time. The origin of their name is unclear but may come from the Latin *gula*, "gluttony," or from "Goliath." Abelard had been referred to as Goliath by the abbot Bernard of Clairvaux (Peter was good at pissing off authority, you'll recall), and thus the term "goliard" could reflect an imagined connection between Abelard and his many students, of whom the goliards may have seen themselves as the descendants.

They were mainly clerical students at various universities, including those of Paris, Oxford, and Bologna, who decided to be a little less pious than they should have been and a little more hell-raising than was acceptable. When not immersed in their studies, they would spend large amounts of time at the local taverns, brothels, and gambling dens, obviously doing serious and intense research on the state of moral decay and hypocrisy in the modern world of *ca.* 1200. Such activities also often led to many a hastily written letter home asking the folks for more money. Some things never change.

Their wild ways led to some wickedly funny poetic and musical satires on a wide variety of topics: church corruption, love and marriage, financial shenanigans in authority, and the benefits of imbibing large amounts of alcohol. One song, *In Taberna*, finishes up with an admission of guilt but little repentance:

No amount of money could pay
The bill for all that we drink
We drink without measure
Only for our own enjoyment.
Everyone criticizes us
And we will soon be paupers
May our critics be confounded
When they are not recorded among the saved!

Not to be confined to just the written word, they were also known for pranks and outlandish behavior. In a scene straight out of Monty Python, a record from St. Remy in Provence states that they would go to mass each dragging a herring on a string behind him. The goal of this game was to try to step on the herring in front of you, while at the same time keeping your own herring from being stepped on (no jokes about red herrings, I promise).

One of the stranger musical works associated with this genre is the *Mass of the Asses, Drunkards, and Gamblers*, a musical and textual parody of the Catholic mass that involved references to all kinds of gambling, winning, and losing, and a share of insults thrown in for good measure. The Catholic exhortation "let us pray" became, in this work, "let us bet." There is also a piece in praise of Bacchus:

I will go to the altar of Bacchus
To him who gives joy to the heart of man
Let us drink
We beseech you, Bacchus, take our clothes from us
That we may be worthy, with naked bodies, to enter the tavern.

Naturally, their wanton ways did not sit well with authorities, in either the universities or the Church. Crackdowns were enacted and various people threatened with expulsion, all of the usual things that impotent authorities do to try to maintain order. But strangely, more often than not, they got away with it, and in time, the Church (wisely) came to view some of their activities as simply a way of blowing off youthful steam.

Despite these activities, there is evidence that most of the surviving lyrics were not autobiographical at all, since many of the known poets were highly educated and well regarded. They were simply using such imagery as social criticism and rhetorical devices for equally sophisticated audiences. The actual students probably didn't write a lot of the surviving songs.

A good collection of goliardic verse and song is in the manuscript known as the *Carmina Burana* from thirteenth-century Germany. This work inspired twentieth-century composer Carl Orff to set some of its poems to his own majestic orchestral music, thus inadvertently creating a soundtrack for dozens of cheesy low-budget fantasy films and an equal number of video games over the last thirty years. The goliards would be amused. Or at least they'd drink to it.

Jehan de l'Escurel (*d.* 1304?)

Hang him high

Little is known about Jehan other than that he was one of the last true trouvères. He was the son of a Parisian merchant and left a large (for the medieval period) collection of songs that reflected the themes of his times. He may also have composed some polyphonic music anonymously in other collections. It is recorded that on May 23, 1304, a certain Jehan de l'Escurel was hanged (along with three other clerics) for "debauchery" and "crimes against women."

It has been traditional to assume that this was the same man as the composer in question. However, there has been a lot of debate about this in recent years, with convincing arguments that the executed man was someone else. The question will probably never be resolved, but it is intriguing to ponder. An equally puzzling topic is the reason for the hanging, as these charges were not normally capital offenses, unless he was a persistent and odious re-offender or there was more to it. Perhaps this Jehan was guilty of some dreadful, Jack-the-Ripper-esque crime that the authorities of the day were too shocked to mention? We'll probably never know, but the idea of a medieval serial killer would make for a good *Twilight Zone* episode, or heavy metal video.

Grimace (late fourteenth century)

Grimace was a French composer living in the second half of the fourteenth century. He is known to have written five surviving songs, and maybe a few more. Nothing is known about his life, but with a name like this, he simply had to be included in this book.

3

The Renaissance

Brought to you basically by the same folks that created the term "the Middle Ages," the Renaissance (a French word meaning "rebirth") was touted in the nineteenth century as nothing less than the fantastic rebirth of humanity after a long, post-Roman dark night of stagnation and ignorance. And plague. And turnips. And monks.

Beginning with innovations in art and architecture in fourteenth-century Italy, the whole thing caught on and spread throughout Europe—not unlike the bubonic plague, but without the open sores and agonizing deaths. Before you could say "rebirth," people were reading the old Greek classics, inventing printing presses, painting realistic pictures with better perspective, making music that sounds more "modern" to our ears, and questioning religious authorities left and right. And it's true; the period between roughly 1350 and 1600 is simply remarkable. The Renaissance probably has more amazing art, music, architecture, and literary master-pieces per capita than any other era in Western history. From Leonardo da Vinci to William Shakespeare, from Rabelais to Michelangelo, the jewels in the Renaissance crown are many and brilliant.

It wasn't all fun and games and lute songs, though. Religious differences tore apart nations, towns, and families as the Protestant Reformation drew huge lines in the sand and divided loyalties everywhere, resulting in dread-ful persecutions from both sides (the Catholic Church launched a "Counter-Reformation" in response to Martin Luther's teachings), massacres, and full-on battles. The witch hunts—surprisingly never that big of a deal in medieval times—came into their own, resulting in the deaths of one hundred thousand or more innocent people (nearly a quarter of whom were men). A horrendous book called *Malleus Maleficarum*, written in 1486 by two absolutely appalling priests, became the how-to manual for this bloody and paranoid phenomenon for the next few centuries. There was a real Dracula who impaled his victims on wooden stakes (we'll meet him later), and a crime family, the Borgias, one of whom became pope. Wars broke out, the Ottoman Empire expanded dangerously into Eastern Europe while effectively ruling the eastern Mediterranean Sea, and monarchies and religious leaders were rocked with scandals. If it was a time of "rebirth," it was a rebirth into the harsh realities of the nearly modern world.

Composers were not spared these unpleasant developments. Just like their medieval predecessors, some of them met with very strange fates and shocking ends.

Antoine Busnois (*ca.* 1430–1492)
The fight club

Busnois ("Boo-NWAH," not "bus noise") was a highly regarded French composer, whose songs many now see as ahead of their time in their complexity, melody, and rhythm. He attracted many patrons, hobnobbed in various aristocratic circles, and ended up in the service of Charles the Bold, Duke of Burgundy, in the mid-1460s. Charles loved two things: music and war. He often dragged his court composers and musicians along with him on his military campaigns—and more than one of them got killed as a result—because he didn't want to be without his favorite music. Remember, this was in the days before iPods, so if you wanted music when you traveled, you had to bring the whole band with you.

This fighting spirit seemed to suit Busnois just fine. Despite serving as a chaplain and a subdeacon at various points in his career, he was prone to violence. He filed a petition for absolution (forgiveness) in Tours, France, in February 1461, confessing to being part of a gang that had beaten up a priest. Not once. Not twice. But five times. Five! Exactly why this particular priest was subjected to getting the stuffing kicked out of him so many times is not recorded. Perhaps "Subdeacon Smackdown" was a new team sport that never quite took off.

This behavior had put him in a "state of anathema," basically the Church's way of saying "you've been bad." For whatever reasons, Antoine decided to celebrate mass while in this state (maybe to commemorate the priest's butt-kicking), which was strictly a no-no. He was then excommunicated—the Church's way of saying "you've been *very* bad."

Some sources credit him with writing the incredibly popular song *L'homme armé*, "The Armed Man." This little tune would be used and reused, strangely enough, as a melody in more than forty masses composed between 1450 and about 1700. It was common to take popular songs and mix them into religious music, especially for the mass, as a way of appropriating a sinful song back into holiness.

Despite Busnois's troubles, things didn't end badly for him. He was able to obtain a pardon from the pope and was reinstated. Presumably, he had learned his lesson and left his priest-thumping days behind him. Indeed, later contemporaries would proclaim his sterling character and suitability to instruct his students in both music and morals. Perhaps all he had really needed earlier on was a good military campaign with Charles the Bold to go kick the butt of a secular enemy and get it out of his system.

Charles himself met a gruesome end, living by the sword and all that, at the Battle of Nancy in January 1477. Things went badly for his forces, and his body was found, riddled with lances, a few days after the battle. His head had been cleaved almost in half by a halberd (an axe on a long pole). Busnois had it easy by comparison.

Gilles Joye (1424/25–1483)

A Rose by any other name . . .

A bit like Antoine, Gilles was a composer and (eventually) a priest who seemed drawn toward behavior that was a little less than priestly. Hired as a singer in Bruges from 1449, he seems to have gotten in trouble on more than one occasion, gaining a reputation for involvement in street brawls.

Who knows? Maybe Busnois beat him up once and he decided to get even. Since these kinds of fights were often the result of too much alcohol, and he was reprimanded for drinking too much, we can assume that he was very fond of his wine or beer. When his local chapter abolished the celebration of the Feast of Fools (a Christmas-time festival of silliness, reverse identities, subversion of the rules, and general blowing off of steam—see the goliards in the previous chapter), he protested by refusing to sing.

In addition to swearing too much, he was also rather fond of ladies peddling the world's oldest profession and is said to have favored one in particular, Rosabelle, whose reputation was well known. He even lodged with her for a time. Prostitution in those days was condemned by the Church, but tolerated by towns and cities as long as it was relegated to certain locations and everything was transacted on the sly.

As a result, he seems to have missed, probably due to fatigue or hangovers, a number of important singing events where he was expected to attend and participate. It may be significant that only his secular songs survive, one of which contains these naughty words:

> What you do covertly concerning "let us multiply"
> As long as it is done secretly, is easily excused
> In the sight of the Most High.
>
> And then, let us do it, my girls, and enjoy,
> It is nothing but good sport . . .

He may also have set two masses to a popular tune, *O Rosa bella*, which would be a perfect inside joke, given the name of his favorite courtesan.

For whatever reason, these offenses weren't held against him in the long run. He was made a priest and eventually a canon of St. Donatian in Bruges in 1459. Whether he continued to see Rosabelle to play "priest and confessor" is unknown.

Henry VIII, King of England (1491–1547)

My kingdom for a song?

Ah, dear old Henry, known to history as a bloated, corpulent, gouty, miserable old tyrant with a passion for turkey legs and beheading wives. And those were his good points! In fact, Henry was very athletic and fit for a good portion of his life, only becoming much less so after a broken leg that curtailed his activities. He only had two of his wives executed ("only"), and one of those, Catherine Howard, certainly was guilty of flagrant adultery—not that she deserved to die for it, of course.

Henry was a very complex man, and numerous biographies have been written about him. The king who married six times, tore apart the religious life of England, ravaged its medieval heritage, and changed English history forever was also a great lover of music, an instrument collector, and a skilled composer in his own right, in addition to being a patron to many fine musicians. By the end of his life, he employed nearly sixty musicians of various kinds.

In his youth, he was admired throughout Europe as the model of the Renaissance Prince, and this included a passion for music. He was noted for his skill on the lute, harpsichord, and organ and also played recorder, sometimes practicing for hours a day. His collection of musical instruments grew, encompassing everything from keyboards (organs, harpsichords, and their variations), plucked strings (lutes and harps), and bowed strings (early violins and fiddles, viols, rebecs) to soft wind instruments (recorders and flutes) and loud wind instruments (shawms, horns, trombones, and bagpipes), scattered around various palaces and official residences.

There are thirty-four extant pieces of music attributed to Henry, found in what is, conveniently enough, titled the *Henry VIII Manuscript*. They are quite good and include instrumental as well as vocal works. If these are all by Henry, then he did indeed possess the considerable skill that his sycophants proclaimed he did. Confirming attributions of pieces to specific composers can sometimes be a tricky subject because music was often attributed to famous people just to increase sales—sixteenth-century marketing through name-dropping.

There is a legend, for example, that Henry wrote the immortal tune "Greensleeves" while pining for Anne Boleyn, who would eventually become his second wife (and the first to be executed). The words "Alas my love, you do me wrong, to cast me off discourteously" were once believed to have been his response to being spurned. Sadly, there's no evidence for his authorship. Some musicologists have even pointed out that the style of the song dates to a later part of the sixteenth century, meaning that it was likely written by that most famous and gifted of female composers: Anonymous.

Henry's musical activities began to fade into the background in his later life, as being a tyrant took center stage (a full-time job, that), but he maintained a keen appreciation for the musical arts until the end.

David Rizzio (or Riccio) (*ca.* 1533–1566)
Sticking the knife in and turning it

Rizzio was an Italian courtier and the son of a music teacher; he progressed through the ranks over time to become a favorite of Mary, Queen of Scots. He was said to be ugly, but possessed great musical talent and a beautiful singing voice.

He made his way to Scotland in 1561 via a diplomatic mission from the Marquess of Moretto. The Scottish Court had no real use for the poor fellow, and he was dismissed, but being the clever man he was, he got in good with Mary's musicians. Rizzio's friend, Sir John Melvil, noted that Queen Mary "had three valets, who sang three parts, and she wanted a person to sing a bass, or fourth part."

Well, hey, what a lucky coincidence! Rizzio just happened to be hanging around, and his voice impressed the queen. His musical skill became legendary in later years. In the eighteenth century he was credited with composing a large number of songs in the Scots language, though these were actually folk songs with no connection to him. More likely, he sang fashionable part-songs in Italian and French, as would be found in any respectable Renaissance court. He was much more a musician than a composer.

The next few years were good for him, and he grew wealthy under royal patronage, even attaining the coveted position of secretary for relations with France, an astonishing achievement that provoked much speculation. Rizzio's rapid rise to power, fame, and fortune did not sit well with everyone, including the queen's own husband, Henry, Lord Darnley—whom, ironically, Rizzio had encouraged Mary to wed. Darnley had aspirations to be the undisputed monarch of Scotland, even over Mary, the lawful queen. Meanwhile, rumors were spreading that Rizzio and Mary were having an affair, probably started by nobles who wanted to drive a bigger wedge between Darnley and Mary.

Incensed by the alleged adultery, Darnley decided to take drastic action. Aligning himself with a group of friends that included Protestants (Scotland at the time was still firmly Roman Catholic in its outlook and laws), they entered the Palace of Holyroodhouse in Edinburgh on March 9, 1566, and demanded that she turn Rizzio over to them. Rizzio, ever the gallant courtier, bravely hid behind her, and she refused. When she was then held at gunpoint, she relented, and Rizzio was given over to the conspirators. It was said that he was stabbed fifty-six times, then thrown down the main staircase of the palace, looted for finery and jewels, and buried within a few hours.

Queen Mary later ordered that he be reburied in the sepulcher of the Kings of Scotland. This was a bad move, politically speaking, for Rizzio had no right to be interred there, and it confirmed for many that the two had been having a most improper relationship. Even Henry IV of France is said to have hinted that Mary (who was quite pregnant at the time of the murder) might have been carrying Rizzio's child. Indeed, after the boy was born (he would grow up to be King James I of England, of the famous Bible version), Henry remarked that he hoped the child was not "David the fiddler's son."

Mary was able to escape from the palace soon after, convincing Darnley to abandon the conspirators; the two fled on horseback. She rallied her supporters and returned a little over a week later to rout those conspirators and send them fleeing for sanctuary in England. Rizzio was given his elaborate state funeral afterward.

As for Darnley, while he was able to obtain an official pardon for his actions, she never trusted him again, and he would be dead within a year. Early on the morning of February 10, 1567, his body and that of his servant were found outside in the gardens of Kirk o' Field, Edinburgh, where he had been staying; he was only twenty-two years old. He was wearing just a nightshirt, which may mean that he had been trying to get away quickly. A gunpowder explosion had rocked the house earlier that night. It may well be that Darnley was fleeing from an assassination attempt and didn't make it too far. Some accounts relate that he and his servant had been strangled, the explosion being used as a cover to do it, but they may have died from the explosion itself. Suspects included the Earl of Bothwell (who would later force Queen Mary into marriage) and even the queen herself.

The violent death of one unfortunate musician set in motion a chain of events that would end in 1587 with Mary's own execution by Queen Elizabeth I for conspiring against the English crown. That in turn inspired Philip II of Spain to launch his Armada against England in 1588, which was thrashed by the English and the elements, humbling Spain and opening the way for England to become a major power in Europe and the New World.

Do North Americans speak English today due to the fate of one little Italian singer? One can but wonder.

Thomas Morley (1557/58–1602)

I spy with my little eye

Morley was one of the many Elizabethan composers who flourished at the end of Queen Elizabeth I's reign. This was also the age that saw the rise of poets like Philip Sydney and playwrights such as Christopher Marlowe (himself murdered horribly with a dagger through the eye) and William Shakespeare (you might have heard of him). Indeed, Morley may have been a friend of Shakespeare's, providing the music to Shakespeare's song "It was a Lover and His Lass," from *As You Like It*. While it's possible, we don't know for certain if his setting was ever performed during the play in Shakespeare's time.

Born in Norwich at the beginning of Elizabeth's reign, he was the son of a brewer. He showed great aptitude for music, eventually studying for his bachelor's degree (the title was quite a big deal back then) at Oxford. He was appointed as organist of St. Paul's Cathedral in London, made a Gentleman of the Queen's Royal Chapel, and even obtained a monopoly on the printing of music near the end of his life. He is often credited with introducing, or at least popularizing, the madrigal in England—the genre had originated in Italy. His most famous contribution was *The Triumphs of Oriana*, a 1601 collection of madrigals composed in honor of Queen Elizabeth I. It includes works by Morley and more than twenty other composers.

He also had a more secretive side. It seems that Morley, like other musicians and poets of the time (including Marlowe), was employed by the government for acts of espionage. Elizabeth's England was a dangerous place, with spies and plots abounding. Many Catholics wanted the Protestant Queen to be assassinated, and her spies were engaged constantly in uncovering these plots, some real, some imagined (the whole issue with Mary Queen of Scots and her alleged plots against Elizabeth is a very good example). Artists and musicians were introduced into this paranoid world, as they traveled frequently to play at foreign courts and could be used as eyes and ears to gain information. They could also travel around England, staying in homes and keeping an open ear for any evidence of plots and treason.

Apparently, Morley once got caught out. In a letter dated October 3, 1591, from the double agent Charles Paget to Thomas Phellippes, secretary to Elizabeth's spymaster Sir Francis Walsingham, we read (with all of those delicious sixteenth-century spellings):

Ther is one Morley that playeth on the organes in poules [St. Paul's] that was with me in my house. He seemed here to be a good Catholicke and was reconsiled, but notwith-standing suspecting his behaviour I enter-cepted letters that Mr. Nowell [possibly the Dean of St Paul's or Henry Nowell, a courtier] wrote to him Wherby I discovered enoughe to have hanged him. Nevertheles he shewing with teares great repentaunce, and asking on his knees forgiveness, I was content to let him goe.

Phellippes's draft reply confirms Morley's activity:

It is true that Morley the singing man employeth himself in that kind of service and hath browht diverse into danger.

It's not quite clear what Morley was doing, beyond seeking to uncover Catholic plots. He certainly didn't comport himself with any Bond-like bravery when he was found out. There are some suspicions that Morley himself may have been secretly Catholic (as was his teacher, the great William Byrd) but nevertheless loyal to Queen Elizabeth. In this case, he would have been a Catholic pretending to be a Protestant pretending to be a Catholic, acting against Catholic plots in the service of a Protestant queen. There's one for Ian Fleming!

John Bull (1562/63–1628)

A master of the organ—his own, anyway

Bull was an exceptional keyboardist who wrote numerous virtuoso pieces for the virginal, a small English harpsichord. Like a number of other artistic talents of his time, he may have been Roman Catholic in his sym-pathies. He may also have served Queen Elizabeth I on espionage mis-sions, like Morley, but it isn't certain. In any case, trouble seemed to follow him. George Abbot, Archbishop of Canterbury, wrote of him in 1613, "the man hath more music than honesty," an observation that seems to be fairly accurate. For all of his talent and skill, John Bull had a number of run-ins with the law that led to him fleeing from England.

He is on record as having been robbed in 1592, and for being quite poor. But his bigger problems came about because of his philandering ways and a breaking-and-entering charge. In 1597 he was elected as Public Reader in music at Gresham College, London, to be paid the amount of £50 a year, a nice sum in those days. One requirement was that such readers had to live in a certain Gresham House. Bull had a problem, in that the rooms assigned to him were still occupied by a previous tenant. Afraid of losing his appointment, he went with a mason and broke down brickwork to gain access to the portion of the house assigned to him. Needless to say, this didn't go over well. Actions were filed against him in the Star Chamber, a court of law based at Westminster Palace, which sounds way more cool than it probably was, but the court's decision is not preserved.

In 1607 he was discovered to have gotten a young woman, Elizabeth Walter, pregnant and was forced to marry her. He also had to resign from his duties at Gresham and seek employment elsewhere.

Eventually his various troubles forced him to leave England permanently in 1613, apparently quickly and in secret. It seems he was still knocking up young ladies and faced charges of adultery from George Abbot. He fled to Flanders and remained there for the rest of his life. Some details are provided by William Trumbull, who was the English envoy to the area:

> Bull did not leave your Majesties service for any wrong done unto him, or for matter of religion, under which fained pretext he now sought to wrong the reputation of your Majesties justice, but did in that dishonest matter steal out of England through the guilt of a corrupt conscience, to escape the punishment, which notoriously he had deserved, and was designed to have been inflicted on him by the hand of justice, for his incontinence, fornication, adultery, and other grievous crimes.

Indeed, Abbot, who had questioned his honesty, also noted that Bull "is as famous for marring of virginity as he is for fingering of organs and virginals." Oh, the possibilities for punning in that sentence!

It seems Bull claimed that he fled England due to religious persecution; authorities had evidence of him being a Catholic and of his refusal to acknowledge King James I as the head of the English Church.

Strangely, he neither confirmed nor denied the charges. In any case, he was never extradited back to England.

He may have learned a bit of a lesson and been less of a troublemaker in Antwerp, eventually finding new employment as a musician and organist and living out his days in relative peace. Or at least he kept his philandering better hidden.

Carlo Gesualdo (1566–1613)

Sticking the knife in and turning it II

Gesualdo is famous for two things: writing very odd music and being the most famous composer-murderer in history. He was the Prince of Venosa and Count of Conza, and a gifted composer and lute player. He seems to have suffered from depression, and this affliction may have been reflected in many of his works.

Gesualdo married his first cousin, Donna Maria d'Avalos, in 1586. She was also of noble birth, being the daughter of the Marquis of Pescara. Their marriage was presumably not all that happy, for in less than two years, she was having an affair with Fabrizio Carafa, Duke of Andria; with a name like "Fabrizio," he must have been the Fabio of his time! Or maybe Gesualdo just sucked as a husband.

In any case, they successfully kept their affair secret from Gesualdo for some time, even though, as is often the case in these things, many others around them seemed to know about it. Unfortunately for the lovers, the proverbial chickens came home to roost in October 1590 at the Palazzo San Severo in Naples.

Returning to the palace earlier than expected from a hunting trip, Gesualdo caught them in a rather compromising position (we don't know exactly which one). Enraged, he didn't just kill them; with the help of servants, he stabbed both of them with a sword multiple times. He killed his wife first, and then, forcing Fabrizio to don her nightshirt, he killed her lover second, shooting him in the head with a pistol to be sure.

The thing about all of this is that, being a nobleman, Gesualdo was immune from any official prosecution—it's always good to be stinking rich and have family connections! However, he knew that his life was still in danger from members of his victims' families seeking revenge. So he fled to the castle that was his namesake—Gesualdo, that is—for safety.

Such a lurid tale spread across the land at a rapid pace, becoming the tabloid sensation of its day. People loved a good bloody tale as much then as now. Rumors circulated that he also murdered his infant son by Maria, swinging him about wildly until the child was dead, because he suspected him of being Fabrizio's. But why stop there? More grotesque stories soon appeared: that he mutilated their genitalia, that an insane monk violated Donna Maria's corpse, and that Gesualdo placed their bloody bodies in front of the palace in a kind of perverse public display. He is said to have also murdered Donna Maria's father after the latter sought vengeance for her death. This was unlikely, though, as Gesualdo hired a whole team of men-at-arms as body-guards to prevent revenge-seekers from getting anywhere near him.

Gesualdo never stood trial for the two murders he definitely did commit. He remarried in 1594 and is said to have beaten his new wife, though thankfully for her, his murderous impulses did not return.

In 1603, two women from his household were tried for witchcraft and confessed after being tortured, adding that he had taken part in their activities. They were imprisoned, but again, it seems he escaped punishment.

He did seem to suffer guilt from his actions toward the end of his life and ordered himself to be beaten every day. He endured this flagellation to drive out his demons and tried to obtain holy relics, such as skeletal remains, that he hoped would cure him of his deteriorating mental condition. The poems to his musical works, many of which were likely written by him, are revealing for their images of pain; they may well have been autobiographical. While mostly concerned with the hurtfulness of love, there is darkness in them that betrays much deeper personal torments. In 1611's madrigal *Poichè l'avida sete* ("Since the insatiable thirst"), we read:

> Since the insatiable thirst
> You have for my sad and tearful humor
> Is not yet quenched, o pitiless heart,
> Let my blood quench it,
> For now it will pour out from my pierced breast
> A river of sorrow

In *Se la mia morte brami* ("If you long for my death"), also from 1611, he declares:

> If you long for my death,
> Cruel one, happily shall I die,
> And after death shall still adore you alone
> But if you want me to stop loving you,
> Alas, if I even think of such a thing,
> Grief kills me and my soul takes flight.

Death is a constant theme, as in *Moro, lasso, al mio duolo* ("I am dying, alas, of sorrow"):

> I am dying, alas, of sorrow.
> And the one who might save me,
> Alas, is killing me and will not help me.
> O sad fate,
> The one who might save me, alas, is bringing about my death.

Are these the words of a man expressing remorse? It is certainly possible. These later madrigals also contain some texts expressing happiness, though they seem muted by comparison to the excessive gloom of the majority of the works surrounding them. The music for these later pieces is remarkable for its experimental harmonies and progressions, quite unlike anything else at the time.

Gesualdo died in 1613, and his second wife, Eleonora, was whispered to be responsible. I doubt that anyone would blame her.

Tobias Hume (*ca.* 1569–1645)

Soldier of Fortune

Captain Tobias Hume was a peculiar eccentric—okay, he was rather weird—a long-lived fellow who saw the reigns of Elizabeth I, James I, and Charles I. Undoubtedly a virtuoso on the viol (rather like an early version of the cello, though they are not technically related), he was also a soldier of fortune who traveled widely across Europe in the service of various monarchs and factions. He was something of a master of flowery speech, declaring of himself:

> I doe not studie Eloquence, or professe Musicke, although I doe love Sense, and affect Harmony: My Profession being, as my Education hath beene, Armes, the onely effeminate part of me, hath beene Musicke; which in mee hath beene alwayes Generous, because never Mercenarie.

He championed the viol as being superior to the lute and published two collections of music, both with colorful names: *The First Part of Ayres or Musicall Humors* (1605) and *Captain Humes Poeticall Musicke* (1607). One piece, "An Invention for Two to Play upone one Viole," does indeed require two players, each with a bow. The smaller musician is to sit in the lap of the larger one so that both play one instrument. Apparently it can be done.

Among Hume's employers were the King of Sweden and the Emperor of Russia, and he served in various battles and squabbles. He seems to have spent many years on the continent before returning to England in 1629. Once back in London, he applied to be admitted to the Charterhouse, a former priory that served as a kind of retirement home for men over the age of fifty "such as had been servants to the King's Majestie or could bring good testimony of their good behavior and soundness in religion."

Tobias didn't seem to take to retirement well, though, even with all that time to write his music. Ever the soldier, he was eager to get out into the field and fight again, though it seems that his mind was going by then. He petitioned Charles I to go on a mission for the King of Sweden, but was apparently turned down (in all likelihood, ignored), probably due to his age and his mental state.

He tried one more time in 1642, having a pamphlet printed wherein he entreated Parliament to allow him to lead an army into Ireland to put down a Catholic rebellion. Entitled *The True Petition of Colonel Hume* (he gave himself a promotion), it makes clear that his grasp on reality was getting looser all the time. He writes:

> I do humbly intreat to know why your Lordships do slight me, as if I were a fool or an ass. . . . I have pawned all my best clothes, and have now no good garment to wear. . . . I have not one penny to help me at this time to buy me bread, so that I am like to be starved for want of meat and drink, and did walk into the fields lately to gather snails in the netles, and brought a bag of them home to eat, and do now feed on them for want of other meat, to the great shame of this land and those that do not help me . . .

If given a navy, he declared, he would bring "twenty millions of money" back to the king. His plea went unheeded, and he died in Charterhouse on April 16, 1645, while the Civil War between Oliver Cromwell and Charles I raged.

Thomas Weelkes (1576–1623)

I drink, therefore I am

Weelkes was a noted composer of madrigals whose works are still performed frequently by madrigal enthusiasts today. His church anthems are also highly regarded. Like Morley, who was his friend when he was a young man, he took his bachelor's degree in music in 1602 from Oxford and moved on to a permanent position at Chichester Cathedral.

Weelkes appears to have lived a fairly unassuming life until he was in his thirties. He was apparently quite fond of drink, a love that gradually increased as he got older. Naturally, this led to some problems with his employer. He was noted for unauthorized and unexplained absences from the cathedral as early as 1609, but by 1613, there is a disapproving record of his drunkenness. By 1616 his behavior was brought to the Bishop's attention, and it was mentioned that he was "noted and famed for a common drunckard and notorious swearer & blasphemer."

The Dean and Chapter eventually dismissed him for being drunk at the organ and swearing during the service—what an experience *that* must have been!

He convinced them that he would mend his ways, for he was reinstated and kept the position until his death. He soon lapsed, however, being reported once again in 1619 for the same behavior:

> Dyvers tymes & very often come so disguised eyther from the Taverne or Ale house into the quire as is muche to be lamented, for in these humoures he will bothe curse & sweare most dreadfully, & so profane the service of God . . . and though he hath bene often tymes admonished . . . to refrayne theis humors and reforme hym selfe, yett he daylye continuse the same, & is rather worse than better therein.

It doesn't seem quite so bad when it's written in such language, does it? Somehow he managed to hold on to his employment in spite of these many offenses; he either had sympathetic employers or was a good bluffer.

Alfonso Fontanelli (1557–1622)

Here we go with the whole wife-killing thing again

Fontanelli, while technically a "Renaissance" composer, nevertheless embraced the evolving musical styles toward the end of his life; there's a lot of overlap in successive musical eras, and aggravation, since we tend to like things in nice neat packages. When a composer straddles more than one era, it makes it trickier to classify the style. We will encounter this issue again in the Baroque chapter.

A skilled madrigalist, Fontanelli was born in northern Italy, and like so many composers, moved around from court to court, also acting in a diplomatic fashion on various occasions. His travels brought him into contact with the notorious Gesualdo, and the two traveled together for a time around Italy.

Maybe it was the association with Gesualdo, maybe it was overly strong Italian grappa, maybe it was heatstroke, but at some point Fontanelli acquired Gesualdo's murderous impulses. In 1601 he discovered that his wife, Maria, was having an affair. However, unlike Gesualdo, he spared his wife and "only" murdered her lover.

He also seems to have suffered consequences, at least initially. If he had hoped that the murder would somehow go unnoticed, he was seriously mistaken. Banished from his patron's lands and stripped of all of his possessions, he found a new home as a butler to Cardinal Alessandro d'Este—interestingly, the younger brother of Duke Cesare, who had banished him. Apparently the cardinal didn't give a fig about murder and overlooked the whole thing. While living at the cardinal's palace, Fontanelli hosted popular Thursday evening musical gatherings and composed an important collection of madrigals.

He ended his life, as was oddly common for these criminals, as a priest, and even more strangely, he died as the result of an insect bite that became infected shortly thereafter. Maybe it was divine judgment. Maybe he was allergic.

Orlando Gibbons (1583–1625)

Brain trust

Gibbons was a short-lived but very talented musician and composer, famous for his works for virginals, organ, and choir. Born into the "Golden Age" of Elizabethan England, he eventually served King James and was the organist at Westminster Abbey. All was going reasonably well for him, when he died suddenly in June 1625. There was some fear that he was a victim of plague, but it seems that stroke was the cause. He merits an inclusion here for the extensive autopsy report preserved in Britain's National Archives. It goes into some detail and is rather gruesome, which makes it perfect to quote at length:

> In the time of his late and sudden sickness, which we found in the beginning lethargical, or a profound sleep; out of which, we could

never recover him, neither by inward nor outward medicines, & then instantly he fell in most strong, & sharp convulsions; which did wring his mouth up to his ears, & his eyes were distorted, as though they would have been thrust out of his head & then suddenly he lost both speech, sight and hearing, & so grew apoplectical & lost the whole motion of every part of his body, & so died.

Death wasn't the end, however. Things were about to get weirder:

Then here upon (his death being so sudden) rumours were cast out that he did die of the plague, whereupon we . . . caused his body to be searched by certain women that were sworn to deliver the truth, who did affirm that they never saw a fairer corpse. Yet notwithstanding we to give full satisfaction to all did cause the skull to be opened in our presence & we carefully viewed the body, which we found also to be very clean without any show or spot of any contagious matter.

But just when they thought they were in the clear:

In the brain we found the whole & sole cause of his sickness namely a great admirable blackness & syderation in the outside of the brain. Within the brain (being opened) there did issue out abundance of water intermixed with blood & this we affirm to be the only cause of his sudden death.

Wow. I suppose they had to be thorough, but "too much information" comes to mind. He was buried hastily at Canterbury for unknown reasons, where a monument to him was also placed in the cathedral. The suddenness of the whole thing came as quite a shock to his friends, but nothing more seems to have been said about the death, leaving it all rather suspicious.

4

The Baroque Era

"Baroque" is actually a slightly derogatory term, originally meaning a "rough or imperfect pearl." In the past it was used to describe art and architecture that were overly ornate, even a bit garish and grotesque.

However, it also refers to a period of music (and art) from the early seventeenth to the mid-eighteenth century, which many consider to be the finest in the history of classical music. It was not a term normally used by the composers of that time, and one of its first appearances was in a negative review of an opera by the eighteenth-century Frenchman Jean-Philippe Rameau. From our contemporary perspective, however, the composers who wrote during these decades form a veritable who's who list of greats: Bach, Handel, Vivaldi, Scarlatti, Pachelbel, Telemann, Monteverdi, and more. Even non-specialists have heard of most of them. Collectively, these fellows have sold untold millions of recordings and concert tickets over the years. To the dismay of music historians and purists, their music also fills countless relaxation CDs.

Music from this era is among the most popular with modern listeners and is often the first introduction for many to the world of classical music, given its great beauty and sheer listenability. Detractors sometimes criticize the repertoire for a repetitive sound or sameness to many pieces. I am reminded of the quip made by a college teacher of mine about a composer who wrote "music by the yard." It is true that sometimes lesser-known Baroque works can seem more like craft than art, but this is precisely why they are lesser known. Those pieces actually *were* works-for-hire, and might have been intended only as background music for a single occasion (a wedding, a party, a coronation, etc.), after which they were shelved and forgotten. The composers who wrote them moved on to other projects, and their B-grade pieces were left to be discovered by musicologists in the nineteenth and twentieth centuries, some of whom probably attached more importance to these works than their own composers did.

By contrast, the masterpieces by Bach, Handel, and others are now thought to be among the greatest glories of Western music history, but even these were sometimes forgotten for decades after their composers' deaths. Bach's music was largely ignored for the remainder of the century; Mozart and Beethoven were said to have admired it, but they did little to popularize it. This sad situation continued until Felix Mendelssohn conducted Bach's *St. Matthew Passion* in 1829 and re-ignited the interest of both the music-loving public and other composers. Handel fared somewhat better in the fame department after his death; no less a composer than Beethoven wrote variations on one of Handel's works in 1797, and Haydn is said to have wept in joy during a performance of the *Messiah*, proclaiming Handel to be the master of them all.

So, read on and see some of the scandalous stories behind the delicious music. And there will be no miserable, overused puns like "going for Baroque" or "if it ain't Baroque, don't fix it." In fact, it's rather appalling how many times these have shown up as album or concert titles over the years. It needs to stop.

Giulio Caccini (1551–1618)

A snitch in time

Caccini, though born at the height of the Renaissance, is more often connected with the emerging Baroque style of the early seventeenth century. As we saw in the previous chapter, there is a lot of overlap between these eras, so there is some confusion and irritation as to how to classify composers. One sometimes simply has to make a call as to where to place a given composer historically—and then end up defending it from the inevitable criticisms of musicologists in tweed jackets.

Back to Caccini. He was a gifted tenor who was influential in the development of the new Baroque style that embraced a different sound than what had been common during the Renaissance. An important feature was the use of solo vocal lines of great emotional depth, accompanied by simpler harmonic chords. This contrasted sharply with the rich, polyphonic music of the Renaissance, with its complex, interweaving melody lines that had their own identities but blended together in dazzling ways. Indeed, it was those innovations in early seventeenth-century Italy that laid the foundations for the standards of modern music theory and composition. Most music students today begin by studying theory that was basically developed at this time.

Giulio was important and he knew it, claiming to have invented a new kind of music. He was also not above spreading news of scandal or stabbing others in the back if he thought he could advance himself. He was able to have some people squeezed out of positions of importance and even tried to head off rivals by having his own works published first. One example of his quest for the musical finish line had bloody consequences: he had learned of an affair between a young noble woman, Eleonora de Medici, and her poet lover, Bernardino Antinori. Eleonora's husband, Don Pietro de' Medici, was a nasty, evil little man who didn't care for her at all and doted on his own mistresses instead—the old double standard.

Caccini, being rather nasty himself, learned of this and saw a way to get in good with Francesco I de' Medici, the Grand Duke of Tuscany—and a very wealthy potential patron—namely, to squeal. Caccini undoubtedly thought that this false show of loyalty would benefit his career, but the consequences were far worse. On hearing about the affair, Francesco related the information to Pietro who, in his fury, apparently strangled the poor young lady with a dog leash (!) in July 1576, and had her lover imprisoned and eventually strangled as well. This was given the a-okay from Francesco. Eleonora's young son, Cosimino, died a few weeks later, allegedly of dysentery, but it's entirely possible that Pietro suspected that the boy was not his and committed another horrible crime.

Francesco attempted to cover the whole thing up by putting out an official story that Eleonora had died in a terrible accident, but few believed it. And these dreadful events came about simply because Caccini saw a way for potential personal advancement.

William Lawes (1602–1645)

A shot in the dark

After the Elizabethan and Jacobean (that's a fancy word for "during the time of King James") eras of music and literature, there was a marked dropping off in the amount of great music produced in England. This was due in part to the political turmoil that ravaged the country in the mid-seventeenth century. The English Civil War and the Commonwealth period that followed saw the rise of Puritanism and its dislike of certain music—and theater, and booze, and most celebrations. When said sticks-in-the-mud finally attained power after the war and executed James's son, King Charles I, fun was officially outlawed. Well, not really, but it must have seemed like it. However, Oliver Cromwell, the Puritan who assumed the status of "Lord Protector" of England (some would argue that he was a "king" in all but name), was known to be very fond of dancing and tobacco. Nevertheless, the theaters were closed and music certainly suffered; Cromwell obviously favored some sins over others.

William Lawes stands out as a shining musical example in those chaotic times. Charles was a talented musician himself, and he and Lawes may have played music together from the 1620s, when Lawes's teacher directed a group of musicians in the employ of then-prince Charles. In 1635, now-king Charles appointed Lawes to the somewhat snooty-sounding position of "musician in ordinary for lutes and voices," a fancy title for one of the king's personal musicians. Composing both religious and secular music for the king, Lawes became highly regarded in London and beyond. He also wrote a significant amount of music for the stage.

Lawes was an ardent royalist, and when Charles came into conflict with Parliament and the civil war began, Lawes enlisted in the army to fight for his king. Charles firmly believed that he ruled by the will of God and was answerable to no one: not Parliament, not the people, and certainly not the no-fun Puritans. This pig-headed position was known as divine right (i.e., that the monarch is appointed by God to rule and can do so unquestioned). It rubbed more than a few people the wrong way, especially in England, where the concept of the monarch ruling by consent of the governed had existed in some form since the days of the Magna Carta in 1215.

For his loyalty, Lawes was given a position in the King's Life Guards, which, by the way, was not set up to protect the king while he went swimming. Maybe there's a television show concept in this: featuring well-toned royal guards running in slow motion across a beach in southern England wearing full seventeenth-century finery, while viol consort music plays—maybe not.

This was supposed to be an honorary position to keep Lawes out of danger. However, in spite of this precaution, a Parliamentarian soldier "casually shot" and killed Lawes, probably during the defeat and rout of Royalist forces at the Battle of Rowton Heath (near the city of Chester) on September 24, 1645. The conflict was chaotic; Lawes was likely killed by incidental crossfire and never saw it coming. Charles was deeply saddened at the loss; as a later writer noted:

> Hearing of the death of his deare servant William Lawes, he had a particular Mourning for him when dead, whom he loved when living, and commonly called the Father of Musick.

Because the English could never resist a good pun, the royalist Thomas Jordan wrote in an epitaph, "Will. Lawes was slain by such whose *wills* were *laws*."

Alessandro Poglietti (early seventeenth century–1683)

A blast from the past

Poglietti was a composer and organist important for his keyboard works. Though he was Italian, he moved to Vienna by 1661 and from then until his death held the position of court organist to the Holy Roman Emperor Leopold I, who honored him with titles and wealth. He inherited estates, and the pope also bestowed a papal knighthood on him; he must have impressed the higher-ups.

His keyboard pieces were frequently early examples of program music—that is, they represented other things in sound. This was a practice that would not become truly popular until the nineteenth century; it consists of a musical work that has a separate narrative, conveyed by the music over the course of one or more pieces. Poglietti's works invite the listener to envision other things: nightingales, hens, roosters, and even a Hungarian Protestant rebellion from 1671.

Alessandro's inclusion here is due to his dramatic death in July 1683, in Vienna. The Ottoman Turks launched a siege against the city, having long viewed it as the key to controlling the region. It was to be one of the last major assaults that the Ottomans would make on Western Europe, though they didn't know that at the time, of course. Their army consisted of an astonishing 150,000 men, and things looked bleak for Vienna, which had only about 16,000 men capable of fighting. Without going into a long-winded history lesson, we can say that Vienna held out, and the subsequent battle (with reinforcements) routed the Turks in what was surely a humiliating defeat. But for a few months before that, the Ottomans methodically pounded the city, trying to wear down its thick walls with their three hundred cannons. Their initial preferred strategy was to dig tunnels underneath the city walls and blow them up, weakening the foundations.

Poor Poglietti was a victim of one of these methods, either obliterated by cannon fire or in the wrong vicinity when an underground explosion hit. He didn't live to see the triumph of the city he'd called home for more than twenty years.

Jean-Baptiste Lully (1632–1687)
Going out with a bang

Lully was noted for his considerable amount of excellent instrumental and ballet music in the service to the rather decadent French "Sun King," Louis XIV. He became very wealthy in the king's service and apparently liked to lord it over his rivals. He did everything he could to hinder them, which led to resentment, even hatred. He had quite a temper, and it was said that he broke violins on the backs of players if he didn't like their playing. Nevertheless, his music was very popular, and he collaborated with the great playwright Molière, with whom he produced several *comédies-ballets*—hybrid works combining music and theater—though the two had a falling out in 1671.

In January 1687, he was conducting a religious piece written to celebrate Louis XIV's recent recovery from an illness. He was using a long staff to hit the floor and keep time, a method common in the days before conductors used batons. He accidentally struck and injured his toe, ultimately causing an abscess. Without the benefit of modern disinfectants and the like, the wound turned gangrenous. Lully refused to have the toe amputated, possibly because he wanted to continue to dance, and the gangrene spread. By March, he was dying.

We do not know how he reacted to the idea of accidentally killing himself, but one story relates that on his deathbed he showed his usual defiance for the opinions of others, especially the Church. As a priest visited him, pressing him to renounce his sinful ways, Lully obliged and tossed the score for his final opera on the fire as a show of penitence for a life of un-Christian behavior. Satisfied, the priest granted him absolution and departed. A friend, horrified by what he had just witnessed, asked Lully why he had destroyed this last work. Lully smiled and explained that he had another copy.

Alessandro Stradella (1639–1682)

A narrow escape, more than once

A noted Italian composer, Stradella is famous for inventing the *concerto grosso* form (no, that doesn't mean the "gross concerto," but rather the "large" one) as well as composing a sizable quantity of vocal and sacred music.

But it's the juicy bits we're interested in here, and Al's life had plenty of them. As a young man in Rome in the late 1660s, he attempted to embezzle money from the Church, but he was discovered and had to flee the city for a while. More infamously, he was also an inveterate womanizer who left a trail of angry husbands, outraged family members, deflowered virgins, and shocked clergymen.

A popular story tells that Venetian nobleman Alvise Contarini once hired him to teach singing to his young mistress, Agnese Van Uffele; you can already guess where this is going. Unable to keep it in his pants, Stradella seduced her and fled with her to Turin. The furious noble sent two assassins after him. When they arrived, the hired killers discovered that Stradella had just finished composing a new oratorio and would be present at the performance the next day at St. Giovanni in Laterano. Seeing this as a stroke of luck, they plotted to kill him at the performance. However, after hearing the beauty of his music, they could not bring themselves to commit the act, and so instead confessed their plot to him, warning him that he needed to leave immediately. Hired assassins with hearts, who knew?

Stradella married Agnese in 1677 in an attempt to bring legitimacy to their relationship. Sources say that agents of Contarini attacked him in Turin and left him for dead, but he did not die and recovered from his wounds. Stradella moved to Genoa in 1678, but there is no further mention of Agnese, so their happiness must have been short-lived. He still had many enemies; in February 1682 a hired killer stabbed and murdered him, probably at the request of one Giovanni Battista Lomellino, who was envious of his popularity and perhaps his ways with the ladies.

John Abell (1653–after 1716/24)

An un-bear-able choice

Abell was a Scottish composer, singer, and lutenist. He found favor with the Catholic King James II of England, being listed as a member of the King's Private Musick—a kind of personal orchestra that played for private royal functions—and earning a considerable amount of money. His fortune was due to change, however, when James was made to abdicate due to his religious outlook and his belief in the divine right of kings. As we saw, this was one of the main reasons that Cromwell and his buddies chopped off the head of James's father, Charles I. Abell, a Catholic himself, was forced to flee England in 1688 with his monarch and take up residence with him in France, as part of a court-in-exile. James never did regain his throne and died in 1701.

While there, Abell was permitted to travel about the continent, and word of his skilled singing spread. When he reached the Polish court, however, he was in for a rather unpleasant surprise. Sir John Hawkins, in his *General History of the Science and Practice of Music* (London, 1776), records the incident vividly:

> Upon his arrival at Warsaw, the king having notice of it, sent for him to his court. Abell made some slight excuse to evade going, but upon being told that he had everything to fear from the king's resentment, he made an apology, and received a command to attend the king next day. Upon his arrival at the palace, he was seated in a chair in the middle of a spacious hall, and immediately drawn up to a great height; presently the king with his attendants appeared in a gallery opposite to him, and at the same instant a number of wild bears were turned in; the king bade him then choose whether he would sing or be let down among the bears: Abell chose the former, and declared afterwards that he never sang so well in his life.

Now that's a monarch who knew what he wanted! In any case, Abell survived the ordeal, left Poland (probably quite happily), and eventually sought permission to return to England, which was granted in 1699. He lived in England for a good number of years more, presumably having no further run-ins with hungry members of the Ursidae family.

Marin Marais (1656–1728)

A stone's throw

Marais is known to modern audiences from the popular French film *Tous le matins du monde*, a fictional biography that describes his troubled relationship with the reclusive and enigmatic composer Sainte-Colombe. He was portrayed by both Gérard Depardieu (as the older man) and his son, Guillaume Depardieu (as the younger one). Marais was a master of the bass viola de gamba and the principal composer of music for it in the early eighteenth century. Though surprisingly little is known of his life, he did father nineteen children, a feat that puts him in the same prolific hall of fame as his younger contemporary, Johann Sebastian Bach, who sired twenty children by two wives. Marais's wife, Catherine d'Amicourt, bore all nineteen of them, the poor dear. This was a remarkable achievement, given the dangers of childbirth in those days.

Speaking of medical risks, Marais was known for writing some unusual program music. Late in his life, he produced an amusing, if probably excruciating, example based on an actual experience he had endured. Found in his fifth book of *Pièces de Viole* (he wrote five such books, containing nearly six hundred pieces), it is called *Tableau de l'Opération de la Taille*, "Description of the Operation of the Stone," a musical depiction of the surgical removal of a bladder stone. Yes, a description of an eighteenth-century surgery, in musical form.

The work is annotated with a number of phrases as it progresses, to aid the performer in expressively interpreting each piece of music. These include such helpful comments as:

- "The appearance of the operating table"
- "Trembling at its sight"
- "Serious thoughts"

- "Knotting the silk restrains for arms and legs"
- "Here the incision is made"
- "The stone is drawn"
- "Blood flows"

Well, it's certainly a switch from *adagio*, *allegro*, and *andante*. One wonders if the musicians were supposed to make appropriate facial expressions at each step of the operation.

This was not the only time Marais ventured into the world of medical thematic programming. In his fourth book of viol pieces he wrote the colorful *Allemande L'Asthmatique*, which sought to simulate in music the wheezing and breathiness of an asthmatic episode. Marais was either something of a musical joker, or was maybe giving the world just a bit too much information about his private life.

Henry Purcell (1659–1695)

You'll catch your death out there

Purcell is rightly regarded as one of the greatest composers the green and pleasant land of England has ever produced, certainly the greatest since the Elizabethan and Jacobean eras. He wrote a large amount of music in his short life and showed promise to become even greater. Only thirty-five at the time of his death, he was at the height of his career. Had he lived, he might have even eclipsed that great German composer and naturalized English citizen Handel.

It is ironic that the popular story of his death, if true, is one of the silliest and most wasteful of tragic accidents that need not have happened at all. Like many a good Englishman throughout time, Henry was said to be rather fond of his drink and of socializing with his friends at the taverns and theaters. These boys' nights out apparently increasingly irritated his wife, but despite her attempts to curtail them, they continued.

Returning late from the theater one night, Henry arrived home to discover that he was locked out. His wife had given instructions to the servants not to let him in, no matter how he protested. She figured this would be a good lesson and would limit his future outings. Unfortunately, she was right. For whatever reason, Henry stayed out too long, and in the cold, damp weather that England is so well known for, he caught a chill that became a fever and worsened. He died on November 21, 1695. The remorse his wife must have felt is beyond comprehension.

Another less fanciful theory is that he died of tuberculosis unrelated to his socializing, an all-too-common killer in those times. Still another story circulated that he died of, or maybe was even murdered by, tainted chocolate; perhaps "Death by Chocolate" is not just a modern dessert phenomenon. Whatever the truth, he made and signed a will leaving everything to his wife (he apparently had forgiven her) on the very day he died, so he must have known that the end was coming soon.

However it happened, classical music was robbed of a singular genius who deserved more time in this world, not unlike Mozart nearly a century later. We can only wonder what both of them would have accomplished had they lived another thirty or forty years!

Antonio Vivaldi (1678–1741)

The Red Priest with a wandering eye

Dear old Tony, most famous for *The Four Seasons*, which incidentally are not salt, pepper, mustard, and vinegar, but rather four concertos in a larger collection of twelve. Known for writing at least one concerto for nearly every instrument known to humanity except the nose flute (and who knows, one may turn up someday), he has also been unfairly disparaged for a lack of originality. Stravinsky quipped that he is "greatly overrated—a dull fellow who could compose the same form so many times over."

Called the "Red Priest of Venice" because of his hair color, he wasn't exactly the model priest the Church was looking for. He was said to be perfectly willing to set aside priestly duties if a musical idea came to mind, even in mid-service! There are also reports that he may have suffered from asthma (now in doubt), and that he could thus be excused from having to celebrate mass because he simply didn't have the breath to intone all the chants and texts. Or it might just have been a good excuse for getting out of doing it.

Somehow he was offered a job in 1703 as the music teacher at the Conservatorio dell' Ospedale della Pietà, a school and home for (mostly) orphaned girls. A good-looking young priest, a school full of teenage girls eager to learn—this has all the makings of one of those bad 1970s European sex comedy films that used to show up on late-night American cable TV. Indeed, Vivaldi was in trouble more than once for behaviors that were, to put it mildly, not suited to his profession. In 1737, he was officially censured. He was known to travel frequently, and among his traveling companions were two half-sisters: one, Anna Giraud (or Girò), was a student of his, and the other, Paolina, was his "nurse." *Carry on, Vivaldi? Confessions of a Baroque Composer?*

Naturally, there was gossip about all of this, but Vivaldi denied that anything improper was happening. He continued to cut shrewd business deals to finance his extravagant and unpriestly lifestyle, making enemies along the way both inside and outside of the Church.

His greatest challenge, though, was the one that afflicted so many artists of all kinds over the centuries: changing tastes and a lack of desire, or even ability, to adapt. By 1741, his music was falling out of fashion, and he could no longer make the money he used to. As a result, he sold off many of his manuscripts to finance a move from Venice to Vienna. The exact reason why he chose this city is not clear, but Anna (with whom he was now openly involved) was an opera singer, and he might have moved there hoping to secure a position to write more operas at the court of Charles VI, bringing both of them well-paid work.

It was a good plan, but nothing came of it. Charles VI died shortly after Vivaldi's arrival in late June 1741, completely ruining his hopes. Vivaldi himself died mysteriously about a month later. The causes are still unknown but may have been some kind of internal infection. Rumors of murder seem unfounded, but no one knows for sure; with his large ego and monetary obsession, he had certainly angered many. Since he was impoverished at the time, he was buried in a pauper's grave. His work was largely forgotten—even the famous *Four Seasons*—until it was revived in the twentieth century.

Benedetto Marcello (1686–1739) and Rosanna Scalfi Marcello (*d.* 1742)

A class act

The sad story of Benedetto and Rosanna may not be of *Romeo and Juliet* proportions, but it does show the cruel way that courtly life, with its rigid social rules and class stratifications, could treat people in unfortunate situations in those earlier times. A noble who was part of Venice's government, Benedetto was a capable composer. He was a younger contemporary of Vivaldi, certainly influenced musically by his esteemed colleague. Rosanna Scalfi was said to be a talented gondola singer—yes, they were boating down the canals back in those days, too. She studied voice with Benedetto from about 1723. Legend says that he heard her singing in a gondola while he was at his window overlooking the Grand Canal and became enchanted with her. She went on to learn composition and became a capable composer in her own right, writing a set of twelve cantatas.

Regardless of how they met, their relationship blossomed and they were wed in a secret religious ceremony in May 1728. There was only one problem: the marriage was never given a civil ceremony, because marriage between a noble and a commoner was not generally permitted unless various legal hurdles were jumped.

Poor Benedetto died in 1739 of tuberculosis, a common enough killer of all classes in those days, and the marriage was declared illegal and null. Rosanna was thus ineligible to inherit his wealth and was left destitute. In 1742 she sued his brother, Alessandro Marcello, seeking financial support, but her suit was rejected, again on the grounds that she had no claim to any of the family's money. Though she was still performing at this time, it seems she died shortly after in poverty, rejected and forgotten.

Francesco Maria Veracini (1690–1768)

A lame excuse

The long-lived Veracini had a few notable mishaps that might have ended his life. The son of a pharmacist and undertaker (presumably if the drugs didn't work for his patients, his father had a back-up job), Veracini was a virtuoso violinist. His bowing technique even impressed the great Tartini, causing the latter to leave the vicinity and lock himself away to practice. Veracini was also noted for being arrogant and a bit eccentric. He traveled far and wide, eventually ending up in the service of the Prince Elector Friederich Augustus of Saxony. As is often the case, those musicians or composers already in the monarch's service resented anyone new coming in, especially someone as talented and conceited as he was.

He began to suspect plots against his life, and after a quarrel about the abilities of some of his German colleagues (which he thought were severely lacking), he took a very strange course of action. As recorded by Johann Mattheson, a printer:

> Moreover here in Dresden a distressing incident has happened to one of our great virtuosos a short while ago. It is, namely, Mr. Veracini, our world famous violinist (who) suddenly became mad and so delirious that he threw himself out of a second storey window on August 13th, 1722, and broke his foot in two places and (also) his hip, and is given little hope for regaining his good sense as well as for the healing of his body. The blame for such derangement of his understanding is due partly to his all-too-great application to music, partly to the reading of chemical (alchemical) writings in which he let himself get so involved that he finally could no longer sleep.

Apparently Veracini's devotion to the occult sciences was making him a bit loopy. Other accounts state that he leapt while fleeing from a fight, because he feared for his life. He may have thought that some desired to kill him out of jealousy for his musical talent. It seems that his arrogance had made him a bit paranoid. In any case, the accident gave him a limp for the rest of his days. He traveled again to London and had considerable success initially, but the failure of his opera *Roselinda* (based on Shakespeare's *As You Like It*) prompted him to leave London and return to Italy in 1745. The ship was wrecked on the crossing of the English Channel and two of his prized violins were lost, but he survived. Perhaps he thought it was an elaborate assassination plot.

Giuseppe Tartini (1692–1770)
The devil made him do it

Tartini was a superb violinist; he had studied at Padua and shown great promise. However, as seems to be a recurring theme among these young Italian composers, the young man soon got himself in trouble over a woman. Originally intending to enter the Franciscan Order and study for the priesthood, he instead secretly married Elizabetta Premazore, a fellow student and (to make things more complicated) a favorite of Cardinal Giorgio Cornaro, bishop of Padua. The cardinal was not pleased and immediately ordered Tartini's arrest. To make matters worse, Tartini's family was unhappy because of the young lady's inferior social class. He fled to Padua and, disguised as the friar he had intended to be, was given refuge in the monastery at Assisi (of St. Francis fame) in Umbria, north of Rome. The cardinal eventually cooled down and forgave Tartini, and he was able to return.

In the meantime, he had developed his violin skills to an astonishing degree. As with Paganini (we'll discuss him in the Romantic Era chapter), rumors circulated about Tartini's seemingly inhuman technical virtuosity and its presumed supernatural origin. In the nineteenth century, some said that he had six fingers on his left hand, which was the only way he could play his own very difficult works.

Tartini's most famous piece is his Sonata in G Minor: *Il trillo del Diavolo*, or "The Devil's Trill," composed in the later 1740s. The details surrounding its origin are rather macabre and fascinating. Tartini himself describes the setting:

One night I dreamt that I had made a bargain with the Devil for my soul. Everything went at my command—my noble servant anticipated every one of my wishes. Then the idea struck me to hand him my fiddle and to see what he could do with it. But how great was my astonishment when I heard him play with consummate skill a sonata of such exquisite beauty as surpassed the boldest flight of my imagination. I felt enraptured, transported, enchanted; my breath was taken away; and I awoke. Seizing my violin I tried to retain the sounds I had heard. But it was in vain. The piece I then composed, the Devil's Sonata, although the best I ever wrote, how far below the one I heard in my dream!

Tartini never had another such dream, and perhaps it's just as well. The piece is still regarded as incredibly difficult and virtuosic by modern violinists, and Tartini's reputation as one of the great violinists in classical music history is well assured. The fate of his immortal soul, however, is not known.

Jean-Marie Leclair (1697–1764)
Sticking the knife in and turning it III

A native of Lyons, Leclair was a skilled violinist who also wrote fine music for both violin and flute. Indeed, he was the first Frenchman to write violin concertos, taking a cue from Vivaldi's works, which had become popular in Paris. His skill on the violin ranks him alongside the leading Italian violinists of the day. Unfortunately for him, he is most often remembered today, if at all, because he was brutally murdered.

He traveled widely but by the 1750s was living in Paris. In 1758 his marriage ended, and for some odd reason Leclair chose to move to the Rue de Careme-Prenant, a bad neighborhood on the outskirts of Paris. Why? He surely had enough money and no real reason to do so. Maybe he wanted to try out the artistic life of squalor for himself, though it would be some decades before this fad really caught on. But for whatever reason, there he stayed, and there his life ended.

On the morning of October 23, 1764, his gardener found him lying in a pool of his own blood; he had been stabbed three times. The crime was never solved, though there are several suspects, including a disgruntled nephew now considered by many to be the most likely candidate, the gardener, and Leclair's ex-wife. After his death, she was entitled to auction his house and possessions to raise money, and no surprise, this is exactly what she did. In fairness, she did also see to it that his works were republished and that his unpublished music saw the light of day, saving it for future generations. But then again, maybe that was just to dispel the suspicion that undoubtedly lingered around her.

John Taylor (1703–1772)

Lights out

"Chevalier" Taylor (one of his preferred titles) was not a composer, but a doctor who, despite having legitimate training, comes off to modern readers as a self-promoting quack. He has the dubious distinction of botching eye operations on the two great giants of the Baroque, possibly killing one of them as a result. The son of an apothecary, he studied medicine and gained a position as eye doctor to King George II of England and others, whether through fraud, bluffing, or sheer nerve. He traveled widely in a coach painted with eyes to promote himself, and while in Leipzig in 1749 he met Johann Sebastian Bach, then in his sixties and suffering from failing eyesight. Bach consented to an operation to restore his sight, which didn't succeed. A second operation proved no better, and by then, Bach was totally blind.

Possibly as a result of these surgeries (infection and such), Bach's health began to deteriorate, he suffered a stroke, and within a year, he was dead. Was Taylor remorseful? Not that we can determine. He probably wasn't even aware that his work could have been a factor.

Back in England only a year later, he paid a visit to the other great master of the late Baroque era, George Frederic Handel. Handel's eyesight was also failing, though the cause is not certain. For reasons unknown—Taylor was already being denounced publicly as a quack—Handel also agreed to an operation, which was just as unsuccessful and his eyesight continued to deteriorate. While Handel would live for another eight years, it would be in darkness. He seems to have contacted Taylor for another operation a few years later, such was the magnitude of the man's ability to bluff in the face of criticism.

Bach and Handel have another curious connection—they were born in the same year, 1685. But despite their admiration for each other's works, they were destined never to meet. Bach once traveled to Halle (near Leipzig) to meet Handel, but missed him by a day.

There is some slight poetic justice to the story of this quack who wrecked the lives of our two finest Baroque composers: Taylor also went blind before his own death in 1772 (some say 1770).

Louis-Gabriel Guillemain (1705–1770)
Sticking the knife in and turning it far too many times

The French composer Guillemain lived in the transitional period between the Baroque and the Classical eras, the so-called Rococo or Galante era. Though little-known today, he was well regarded in his own time. From 1737, he was a *musicien ordinaire* to King Louis XV and was said to be one of the highest-paid musicians of the court, even performing in private concerts for the king and queen, though there is evidence that he may have suffered from stage fright when appearing in front of larger audiences and tried to avoid those situations.

As can happen to those of humbler backgrounds who quickly come into large incomes, he eventually gave himself over to an extravagant lifestyle and spent too much money, probably in an attempt to keep up with those around him who were wealthier. As his debts piled up he began drinking, heavier in his later years. He was able to keep ahead of troubles for some time, but there is a mystery surrounding his death. It is possible that his drinking killed him, but there were rumors of a far darker fate. Many believed that he had committed suicide by a dreadful, bloody death in which he stabbed himself fourteen times. The very thought of self-inflicting that kind of harm is staggering and horrifying.

Could he really have done this to himself in a fit of drunken madness, despondent over debts that he couldn't pay? Or was he savagely murdered by one of his many creditors?

While he was given a proper burial—which would tend to rule out suicide because committing suicide prevented one from being buried in hallowed ground—it was with great haste: on the day he died, in fact. It could be that this hasty action was an attempt to hide something, such as a murder or an illness. We will never know the truth, but the fact that this rumor exists at all says that some believed it. Given how difficult it is for awful secrets to be kept quiet, it's certainly possible that poor Louis-Gabriel went to his grave in a truly terrible way.

5

The Classical Era

While the whole of Western music has been labeled "classical" in modern designation, the actual "Classical era" in music history refers to a period from the later eighteenth century into the early nineteenth, between the Baroque and Romantic periods. Its giants were Haydn, Mozart, Beethoven, and sometimes Schubert, collectively known as the "First Viennese School" since they all lived and worked in and around Vienna at various times. Schubert, whom we will look at in the next chapter, is also considered an early Romantic. So the Classical era encompasses roughly 1750 to 1820 or 1830, depending on whom you consult. As is the case for all of these dates, we shouldn't assign arbitrary starts and cut-offs to artistic eras. Bearing that in mind, these are the years in which the four composers above wrote the majority of their work.

This musical style coincided with the rise of neo-Classicism in architecture (i.e., the resurrection of Greco-Roman styles); this is why you see so many Greek- and Roman-looking buildings in London, Paris, and Washington, DC, from that time. Also included in the package were Enlightenment philosophy, the beginnings of the scientific method, intense debate over political systems, and—as a result of that—the American and French Revolutions. Those last two were obviously not so great for King George III and the French aristocracy, but they did fuel democratic ideals and the creation of political systems that are still with us, for better and worse.

During this time, orchestral music started to become "bigger," longer, and more epic in scope. Even the orchestras themselves were increasing in size. The piano replaced the harpsichord as the keyboard instrument of choice—both for soloists and in groups—because it offered more range and volume, more of the "expression" that all those just-on-the-edge-of-Romanticism ears desired. Instruments like the clarinet appeared, to be followed by many new inventions and innovations in the nineteenth century. Classical music became quite "classical."

Frantisek Kotzwara (1730/31–1791)

All choked up

Known as František Kočvara in his native Prague, this fellow was a skilled double bass player and composer. He seems to have traveled considerably, finally finding a home in London where his works were published from the 1770s. He left little of note except one popular composition, *The Battle of Prague*. More notable is the manner of his death, which was quite shocking for the time and hints at some very dark fetishes indeed.

It seems that on September 2, 1791, he visited a prostitute, one Susannah Hill, at her lodgings in Westminster; he had a history of visiting such ladies in his travels. After dinner and alcohol, he paid her two shillings and bluntly asked her to castrate him. Exactly what was in those drinks, we don't know. Anyway, she refused but didn't want to lose his money, so she agreed when he asked her instead to fix a noose about his neck and tie the other end to a doorknob, so that he might be partially strangled while they engaged in the act. At some point, however, things went wrong and he died in one of the first recorded cases of erotic asphyxiation. Poor Susannah was brought to trial on a murder charge but was acquitted; the jury believed her when she insisted that it was an accident.

The account was considered too scandalous to report to the Georgian public, and the judge ordered the trial details to be destroyed. Naturally, they soon found the light of day anyway, since who could resist a story like this? A few years later in 1797, a pamphlet with the inventive title of *Modern Propensities; or, An Essay on the Art of Strangling* circulated. It depicted a drawing of the young lady and Kotzwara on the front cover, he with a noose about his neck and looking mightily pleased, she flashing an equally large smile as she puts the noose in place. This particular fetish survived into Victorian underground society, and respectable and wealthy gentlemen could secretly visit "Hanged Men's Clubs" to engage in hoped-for arousal by similar techniques. Needless to say, this sometimes also went horribly wrong, and the need to hush it all up must have been even greater than in the eighteenth century.

Franz Joseph Haydn (1732–1809)

Dude, where's my head?

"Papa" Haydn (as his friends and students knew him) lived a long, productive, happy, and secure life, being in the service of the same patron (the Hungarian Esterházy family) for most of his years. He was born when Handel and Bach were at the height of their creativity, outlived his younger friend Mozart by nearly eighteen years, and lived long enough to see the young Beethoven (his pupil) established as a great composer in his own right. Yes, his was a life of contentment, job security, and stability.

So why is he listed here? Well, the interesting thing is what happened after he died. Haydn was given a memorial with great honors in French-occupied Vienna on June 15, 1809, two weeks after his death. Mozart's Requiem was performed at the service, and it was apparently all very moving. He was interred in a churchyard near where he had lived. In 1820, Prince Esterházy ordered that his remains be exhumed and reburied in the parish church at Eisenstadt, which was done on November 7.

There was one slight problem, however: poor Haydn's head was missing. It had apparently been stolen a few days after his death by his friend and admirer Joseph Carl Rosenbaum and prison governor Johann Nepomuk Peter. Just thinking about how that must have been done is enough to turn the stomach. Indeed, Rosenbaum noted in his diary that as he entered his carriage after the decapitation, head in hand, the smell was so bad that he nearly vomited. They were devotees of the pseudo-science of phrenology, which we will discuss in more detail in Part II, and sought out the skulls of the famous and talented. After residing in private hands for many decades (it must have made a splendid conversation piece), Haydn's noggin was given to the Gesellschaft der Musikfreunde ("Society of the Friends of Music") in Vienna in 1895.

Needless to say, this was all a bit embarrassing for the establishment back in 1820. Rosenbaum sent a skull to the prince to be buried along with the body in the new location. A slight problem: it turned out afterward that this wasn't Haydn's head, which Rosenbaum had no intention of relinquishing. After acquiring it, the Friends of Music were destined to possess it until 1954, when it was finally reunited with its body after nearly 150 years. It's ironic that a man who lived such a placid life compared to many of his colleagues would have to endure such a strange and ghoulish drama after his death.

A few other unanswered questions remain: What did the Friends of Music actually *do* with the head for all of those years? Presumably it wasn't just on public display. And most chillingly, just whose skull rested with Haydn's body for 150 years? In case you're wondering, that second mystery skull still resides with the composer's body.

Johann Anton Fils (1733–1760)

Step into my parlor

The young Fils (or Filtz) was of German origin, having for a long time been thought to be a Bohemian (that's a Czech, not a free-living, rebellious young person). He was talented and prolific, producing no fewer than thirty-four symphonies and thirty concertos in his short life, as well as many other works. He had a wife, a young daughter, and an enviable and well-paid position as cellist to the electoral court at

Mannheim. Everything was going swimmingly, except that he died at the young age of twenty-six, narrowly missing admission to the 27 Club (see Part II).

The exact cause of death is not clear, but the strangest accounts say that it was due to his habit of eating live spiders, as one does. Presumably consuming them for health reasons, or perhaps as some bizarre delicacy, he is said to have remarked that they tasted like fresh strawberries. If the story is true (the eating, not the strawberry taste), perhaps some venomous arachnid ended his life. This seems a very nasty way to go, especially since it was self-inflicted.

Just remember to be wary of those new health food fads.

Johann Schobert (*ca.* 1735–1767)

Funny fungi

Schobert's exact birth year seems uncertain and has been listed as anywhere between 1720 and 1740, with a cautious consensus of 1735. Beginning in 1760 he was a harpsichordist in the service of the Prince de Conti in Paris. He had interactions with the Mozart family, specifically the father, Leopold, who reportedly said that his children could play Schobert's music with ease. When you consider that one of his children was young Wolfgang Amadeus, who was already composing by the age of four, his statement isn't quite as insulting as it first seems, though he probably meant it to be.

Actually, Wolfgang was fond of Schobert's work from childhood. However, papa Leopold also stated that "Schobert is not at all the man he is said to be—he flatters to one's face and is utterly false," so their relationship was certainly a bit complicated! Regardless, Wolfgang would teach his music for years, and he even quoted some of Schobert's melodies in his own works.

Yes, everything was going well enough for Johann and his family until a disastrous encounter with some of the local flora. He had picked some wild mushrooms, cooked them, and served them to his wife and child, as well as to himself. Apparently a local tavern keeper had warned him against doing this without proper knowledge, and he was right. The mushrooms were poisonous and killed all three of them, plus a servant and others. Mycology was not one of his strong points.

Josef Mysliveček (1737–1781)
The nose knows

Mysliveček, as his name implies, was a Czech composer of the transitional period between Baroque and Classical. Born in Prague, he eventually found his way to Italy, and to a decent amount of acclaim. His admirers included the young Mozart, who arranged one of his works for voice and piano. Indeed, the two became good friends and corresponded for years. His operas were well received, and he even acquired a pet name: *Il divino Boemo*, "the divine Bohemian," which sounds like the name of a contemporary hipster coffee shop or a vegan restaurant.

Like many composers who would come after him, he was doomed to the "been there, done that" fate; people simply grew tired of his music. Tastes and styles changed and he didn't keep up with the changes, or rather, just fell out of fashion. The money and fame dried up, and he died a pauper in Rome.

Something strange happened a short time before his death. During a surgery, his nose was burned off. Now, one probably would not elect to have this procedure done voluntarily, so there has to be a reason. Sources conflict, but there seem to be two possibilities. The first is that it happened accidentally during a treatment for syphilis, and that the intention was never to remove the nose. Why they were poking around in his nose to cure the pox is a mystery, though it may have been to remove growths, and it all got a bit carried away. It is also sometimes possible for the nose of a person with advanced syphilis simply to fall off on its own, so maybe they were poking around for some other reason and—oops!

Syphilis would be the scourge of many a tragic nineteenth-century composer living out the fantasy of the "Romantic life," as we shall see in the next chapter; maybe Josef just wanted to get a head start. He did have a reputation for promiscuity during his "Mozart years," so perhaps there is some truth to the idea.

The other theory is that the operation was an attempt to treat a dental infection he contracted after a coach accident (perhaps a door hit him in the mouth?) and had nothing at all to do with syphilis. Another source even suggests that he had bone cancer. Regardless of the cause, it seems that the nose removal was an unintended consequence, and it's perhaps just as well that he didn't live long afterward.

Jean-Baptiste Krumpholtz (1742–1790)

Cry me a river

Krumpholtz was a minor composer not well known nowadays, maybe because his last name sounds a bit like a Bavarian pastry. He was revered in his time as a skilled harpist, indeed one of the greatest of the later eighteenth century. He served in the employ of the Esterházys, a wealthy Hungarian noble family of ancient lineage who were great patrons of the arts. Haydn, who was also under their patronage, gave him lessons in composition during his stay. Eager to improve the structure and sound of his instrument, he was responsible for working on some new innovative designs for the harps of his time with Jean-Henri Naderman, a well-known harp maker.

His wife, Anne-Marie, was also a virtuoso harpist and had been his student. With the apparent thought that she could do better than poor Jean-Baptiste, Anne-Marie began an affair in 1788 with pianist and composer Jan Ladislav Dussek and allegedly ran off to London with him a year later. Dussek was eager to escape the dangers of revolutionary France, and taking refuge in England with someone else's young wife seemed an appealing alternative.

Dussek was apparently quite proud of his good looks, or at least his profile. When performing, he turned the direction of the piano by 90 degrees. Previously, pianists had faced the audience. But with this new configuration, audiences now viewed him in profile and thus were spared none of the thrill. Interestingly, the idea caught on and is still the pre-ferred positioning of pianists on stage to this day, regardless of how dash-ing (or not) their profiles may be. Dussek grew tired of Anne-Marie and abandoned her in 1792. He married the singer (and yet another harpist) Sophia Corri in that year but also left her by the century's end. He was a bit of a jerk.

Back to Jean-Baptiste: he was so despondent over the whole thing that he jumped into the frigid waters of the Seine in Paris in February 1790 and drowned or froze to death.

John Stafford Smith (1750–1836)

The god of wine and the wrath of grapes

Smith was an English composer, organist, and one of the first musicolo-gists. He had a keen interest in early music, which is rather amusing if you think about it, considering that music from his own time is often considered an important part of the early music repertoire today. Smith's interest lay in medieval and Renaissance music; he studied various man-uscripts and produced several editions, including songs from an old trouvère manuscript that sadly was destroyed by fire not long afterward. In 1779 he produced what is considered the first scholarly edition of early music to be printed in England, *A Collection of English Songs Composed about the year 1500. Taken from MSS. of the same age.*

Smith's other big claim to fame is the composition of the song "To Anacreon in Heaven" for a gentlemen's club, the Anacreontic Society, to which he belonged and which consisted of many amateur musicians devoted to the promotion of music, along with a celebration of good drink. Anacreon was a sixth-century BCE Greek poet whose words cel-ebrated the stereotypical wine, women, and song. You may have heard this little ditty. The words of the first verse are:

> To Anacreon in Heav'n, where he sat in full Glee,
> A few Sons of Harmony sent a Petition,
> That He their Inspirer and Patron wou'd be;

When this Answer arriv'd from the jolly old Grecian
"Voice, Fiddle, and Flute,
No longer be mute,
I'll lend you my Name and inspire you to boot,
And, besides, I'll instruct you like me, to entwine
The Myrtle of Venus with Bacchus's Vine."

Doesn't ring a bell? This tune was later used by Francis Scott Key for his poem "Defence of Fort McHenry" during the War of 1812. It was later retitled "The Star-Spangled Banner." Yes, the American National Anthem (officially designated in 1931) is a tune that was originally a British drinking song. Enjoy thinking about that for a while.

Smith lived a long life without conflict or troubles. At his death, his remarkable and vast library, which likely contained many priceless volumes (2,191 devoted to music, over 500 of which were manuscripts), was passed to his daughter, who was declared insane in 1844. And what happened to these precious works? Infuriatingly, they were not acquired by a university, such as Oxford or Cambridge, nor were they bought by the British Library. The books were auctioned off to private collectors, and many were undoubtedly lost forever over the next century. No adequate catalog of the collection was even made.

There was one ironic twist to the end of his long life: he died at the advanced age of eighty-six, not from old age or illness, but allegedly by choking on a grape pip which had become stuck in his windpipe. You may recall that a similar tale had long been told about the death of Anacreon himself, so Smith was in good company. It seems that Bacchus's vine did him in after all.

Wolfgang Amadeus Mozart (1756–1791)

An end shrouded in mystery

Dearly beloved Mozart, along with Beethoven, is probably the most famous composer in history. Even people who know nothing about classical music have heard of him, and some of them even know how to pronounce his name. His story is irresistible: a young musical prodigy gifted beyond all belief, adored by the courts of Europe as a boy, but as he grows up he is increasingly ignored and neglected, has family and financial problems, turns to drink, burns out, and dies at the age of thirty-five, buried in a pauper's grave. He could be a model for the Romantics that followed.

Someone should make a movie based on his life, or at least a play.

In reality, some of these biographical details are not as true as many believe. He was deeply devoted to his wife and father, and his money troubles had much to do with his wife's poor health and the need to maintain a fine wardrobe to impress potential patrons. The legend of his being buried in an unmarked grave for the poor is not entirely correct either. In 1783 the Emperor Joseph II declared that cemeteries in Vienna's city limits were to be closed and that new burials were only to be allowed outside the city at new sites. This new regulation was not only for the poor, and it was common for bodies to share graves, which would later be reused.

However, Mozart did have some eccentricities that were legendary in his own time. His love of scatological humor and his inappropriate behaviors have led to many theories about underlying conditions. A 2007 paper in the *Journal of Neurology, Neurosurgery, and Psychiatry* explored the possibility that he may have had ADHD, OCD, or even Tourette's syndrome, as many of his actions were consistent with these diagnoses. It's difficult, however, to prove medical theories when looking back across the centuries. He may well just have been a socially clueless young man whose extraordinary gifts prevented him from having anything like a normal childhood.

Speculation about Mozart's untimely demise has filled dozens of books with analysis, history, rivalries, marital difficulties, conspiracy theories, juicy facts and hypotheses, and just plain made-up nonsense. It's right up there with the "did Shakespeare write Shakespeare?" debate. The wonderful film *Amadeus*, based on Peter Shaffer's play, explores this all in delicious detail, playing up the rivalry with the less-talented Salieri (which was only true to a point; more on Salieri below) and implicating him in the young man's death.

So what was the actual cause of this most gifted musician's death? There are many theories. Although initially recorded as a severe miliary fever—a kind of contagious, epidemic sweating sickness—later researchers have suggested that the cause of death was Schönlein-Henoch syndrome, rheumatic inflammatory fever, exhaustion, etc. The list goes on.

A number of suggestions—including uraemia, Bright's disease, nephritis, and renal failure—are symptomatic of kidney disorder and failure. This is usually thought to be the likely cause of his death, though the debate continues because no one can resist speculating. There are plenty of medical journal articles that discuss Mozart's death in minute detail, for anyone interested in getting into complex medical terminology and gory details.

But what did Mozart himself think was happening in his last months as his health deteriorated? Well, he may have believed that he was being poisoned, and he knew he wouldn't last long. Having been sickly at many times in his life, he apparently had long believed that he would die young. He was right.

A commission from a mysterious benefactor to write a Requiem Mass (a mass for the dead) came to him in July 1791. In fact, the offer seems to have come from a certain Count Franz Walsegg, a wealthy amateur musician, or rather a wannabe. He had the very unpleasant habit of commissioning works from composers, paying them well, and then trying to pass off their work as his own; in short, he was a musical plagiarist. Guess who was next on his list?

Mozart took the commission from the stranger at his door. Since he was rather superstitious, some say he came to think that this messenger was Death himself. Believing that he was writing his own Requiem, he struggled with finishing the work; he thought that once it was done, he would be done, so to speak.

At the same time, he was finishing his wonderful opera *The Magic Flute*. This whimsical and strange work contains rich Masonic symbolism (Mozart had been a member of a Masonic Lodge since 1784), though there are no outright references to Freemasonry. Nevertheless, as his health deteriorated, he may have suspected that the Masons were not happy with his having "disclosed" such themes in a symbolic way in a mere comic opera, and that they might be responsible for poisoning him.

This suspicion, coupled with the mysterious request for the Requiem, could have fueled his superstitious imagination. In his last days he became obsessed with the death mass, though ultimately he died before its completion. His widow, Constanze, gave the unfinished work to Mozart's pupil, Franz Xavier Süssmayr, who had discussed with the composer how the remaining structures were to be written and organized. He completed the piece and it became Mozart's last composition, part his and part his student's.

Constanze eventually presented the piece to the unscrupulous count, but not before making a copy and publicly announcing that her late husband had composed it, thus thwarting Walsegg's unethical scheme. A lawsuit on his part (talk about sour grapes!) was headed off when she bought back the rights from him, thus saving a masterpiece from oblivion, or at least from getting the eighteenth-century lip-syncing treatment.

Though Wolfgang only partially composed the Requiem, it stands as a triumph. It is a momentous work and a fitting conclusion to his short, brilliant life. But his story doesn't end here. After his death, his skull—like that of his younger counterpart Beethoven—may or may not have taken a very strange journey, as we will see in Part II.

Antonio Salieri (1750–1825)

So what is the real story here?

Salieri is remembered mostly as the less talented composer who did not like Mozart, kept up an intense rivalry out of jealousy for the younger man's talent, and may have had something to do with his early death. The story that circulated at the time was revived in the nineteenth century and made into a fabulous play and film in the twentieth, but is any of it actually true? In all honesty, it's highly unlikely.

The first whiff of this whole sordid tale seems to have come from Mozart's father, Leopold, who was always both eager to see his son prosper and suspicious when things didn't work out for him. He believed there were secret organizations of "Italians" making things difficult for his son and impeding his career. Bear in mind that this was well before *The Godfather*. There isn't any real evidence for this suspicion and certainly nothing to connect Salieri to any such group, even if it did exist.

Perhaps Leopold's paranoia stemmed from the fact that in 1781, his son applied to be the music teacher of the young Princess of Württemberg, a lucrative court appointment. Salieri, known as a good voice teacher, was chosen instead. The following year, Mozart applied for the position of the piano teacher and was again passed over. These rejections set off red flags in Leopold's head, but the fact is that many qualified musicians applied for such posts. His suspicions rubbed off on his son, as evidenced in letters between them complaining of the possibility of Salieri meddling to hinder the younger man's career. However, Mozart and Salieri seemed to have been respectful colleagues, if not great friends.

Interestingly enough, there are several incidents where Salieri actually helped to further Mozart's reputation and career. He actively revived Mozart's opera *The Marriage of Figaro* in 1788 and saw to it that his masses were performed at the various coronation festivities of Emperor Leopold II in the year before Mozart's death. The two even composed a work together—a cantata known as *Per la ricuperata salute di Ophelia*—written to celebrate a well-known soprano's recovery from an illness. Amazingly, it was rediscovered in Prague's Czech Museum of Music in November 2015 long after it was assumed to be lost. Salieri may have conducted Mozart's Symphony No. 40 in G Minor and was apparently greatly impressed with *The Magic Flute*.

So, other than Leopold's sour grapes, where does this rivalry legend come from? There may have been an element of German and Austrian nationalism at work, which at the turn of the nineteenth century was in full swing as the Romantic Movement got under way. Some undoubtedly wanted to exclude foreign (in other words, non-Germanic) musicians and their influence. Maybe a reason needed to be found to explain the loss of the genius at such a young age, and Salieri, the foreigner, was just the convenient patsy. The ironic thing is that even though Salieri was from Italy, he spent most of his life in Vienna and his music is much more influenced by German styles than Italian ones.

Nevertheless, rumors were whispered that he had murdered Mozart out of jealousy and rage, and it was said that on his deathbed he confessed to the crime. However, the doctor and two nurses who treated him (all of whom were German, incidentally) denied that he had ever made such a confession.

In any case, Mozart's music continued to be popular, and it's possible that Salieri's was deliberately neglected, which is a shame because it is considerably better than many have been led to believe. In fact, it was rather dumbed-down for *Amadeus* in order to show the supposed contrast between the two.

Not long after Salieri died in 1825, Russian writer Alexander Pushkin (yes, the story had reached that far!) wrote his "tragedy" *Mozart and Salieri*, a play that was conceived as a kind of study on the deadly sin of envy. This work helped to keep the rumor alive in the minds of nineteenth-century music aficionados and literature buffs. As long after the incident as 1898, Russian composer Nikolai Rimsky-Korsakov made an adaptation of Pushkin's play as an opera of the same name, perpetuating the story. Fast forward to our time, with the play and movie *Amadeus*, and the legend lives on as strong as ever.

In the end, it seems that Salieri just got a bum rap. He was neither as incompetent as many people believe nor overly jealous of Mozart, at least not enough to try to murder him.

Jakub Jan Ryba (1765–1815)

Razor's edge

Ryba, a Czech music teacher and composer, is little known today. In his own time he was an important early promoter of the Czech language in his music, one of the first composers to feature it in his art songs. He was regarded for his religious music, and his Christmas mass, *Hej, mistře* ("Hail, Master"), is still performed in the Czech Republic.

Ryba had an unsettled life. Though he had aspirations to compose full time and become famous, his father (also a musician) brought him back to reality and ordered him to take up teaching positions for a more stable income. It was a case of the usual concerned, if overbearing, parent.

Ryba frequently argued with his superiors over various matters and was fired from his first job. Nevertheless, he was devoted to teaching and eventually secured another position, though the conflicts continued with councils and clergy. His work was poorly paid and his requests were frequently ignored, sending him ever deeper into despair. Finally, he couldn't take it any longer. After attending mass on April 8, 1815, he wandered into a forest near the town of Rožmitál.

His body was found sometime later. He had cut his own throat and had a copy of *Essay on Peace of Soul* by Seneca the Younger with him. A favorite author of his, Seneca (4 BCE–65 CE) was a famous Roman statesman and philosopher forced to commit suicide after being implicated in a plot to assassinate Emperor Nero; he was probably innocent, but as we saw earlier, Nero wasn't exactly popular. Seneca opened his veins to bleed to death: a calm, if unsettling, way to go.

Since Ryba's death was a suicide, he could not be buried in hallowed ground and so was interred in a plague cemetery where, as you can imagine, bodies were hastily disposed. Did he take Seneca's fate as a model for his own?

Ludwig van Beethoven (1770–1827)

Hear, hear

Beethoven, mighty Beethoven. This tragic titan is the most famous composer in the world, regarded, along with Bach and Mozart, as the greatest of all of them. Everyone knows the opening eight notes of his immortal Fifth Symphony, and most are familiar with pieces like the *Moonlight Sonata, Für Elise,* and the "Ode to Joy" section of his Ninth Symphony. Bridging the transition from late Classical to early Romantic, his late string quartets are regarded as some of the finest "classical" music ever written. Most people know how, incredibly, he struggled with the loss of his hearing and spent the last many years of his life completely deaf, yet was still able to "hear" the music he wrote in his mind perfectly.

But there was much more to Beethoven's harsh, difficult, and sad life. It was filled with incredible drama, anger, passion, and quite simply ridiculous turns of events. If anyone crafted a fictional character with a similar biography, they would immediately be dismissed for dreaming up something so improbable and melodramatic; the publisher would probably want the advance returned.

Beethoven's unkempt home, his wild shock of hair, and his angry outbursts were the stuff of legend in his own lifetime, all with varying degrees of truth. Despite this chaos (or perhaps because of it), he achieved unparalleled levels of creative and artistic greatness.

Literally millions of words have been written about the man, his music, and his life, and the short summary provided here can hardly do him justice. But since we're focusing mainly on the bizarre, the grotesque, and the unbelievable, here is a snapshot of the high points, or low points, really. Unfortunately, there are a lot of them.

It seems that poor Ludwig got off to a bad start right from the beginning. He was born in Bonn, Germany; his father Johann was an alcoholic, and probably abusive. Seeing his son's musical talent, he may have attempted to exploit him as a new Mozart-like child prodigy, sending him to various tutors for music lessons, one of whom, Christian Gottlob Neefe, did indeed compare him to Mozart. The young Beethoven pursued music, eventually meeting Mozart and studying with Haydn, both of whom were impressed with the young man's talent.

His mother died of tuberculosis when he was sixteen, and at eighteen, he petitioned a court to grant him half of his father's salary—Johann was a court singer, and his voice was failing—to care for his younger brothers, as their dad had a tendency to wash away his sorrows (and money) at taverns. Ludwig was unmoved when his father died a few years later. Johann's employer, Archduke Maximilian Francis, noted bluntly that his death had resulted in a loss of revenue from the alcohol tax.

Despite his harsh upbringing and his understandable distrust of authority, Beethoven seemed on track to make a great name for himself as early as the 1790s: he was performing concerts, taking on very wealthy and high-ranking students, enjoying the patronage of the rich and famous, traveling and performing, and even having his music published. Yes, everything was going his way . . . except that sometime before 1800, he began to notice that he wasn't hearing things as well. Undoubtedly, he put it down to other causes at first, but when the awful truth began to dawn on him, he must have resisted it bitterly, even desperately. The one sense he needed above all others, and here it was, fading away from him. Doctors were of no real use; some told him to take cold baths, others told him to take hot baths—neither helped.

By 1801, he was suffering from fairly severe tinnitus, a constant ringing in the ears like what one might experience after being at a loud event, such as a modern rock concert. For poor Beethoven, this condition was permanent. As his talent and reputation grew, his hearing worsened. Painfully aware of it, he wrote at the age of thirty-one that life was withering and fading away. This depression would haunt him for the rest of his life, causing him to cease composition for long periods at a time.

By 1818, he was completely deaf and had to communicate with people by writing to them and having them write back in "conversation books" that he carried around. There is the famous story of the 1824 premiere of his Ninth Symphony, which received a rapturous response from the audience. He was facing away from the crowd and had to be turned around to see that they were giving him an ovation, since he could not hear even the smallest part of it. All of his last and many of his greatest pieces were written entirely in his "mind's ear."

This alone would be a tragedy enough to wear down most composers, but his life was constantly assaulted with other disappointments and severe stress. His deafness eventually precluded him from performing live, which could be a lucrative means of funding a musician's life. The alternative—relying on aristocratic patronage—was not always his strong point, as his temper and brusque manner alienated many. Indeed, Beethoven was among the first of the great "suffering Romantics" that we will encounter in the next chapter. Teaching was also impossible, since he could not hear his students' progress. He increasingly withdrew from human contact.

Beethoven soon faced new shocks and disappointments, such as when his hero Napoleon had the audacity to declare himself emperor in 1804. Beethoven was furious. He had dedicated his Third Symphony to him. At first, Napoleon seemed to be a liberator and one of the people, but he now showed that he was just as power-mad and greedy as anyone the French Revolution had wanted to replace. Originally entitled the *Bonaparte* Symphony, the work was renamed the *Eroica* ("Heroic") Symphony on publication, the title by which it is still known today.

It follows almost naturally that such an unfortunate fellow would have major woman troubles all of his life. Being born of common rank, he was always falling for ladies who were too far above him in social position, still a serious issue at the time. Alternately, his admiration was simply unrequited; being deaf, temperamental, and eventually a hard-drinking slob didn't exactly endear him to a lot of Vienna's genteel, eligible females. It is truly sad, for he genuinely wanted someone to love but was always denied. It's not even known for certain if he ever had sexual relations with a woman.

The fictional film *Immortal Beloved* explores some of the various romantic possibilities he encountered in his life; the title is based on a letter he wrote in July 1812, addressed to a mysterious "Immortal Beloved" (German: *Unsterbliche Geliebte*). Never sent, it was discovered among his possessions after his death. The identity of the addressee is unclear, though several women have been proposed as candidates. Indeed, it's possible that Beethoven may have been loved by one or more women, who were simply not in the social position to express it openly. In any case, he never married and lived alone for the most part (changing residences in Vienna dozens of times throughout his life).

For some time he was financially well off, but emotionally, things continued their downward spiral. His younger brother Carl died in 1815, and Beethoven was named as guardian of Carl's nine-year-old son, rather confusingly named Karl. The only problem was that Carl's widow—the boy's mother, Johanna—was still alive, and an amendment to the will made by

Carl the day before he died decreed that she should have co-guardianship of the boy with Beethoven. For reasons that may have had to do with his need to have a family of his own, he decided that a slander campaign against Johanna was in order. He accused her of theft (she had once been jailed for embezzlement), prostitution, and a number of other crimes, and was ultimately successful in gaining sole custody of the boy. The battle continued for over four years, however, and custody was tossed back and forth like a ball.

Young Karl eventually came to loathe his uncle and desired to return to his mother. At the age of twenty, he tried to commit suicide with two pistols, shooting himself in the head. As it turned out, he was only wounded and was eventually able to return to his mother's home and care.

Beethoven was suffering from the effects of excessive drinking in these last years, and his musical output was sporadic, though still brilliant. The exact cause of death, as is the case with so many of these composers, is disputed. Cirrhosis was likely a contributing factor. Recent theories have suggested that lead poisoning may also have been involved, due to the presence of the metal in a sample of his hair, but this theory has also been disputed as unfounded. Historical forensic science is always tricky.

In any case, Beethoven left the world in March 1827 during a thunderstorm, an appropriate ending for a stormy, turbulent life. He had made many enemies over the course of fifty-six years, and he never found the loving wife or family he so desired. Nevertheless, people flocked to pay their last respects, including fellow composer Franz Schubert, who admired Beethoven above all others (and who would die soon after; more on him in the next chapter). His funeral, or at least the procession of the coffin, was witnessed by thousands.

Destined to endure two strange post-mortem incidents, the poor fellow couldn't rest even in death. The first was a bizarre run-in with later composer and corpse-obsessive Anton Bruckner, who will be covered in the next chapter, and the second involved the possibility of some fragments of his skull ending up in far-away California. This strange afterlife journey is detailed in Part II.

6

The Romantic Era

Ah, the Romantic era: gothic mansions holding dark secrets; bleak empty moorland in stormy weather; Byron and Shelley; Hegel's dialectic and Marx's communism; the Industrial Revolution; morally challenged poets in blousy shirts, wasting away from consumption and alcoholism! Here at last is the vision mentioned earlier, embodied in these tragic geniuses who were misunderstood and even despised by the very people they sought to cultivate as admirers. Well yes, some of them *were* rather weird. The era also embraced the idea of Weltschmerz, a word coined by German writer Jean Paul. It describes a feeling that the real world can never match the ideal world of the mind, a perfect description of the early Romantics.

This era firmly brought in several modern concepts: music was increasingly performed for the general public, as opposed to the aristocratic patrons and invite-only audiences that had characterized so many concerts of earlier times. Program music, the idea of a composition based on an external idea (a story, a theme, or a poem) became popular. Extreme virtuosity in technique (Liszt's piano pieces, for example) was highly appreciated. Long and extended works with recurring themes (Wagner's *Ring Cycle*, anyone?) and symbolism in sound were equally popular. And oh yes, there was that classic: the musician needing a day job to make ends meet. Actually, we could have done without that one. From the Romantic notions of a return to nature in the earlier part of the century to the increased industrialization of the Western world by the end of it, this era brought profound and permanent changes to the way that music was conceived, performed, and experienced.

In a time of great cultural upheaval, revolution, nationalism, scientific progress, and creativity, what better way to start this chapter than with that topic near and dear to so many musicians' hearts, or rather, elsewhere: social diseases!

The Syphilis Scourge

A pox on your houses!

The life of the musician: adoring and screaming fans, groupies galore, and crowds of young teenage girls desperately mobbing the star for a piece of autographed sheet music or piano strings. Yes, this really happened.

All very enticing, no doubt, but the problem was that in the nineteenth century (and earlier)—before the advent of antibiotics and penicillin, before latex shields offered their protection to the adventurous—there were great risks in such carousals. The number of artistic types that contracted some form of VD is extensive and includes a sampling of well-known and loved composers who succumbed to the dreadful effects of syphilis at some point in their lives.

The remarkably gifted and prolific young Franz Schubert (1797–1828) is often labeled as the last of the great composers of the Classical Era and a harbinger of the Romantic. In his short life, he wrote an astonishing number of songs (in excess of six hundred) as well as orchestral music.

Despite being something of a musical icon, he seems to have had romantic difficulties and to have enjoyed the company of ladies-for-hire. Others at the time suggested that, given his seeming preference for male company, he may have been homosexual in a city that was relatively tolerant of it—Vienna. In any case, he may have contracted syphilis as a young man, as his later health problems seem to indicate that he suffered from it. Treatment for the affliction in those days mainly involved taking doses of mercury. Lovely. The result of this approach was often death by mercury poisoning before syphilis took its toll. Indeed, some of Schubert's final symptoms are characteristic of such poisoning. Like Purcell and Mozart, he left this world at far too young an age, and again we have to wonder what he might have accomplished had he lived for another thirty years.

Domenico Gaetano Maria Donizetti (1797–1848) was a noted composer of operas, along with his contemporaries Rossini and Vincenzo Bellini. These three set the stage, so to speak, for the later Italian masters such as Verdi and Puccini. Donizetti's personal life was marred by tragedy: two children died at birth, another survived for only eleven days; in 1837, within a year of both of his parents dying, his wife also died after giving birth to a stillborn child. She may have contracted a syphilitic infection from her husband that caused complications. He moved to Paris the following year and enjoyed success despite his personal losses. At the height of his career in the early 1840s, he began to exhibit signs of syphilis and may have also suffered from bipolar disorder. By 1846, he was committed to an asylum in Paris, the only place where such unfortunate individuals could be sent in those days. He was eventually sent back to his hometown of Bergamo in Italy, where he died in 1848, insane.

Robert Schumann (1810–1856) was one of the great composers of the first half of the nineteenth century, and he embodied the new Romantic style in his works and in his life. He was known to be very moody, frequently falling into depression before becoming euphoric, a sign of bipolar disorder. To make matters worse, he contracted syphilis at the age of twenty-one. Despite his various conditions (or perhaps because of them), he produced numerous songs and song cycles, a large quantity of piano music, and many other important works.

In the 1840s, probably as a result of his worsening illnesses—both mental and physical—he reported that he began to hear a continuous "A" note sounding in his ears. By the early 1850s, this note was joined by voices and what he described as angelic music. In time, the voices became demonic, and he began to hear messages from the dead, either from Schubert or Mendelssohn, who dictated a musical theme to him. In reality, this theme was one that he had composed and used in previous works.

By 1854, he attempted to commit suicide by jumping from a bridge over the Rhine. He was rescued and taken to an asylum at his own request, where he was to remain with worsening symptoms until his death in July 1856. There is evidence that he may have been suffering from mercury poisoning treatments, which only made any other existing conditions that much worse. An autopsy from the time indicates that he may have also had some kind of brain tumor, as if things weren't already bad enough.

His wife, Clara, survived him by forty years and was later the object of love and affection from Johannes Brahms, whose career she had helped when he was young. Schumann's Violin Concerto was to remain unknown to the world for decades after his death, until it was recovered in a most unusual way, as we shall see in Part II.

Niccolò Paganini (1782–1840)

The devil made him do it II, or why does the devil get all the good tunes?

You have to hand it to violinists. They seem to have been the rock guitarists of their time, bold, flashy, and talented. Everyone wanted to see what a skilled composer or musician could do on the instrument, especially if they were just a little too good to be true, as in the case of Paganini. Then, the rumors could start flying about supernatural assistance from the Prince of Darkness.

Paganini was perhaps the greatest violinist in Western music history. His works for the instrument are so demanding and difficult to play that even today violinists consider it a peak of achievement to master his compositions. In his own time, such exceptional talent not only drew admiration, but also aroused suspicion as to just how a mortal man could be so gifted. It seems a strange thing that when looking for the source of genius, many often detect the whiff of brimstone rather than the halo of the angelic.

As Paganini's fame spread, so did the rumors. He began to be known in some circles as a *Hexensohn*, or "witch's brat." It was whispered that his abilities came from having sold his soul to Satan in exchange for almost magical musical powers.

Paganini did nothing to discourage these rumors, figuring, like today's heavy metal bands that use satanic imagery, that there was no such thing as bad publicity. He dressed in black, wore his hair long, and sometimes arrived to performances in a black coach pulled by four black horses. He was tall and thin, emaciated even, and by 1828, he had lost his teeth. Doctors assumed that his various illnesses were due to syphilis (again!) and prescribed mercury treatments, which loosened Paganini's teeth to such an extent that they eventually had to be pulled. This only added to his gaunt and ghoulish appearance. Alice Cooper, King Diamond, and Marilyn Manson are latecomers compared to this guy.

Yes, Niccolò knew all about PR and how to work an audience. Indeed, audience members would remark how they had never heard nor seen anything like him, and as a result, people flocked to see this mystery man and hear his astonishing talent.

In looking for less supernatural explanations for his skill, several medical conditions have been suggested. Among them is Ehlers-Danlos, a genetic disorder causing much greater mobility in the joints due to a collagen synthesis defect. If he did have this condition, it would have allowed his finger joints to be extremely flexible. It was said that he could play three octaves across the violin's fretboard without shifting his hand position. He was also described as having very long arms, legs, and fingers. This might have been due to a condition known as Marfan syndrome, a disorder of the connective tissue.

If he did make a diabolical pact, the devil came to collect his part of the bargain in 1840. Paganini was dying of cancer of the larynx, though other accounts say that he died of an internal hemorrhage. He apparently refused to see the bishop when he came to visit, insisting that he was not dying and did not need last rites. Maybe he was just trying to keep up his image.

In any case, the Church took the whole thing so seriously that it refused to let him be buried in consecrated ground. It took some five years for his family to be able to persuade the pope to move his body to a hallowed resting place, but his remains were not interred until 1876 in

Parma. Maybe in some warm place, Niccolò and Old Nick are fiddling together even now.

Carl Maria von Weber (1786–1826)

Throwing his voice

A leading figure in the early German Romantic movement, Weber was known for his clarinet works and operas. As a result of his early promise, he was appointed Kapellmeister ("chapel master") in Breslau in 1804, at the age of only seventeen. This appointment naturally led to some resentment among his older colleagues.

As a youth, he was gifted with a beautiful singing voice, but he was destined for a cruel fate. One evening, he casually drank from a wine bottle. What he didn't know was that his father was using the bottle to store an engraving acid used in lithography. The effects of such a substance on the body don't bear thinking about. It nearly killed him, and he took two months to recover. The ultimate result was that his voice was ruined, and he could no longer sing.

In spite of this, he pressed on as a composer. Although he created many acclaimed works, he also made enemies through his ambition and racked up debts for his rather lavish lifestyle. Alas, he was destined for another cruel fate, dying of tuberculosis at the young age of thirty-nine.

Hector Berlioz (1803–1869)

Sex, drugs, and black masses

Berlioz's odd life and artistic creations could merit a chapter all of their own. He is most remembered for his *Symphonie fantastique*, which by his own admission depicted visions of an opium trip. It was probably inspired in part by Thomas de Quincey's *Confessions of an English Opium-Eater*; now *there's* a tabloid title! Whether or not the *Symphonie* is intended to be autobiographical is unclear, but there are obvious references to events in Berlioz's own life, fueling suspicion that he created the work under the influence of the drug, like Samuel Taylor Coleridge did in writing his poem "Kubla Khan."

The symphony describes a lovesick young artist's haunted dreams about an unattainable woman. The work follows his journey in seeking refuge for his pain, first in religious belief, and then by escaping into the countryside. Writing to his friend Humbert Ferrand, Berlioz described the macabre story that unfolds:

> In a fit of despair he [the lover] poisons himself with opium; but instead of killing him, the narcotic induces a horrific vision, in which he believes he has murdered the loved one, has been condemned to death, and witnesses his own execution. March to the scaffold; immense procession of headsmen, soldiers and populace. At the end the melody reappears once again, like a last reminder of love, interrupted by the death stroke.

> The next moment he is surrounded by a hideous throng of demons and sorcerers, gathered to celebrate Sabbath night. . . . At last the melody arrives. Till then it had appeared only in a graceful guise, but now it has become a vulgar tavern tune, trivial and base; the beloved object has come to the sabbath to take part in her victim's funeral. She is nothing but a courtesan, fit to figure in the orgy. The ceremony begins; the bells toll, the whole hellish cohort prostrates itself; a chorus chants the plainsong sequence of the dead [the Dies irae], two other choruses repeat it in a burlesque parody. Finally, the sabbath round-dance whirls. At its violent climax it mingles with the Dies irae, and the vision ends.

This was wild stuff to be sure, and it must have been very shocking when it was first performed. Reaction was mixed. Mendelssohn was disgusted by the themes and called the piece "utterly loathsome," while the young Franz Liszt hailed it as a work of genius.

It seems that it was partly autobiographical, for Berlioz himself was smitten with an Irish Shakespearean actress, Harriet Smithson, whom he had seen perform in a Paris production of *Hamlet*. Despite his attempts to gain her attention and favor, she spurned him as a young upstart, refusing to meet him. Apparently in response to this rejection, he composed the *Symphonie*, which was his first major work. He may have written the shocking finale at least partially because of rumors that the actress was having an affair with her manager, and thus Berlioz, in his anger and frustration, damned her to hell symbolically.

The story doesn't end there. In 1830 he met Camille Mokke, a young lady who seemed determined to win him over just to prove that she could. She succeeded, and the two were engaged. Around the same time, Berlioz won a prestigious award, the Prix de Rome. In December 1831, he left France and journeyed to Rome, required to spend the next two years in the city by a clause in the Prix. Not a bad deal, really!

However, during his time there he received an unhappy, and perhaps even cowardly, letter from Camille's mother informing him that she was calling off their engagement. The young lady would instead marry a man confusingly also named Camille (which must have made for very interesting wedding invitations), one Camille Pleyel, a wealthy manufacturer of pianos. Spurned again, Berlioz was furious. In a fit of rage he began plotting the murders of not only his ex-fiancée, but of her mother and Mr. Pleyel as well.

He set about planning everything in detail, including purchasing women's clothes—a dress, wig, hat, veils, and so on—as a disguise to gain entry into their home. He stole a set of pistols with which to carry out the murders and ensured that there was enough ammunition for him to kill himself afterward. Since sometimes such guns would jam, he also purchased laudanum and strychnine, to make sure that he could finish himself off.

Everything was set for a grand plot that could have gone down in the annals of music history as a crime equal to Gesualdo's. He was ready to return to Paris; it was all in place, except for a small problem. After he reached Genoa, he realized that he had left his drag disguise in the carriage. First he tried to find replacement clothes; then one afternoon he decided to end it all by jumping off a cliff into the sea, a bold and dramatic act that would make a statement and epitomize the Romantic ethos—except that he landed in the water near a fishing boat and was promptly rescued. Nevertheless, he vowed to carry out his plan and continued his journey, ending up in Nice. By this time, he was having serious doubts and eventually abandoned the entire plan. He had decided that it was foolish, that Camille was a child, her mother was odious, and that they were not worth his time. He still had music to compose and didn't want to be remembered by posterity as a monster. Well, all right, then.

Back in Italy, he wrote *Lélio*, a piece inspired by his determination to get over Camille and reclaim his life. The work consists of symphonic music with narration. It is a sequel to the *Symphonie*, an awakening from the nightmare, with Camille symbolically offering a way out of the nightmarish dream of the earlier piece, though it also references Smithson.

When he eventually returned to Paris and rented rooms, Berlioz discovered that Smithson was in the city. Convinced that fate was guiding him, he tried once again to contact her and had a third party invite her to a concert that featured *Lélio*. This time, Smithson consented. When she heard the performance, she realized that she had been a great inspiration to him. She met Berlioz, and amazingly, they ultimately married in 1833 despite language barriers and family opposition. There was no happy ending, however, for he soon realized that the reality could not match the ideal he had created in his mind.

Eight years later, the magic had worn off completely, and Berlioz had a new mistress, Marie Recio. His wife didn't approve, naturally, and took to drinking; they separated two years later, in 1844. Ten years after that, poor dejected Smithson died of a stroke (or rather, several), and Berlioz finally married Recio. In 1862, Recio herself died of a heart attack, and Berlioz consoled himself by falling in love with a young woman named Amélie; this story just keeps on going. She died in 1864 after breaking off their relationship, and he would soon lament that he had no more hope; all he had left was contempt for humanity and its cruelty. He wondered why Death would not take him away.

In 1864, Smithson's remains had to be disinterred from Montmartre cemetery to make room for a new street; Berlioz was present for the disinterment. He died in 1869, lonely, unfulfilled, and broken.

Frédéric Chopin (1810–1849)

I left my heart in . . . Warsaw?

A moody and temperamental man who lived a life of artistry and drama and died young from tuberculosis, Chopin embodied the ideals of the Romantic age—well, maybe the TB wasn't so ideal. His virtuoso piano music helped to establish the instrument as a perpetual favorite of the nineteenth century. He traveled widely and entertained a series of lovers, the most famous being the author Aurore Dudevant, better known by her pen name George Sand.

In an attitude befitting one of these stormy times, Chopin had a morbid fear of being buried alive. So much so that he left strict instructions for his heart to be cut out upon his death as an insurance policy against his reviving and finding himself in a tight situation six feet under.

After his death, his sister carried out his wish. She placed his heart in an urn that was delivered back to Warsaw. There, it was sealed in a pillar in the Holy Cross Church on Krakowskie Przedmieście. Beneath the heart is a grimly amusing inscription from the Bible, Matthew 6:21: "For where your treasure is, there will your heart be also." His heart is still there, even though the church was nearly destroyed in World War II and had to be completely rebuilt. The rest of his body is buried in Père Lachaise Cemetery in Paris.

On his deathbed, Chopin showed a bit of humor. In his last request, he stated, "You will play in memory of me and I will hear you from beyond . . . play really good music, Mozart, for instance."

Franz Liszt (1811–1886)

Bring back my body for me

Liszt's reputation as one of the supreme pianists of the nineteenth century is quite secure. He wrote an astonishing amount of virtuoso piano music. As a young man, he was loved like a pop star, with young women swooning in his presence. It was said that his adoring fans collected broken strings from the pianos he played and had them made into bracelets. Ladies even collected his used cigar butts and wore them in their cleavage. Seriously. He happily availed himself of such attentions (and seems to have escaped the syphilis curse), but by later life, he had taken minor orders in the Catholic Church and lived out his days as a priest.

Liszt's life was long and complex, but it is the macabre circumstances surrounding his death that are so interesting. He had remained in remarkably good health throughout his life until a fall down some stairs in 1881. After this accident, he began to be plagued by a number of ailments, including heart problems that finally led to his death, though the official cause was listed as pneumonia. One theory is that shortly before he died he was given two injections near the heart. It was a practice to give such shallow injections of camphor to warm an area of the body, following this with a massage. However, if the camphor was accidentally injected into a frail heart, it could induce a heart attack. In any case, Liszt died shortly afterward.

Then things became truly gruesome. Lina Schmalhausen, a one-time pupil of Liszt, recorded the horrific events in a recently discovered diary. The day after his death, a local barber arrived to embalm the body (barbers often doubled as surgeons; more on them in Part II). However, the poor man had never embalmed a body, and didn't know what to do. He ended up cutting it apart in his attempts, and by the time the damage was done, Liszt's body was so bloated that it became unrecognizable. Consequently, no one was even allowed to view it. By the next day, bowls of chlorine had to be set nearby to mask the odor of the rapidly decaying corpse, and it was quickly removed.

Liszt died in Bayreuth, a town famous for its association with Wagner both then and now. He had never been enthusiastic about the association because he was treated there as something like a second-class citizen in the shadow of the Wagnerian colossus. It might also have something to do with the fact that one of Liszt's illegitimate daughters had an adulterous affair with Wagner for some time before they were eventually married. Wagner's musical fame would eclipse that of Liszt for decades afterward, due in no small part to the efforts of the town that wanted to promote Wagner at the expense of other composers. Liszt, aware of this bias, once remarked of Bayreuth, "if only I do not die here." So much for last wishes.

Charles-Valentin Alkan (1813–1888)

Racking up fame

Alkan was a French pianist and composer, regarded as having some of the finest piano skills of any musician of his time. Even the great Liszt claimed that Alkan had the best technique he had seen. Despite his acclaim and a wide circle of friends, by his mid-thirties he was increasingly antisocial, and by 1850 he had withdrawn almost completely from public life, making only very occasional public appearances. He noted that he seemed to become more and more misanthropic as he got older, and though he continued to play and compose, nothing much gave him pleasure any longer. Nevertheless, he was deeply devoted to his Jewish faith and pursued an intensive study of the Talmud and the Bible.

His end came about in an odd way, as two different stories recount. One says that as he reached for a volume of the Talmud from a high shelf, the bookcase fell on him, killing him instantly. This story seems to have been popularized by pianist Élie-Miriam Delaborde (long assumed to be his illegitimate son). But this appears to be an apocryphal tale based on an urban legend wherein an eighteenth-century rabbi named Aryeh Leib ben Asher Gunzberg met a similar fate. In fact, his death seems to have been even stranger. Something fell on him, to be sure, but it was a heavy *porte-parapluies*, a kind of coat and umbrella rack, and he died while trapped underneath it.

Another legend circulated about him after his death that took a rather cruel shot at him for his reclusive nature. It was said that the magazine *Le Ménestrel* printed an obituary that read, "Alkan is dead. He had to die in order to prove his existence." Actually, there was no such obituary printed in the magazine, and the source of the legend is unknown.

Anton Bruckner (1824–1896)

When a body meets a body

Bruckner was an odd fellow indeed. He had limited critical success as a composer until 1884, when he was nearly sixty and produced his seventh symphony to great acclaim in Leipzig. For the last fifteen years of his life he lived in Vienna, encountering hostility there owing to his allegiance to Wagner's music and the presence of anti-Wagner factions in the city; it was sort of like showing up to a Red Sox game wearing a Yankees cap. His symphonies were denounced as unplayable and even sabotaged when the Vienna Philharmonic Orchestra performed them at all. For his third symphony, for example, he couldn't find a conductor willing to take on the task, so he conducted it himself. This led the orchestra members to mock him by playing out of tune, adding odd extra notes, not repeating phrases where required, and even laughing at him. Despite this blatant rudeness and disrespect, Bruckner was highly regarded as an organist, though strangely he never wrote any major works for the instrument.

A simple and humble man, deeply Roman Catholic, he nevertheless had at least one nervous breakdown and may have suffered from other emotional problems. He never married, though he proposed to a number of young women over the years, all of whom rejected him. Some scholars suspect that the poor man died a virgin.

His piety was such that he was said to fall to his knees and pray whenever he heard church bells ringing. This happened even when he was giving lectures; it probably gave his students some time to catch up on their note taking. In later life, he kept a detailed record of his daily prayers. He was also afflicted with a condition known as numeromania, a compulsion to count everything. Some have asserted that this obsession with numbers can be heard in his musical repetitions and even the great lengths of his symphonies; his eighth symphony can run for an hour and a half or longer depending on the individual performance preferences and interpretations. This is far longer than most comparable symphonies from the later nineteenth century.

Bruckner also had an obsession with dead bodies; it may have been a kind of obsessive-compulsive disorder. He left instructions that his own corpse be embalmed. It would be tempting to think that he had heard of the Liszt debacle, whose funeral he had attended, though it's unlikely since that whole mess was kept quite secret. He also commissioned a photograph of his deceased mother on her death bed, which he kept in his teaching room.

A remarkable story that illustrates his obsession comes from a time when Beethoven's body was exhumed from its resting place in Währing Cemetery to be reburied in the new Central Cemetery in 1888. Bruckner's pupil, Carl Hruby, related later that both he and his teacher attended the event. Exhumers had decided to open the coffin in the cemetery (another account says that they moved the body to a nearby chapel) and Bruckner hastened to get a closer look. As officials were taking skeletal measurements, he managed to push himself forward to get a view of the bones. Bruckner became transfixed with the corpse, staring down at it, moved by the sight. In some accounts, he cradled the skull in his arms and kissed it before being pulled away.

On the journey home with Hruby, he noticed that one of the lenses of his pince-nez (nineteenth-century eyeglasses without earpieces) had fallen out, presumably into the coffin. He was overjoyed, knowing that the lens would be reburied with Beethoven and stay with his body forever.

Apparently he did the same thing when Schubert was exhumed for the same purpose, and after seizing the skull, refused to release it until he was allowed to place it back in the coffin himself. In both instances, he was forcibly ejected from the gathering.

These were not the only corpses Bruckner desired to see. When he heard that the body of Emperor Maximilian of Mexico, whom he greatly admired, might be on display, he wrote to a friend, desperately trying to get a chance to see it and wanting to know when it might be viewable. He didn't want to miss out on the opportunity. Given Bruckner's deep Catholicism, some musicologists have suspected that his fixation on these various bones (always of people he admired) was some form of relic veneration. But it certainly cast him in a strange and even morbid light, so it's no wonder he was continually rejected for marriage.

Camille Saint-Saëns (1835–1921)

The apes of wrath

The long-lived Saint-Saëns was a brilliant musician, seen today more as a solid representative of the French style of composition of his time than as an innovator with a new style. This would later be held against him by some of his younger contemporaries, and he would defend his own style while attacking theirs.

Saint-Saëns was an exceptionally gifted child prodigy. His father was a French government clerk who died when the son was only three months old. He showed great early musical promise and was studying piano by the age of three; most of us can barely even remember what we were doing then! He began the study of proper composition at seven; he must have seemed like a reincarnation of Mozart.

Indeed, he gave his first public recital at the tender age of ten at the Salle Pleyel, a concert hall in Paris; again, most of us were probably in a spelling bee or a school play at that age. However, this was not some simple children's concert. He performed Beethoven's Piano Concerto in C Minor and Mozart's Concerto in B-flat from memory. Yes, that means with no sheet music. To further astound the audience, he offered to play any number of Beethoven's piano sonatas from memory as an encore. Word of this remarkable talent spread quickly, and he was well on his way to a successful career. As if all of this weren't enough, he showed tremendous aptitude for Latin, Greek, and various scientific disciplines. Indeed, when he sold the publishing rights to some of his pieces in 1858, he used the money to buy a telescope.

Despite the many gifts and accolades that he would receive throughout his career—including being awarded the Grande Croix of the Légion d'Honneur—his personal life was marred by tragedy. In 1875, he married a woman half his age, Marie-Laure Truffot. His mother strongly disapproved, and the marriage was rocky. In 1878, their two sons died within six weeks of each other, one from an illness, the other by falling out of a fourth-floor window. This devastating loss would ultimately end the marriage, since he blamed his wife for being negligent. While they were on holiday in 1881 he simply abandoned her, and they soon separated, though they never divorced. Saint-Saëns's mood had certainly darkened, but he was able to gain some refuge in his friendship with the composer Gabriel Fauré, to whose children he became a kind of loving uncle. However, his mother died in 1888, which sent him into a state of depression; at one point he almost became suicidal. He sought refuge in North Africa, primarily Algeria. He would return to Algiers several times and died there in 1921.

Throughout his life he made many friends and many enemies. His remarkable talent undoubtedly led some to resent him, but his compositional style was conservative and hardly ground-breaking, which caused others to criticize his lack of innovation, especially from 1890 onward. He disliked Debussy's music, for example, saying that his *L'après-midi d'un faune* "cultivated the absence of style, logic, and common sense," and calling another of his pieces an atrocity. The feeling was mutual. Debussy felt that Saint-Saëns's music was far too traditional and sentimental, stating in the journal *La revue blanche* in 1901, through the voice of his fictional character Monsieur Croche, "Is there no one who likes Saint-Saëns enough to tell him that he's written enough music and would be better employed in his lately acquired vocation of explorer?"

Saint-Saëns willingly admitted to some conservatism in his music, writing in 1890:

Mea culpa! I am accused of not being decadent.

My Muse dares not put the tooth in unripe fruits

Saint-Saëns and fellow composer César Franck were also famously at odds over differences in composition. And, on hearing Darius Milhaud's experimental 1919 piece *Protée*, Saint-Saëns said, "fortunately, there are still lunatic asylums in France."

He seems to have gotten himself into a bit of a political problem during the First World War, being forced to publicly declare that he rejected the music of Wagner since it was part of a German propaganda campaign. A *New York Times* article from March 4, 1917, reported on this in detail:

> Goaded by accusations of looking with a too friendly eye on Richard Wagner, Camille Saint-Saëns, the famous French composer . . . insists that he is one of those who believe that Frenchmen must fight the German influence wherever they find it, even if it come beneath the disguise of art. In a book which he entitles "Germanophilie," Saint-Saëns warns his fellow-countrymen that the Wagner music-dramas are among the most insidious and dangerous of the weapons used by Germany for the enslavement of France, and he calls upon the French to cease pretending that they like the Wagner operas and to lavish their admiration on the works of French composers instead.

He described three categories of Wagner fans: maniacs, those who are like opium addicts, and those who genuinely like art, but he warned that all must be prepared to give it up. Whether he truly believed this or was simply saving his own behind in a dangerous time is not clear. He took pains to point out that he had, as early as 1881, supported Wagner's work, but not the idea of German nationalism and colonialism.

Saint-Saëns obviously had strong opinions about musical innovation. During the infamous première of Stravinsky's *Rite of Spring* on May 29, 1913, he was reported to have stormed out, appalled at the use of bassoons in a high register, allegedly saying, "If that is a bassoon, then I am a baboon!" His social skills were clearly not always his best feature.

Modest Mussorgsky (1839–1881)

I'll drink to that

The Russian composer Mussorgsky is known these days for works such as *Night on Bald Mountain* and *Pictures at an Exhibition*, the latter of which was originally written for piano, though most modern listeners are probably more familiar with the orchestral version made by French composer Maurice Ravel. Although Mussorgsky was born into a relatively wealthy family, his life was troubled and short, largely due to one of those great Romantic afflictions, alcoholism. Indeed, he was described as having a particularly bad case, historically known as dipsomania, an uncontrollable urge to drink alcohol. This may have been brought on by an early military career and the brutality that was endemic to it, and was made worse by the death of his mother in 1865.

In any case, he also showed promise in music, though his work was frequently interrupted due to a number of things, including a possible spiritual crisis and another of those great Romantic ills, money troubles. He could be quite unfocused; he started a good number of pieces and abandoned them, leaving them unfinished at his death, though several other composers, most notably his friend Rimsky-Korsakov, set themselves the task of finishing or editing his incomplete works.

One of his most haunting works is his *Songs and Dances of Death*, four pieces for bass voice and piano that set poems by Arseny Golenishchev-Kutuzov. Each song describes death in a familiar manner, rather than one that is mythic. They are moving and poignant:

- *Lullaby*: A mother holds her infant, who is dying of an illness. Death appears, offering to relieve the tired mother and rock the baby in its cradle while she sleeps. The mother protests, but Death rocks the child into eternal sleep.

- *Serenade*: Death appears as a suitor at the window of a young dying lady and offers to be her knight, the one that will take her away.

- *Trepak*: A drunken man stumbles into a forest during a blizzard, where Death offers to dance a Trepak, a traditional dance, with him. After this, she suggests that he lie down so that he may be "warmed" by a blanket of snow and drift off to eternal sleep, dreaming of summer.

- *The Field Marshall*: Death circles the battlefield after the battle, like a proud commander, and declares that she has truly won. Death will now see all of the soldiers march, count them, and see that their bones lie in the earth, from which they will never leave.

Trepak was in some ways an ominous foreshadowing of the composer's own fate, while describing a much wider societal problem. Indeed, Mussorgsky's drinking was not only a personal concern; it seems to have been part of a cultural and social idea that the artists of his time were expected to indulge in drink as a means of protesting the established order. Rock and roll really has nothing on earlier generations, who were flipping off the Man with just as much enthusiasm. These "worshippers of Bacchus" believed that it was essential to their creativity and way of life to be as drunk as possible, as often as possible. Mussorgsky spent his nights in a low-life tavern in Saint Petersburg, joined by other artists who praised their own inebriation.

Obviously, this self-destructive behavior couldn't last too long. By February 1881 he was reduced to begging, despite the help of his few remaining friends. He suffered a seizure, followed the next day by three more. He was taken to a military hospital, where he showed some improvement for a while. There is even a famous painting of him from this time, his nose as red as Rudolph's from the years of alcohol abuse. He seemed to recover a bit, but only temporarily. In March he finally died, at the young age of forty-two.

After his death, some viewed him a radical (his opera *Boris Godunov* was rejected for a court performance by the tsar himself), while others saw him as an amateur and a dilettante with unrealized potential. More recent studies have shown that he was indeed very original, with a unique style and a life cut short like so many before and since.

Pyotr Ilyich Tchaikovsky (1840–1893)
I'll drink to that II

The debate surrounding Tchaikovsky's mysterious death has been long, protracted, and (mostly) unresolved. Whole studies have been devoted to it, and even non-specialists have probably heard something about the controversy. It comes down to a few possibilities: Did he die accidentally of cholera by drinking contaminated water, or did he commit suicide by ingesting poison or deliberately drinking unboiled water? A third possibility suggests that he was murdered. Different theorists have produced convincing arguments for each of these stories, though the suicide hypothesis is fading from popularity.

The beloved composer who gave the world the incomparable ballets *Swan Lake*, *Sleeping Beauty*, and *The Nutcracker* lived a sad and tortured life, forced to hide his homosexuality from a very disapproving society. Indeed, disclosure could have resulted in his deportation to Siberia.

Tchaikovsky was afflicted by sadness and haunted by fears of the approaching end for most of his life, understandable under the circumstances. He tried to suppress his natural inclinations not just out of fear of persecution, but also because of the prevailing moral tone of the time. Some scholars have questioned how much shame he felt, saying that he was comfortable with his nature but wisely kept it secret.

He tried to hide his orientation by marrying one of his composition students, Antonina Miliukova, in 1877. Perhaps he hoped that by doing so he could maintain a suitable respectability in the public eye and continue to have relationships with men in private. As might be expected, the marriage was a disaster. Shortly after, he nearly had a nervous breakdown. It seems he then tried to give himself a case of pneumonia by walking into the freezing River Moskva in St. Petersburg. When this failed, he fled from his wife and finally did suffer the breakdown, as well as an acute case of writer's block for some time afterward. They formally separated but were never divorced, owing to the strict laws of the time.

Antonina did not fare much better, and her mental health declined over the years. She was finally declared insane in 1896, dying in 1917 in an asylum. Recent research has suggested that other factors may have been in play; she seems to have been aware of her husband's orientation, and he may have married her both in an attempt to "cure" himself and for the financial security that she brought.

In any case, Tchaikovsky left Russia after this and traveled in Europe (primarily Italy) in the hopes of lifting his mood, a tactic that succeeded to some extent. He secured the support of several wealthy patrons, including the tsar himself, freeing up his time to compose since he did not have to teach and scrape out a living. He even traveled as far as the United States, performing in Carnegie Hall in 1891.

Stress and depression took their toll, however. From insomnia to migraines, he had constant physical complaints. He also showed more than a little of the behavior of a hypochondriac. By 1893, he was in despair. He wrote early that year, "my faith in myself is shattered, and my role is ended." His last symphony was the *Pathétique*, which means "passionate" rather than "pathetic." Some have called it a musical suicide note because it references material from the Russian Orthodox Requiem (mass for the dead), and its finale is specified as a *morendo*, a "dying away." However, scholars now mostly reject this theory.

What is known is that Tchaikovsky died in St. Petersburg on November 6, 1893, only nine days after the premiere of his *Pathétique* Symphony. It's the circumstances surrounding his death that make the story intriguing. Cholera, like typhoid and a few other scourges, periodically surfaced to decimate nineteenth-century communities. An epidemic was occurring at the time, and the official explanation was that he drank unboiled water, contracted the illness, and died. Whether or not this was an accident has been the subject of debate. He was certainly depressed enough to commit suicide, but did he? He had actually been rather pleased with the results of his latest symphony (creatively speaking anyway—it had a lukewarm critical reception) and thought that it was among his best works. He told a friend that, for the first time in his career, he felt completely content about one of his compositions.

A story that has gained popularity more recently was that Tchaikovsky had been conducting a secret affair with a male member of the aristocracy. When the man's uncle discovered this, he threatened to "out" Tchaikovsky to the tsar in a letter. When his former institution, the St. Petersburg School of Jurisprudence, heard about this, they were afraid of what it would do to the school's reputation. They convened a "jury" that tried him *in absentia* and found him guilty, demanding that he kill himself to preserve their honor.

This version of events is certainly not the final word, but it makes for a fascinating and tragic story. We may never know the exact details. As so often seems to happen with Romantic-era composers, Tchaikovsky's misery translated into gold after his death. He is now one of the most popular and beloved composers of all time. No one really cares about his personal life; all they know is the beautiful musical legacy he left to the world.

Karel Komzák II (1850–1905)

Going off the rails

Komzák was a Bohemian composer. Born in Prague, he spent his early years under the tutelage of his father, Karel Komzák I (obviously), who conducted military bands. Not widely known today, he was famed in his time for his dances and marches, music forms that were all the rage in Vienna. Indeed, living in that grand city had long been a goal of his, and in 1882, he was appointed to direct the musicians of the 84th Infantry Regiment. He introduced string instruments into his orchestra, not a common practice at the time, and he and his band became famous for their skilled performances. He eventually toured widely, going so far as to perform with the Wiener Farben Orchestra in the 1904 World Exhibition in St. Louis, Missouri.

By now, the reader must know that something dreadful was about to happen, and indeed it did. On Easter Sunday in April 1905, some months after returning from Missouri, Komzák was at the train station in Baden, a spa town southwest of Vienna where he had been living since the 1890s. The train he wanted to take was just leaving and he attempted to run alongside and jump aboard, like in a scene out of an action movie. Of course, this didn't work out. He slipped and fell directly under the wheels; the result does not bear thinking about.

Ernest Chausson (1855–1899)

A very short Tour de France

Chausson was another Romantic Frenchman (is there any other kind?) who hobnobbed with many of the artistic bigwigs of his time. Beginning in 1886, he was secretary of the Société Nationale de Musique. Among the composers with which he rubbed shoulders were Gabriel Fauré and Claude Debussy; he was also acquainted with the painter Claude Monet.

We don't know how great he might have become, because he died just as his career was taking off. He qualifies as a contender for the most ridiculous death recorded in this book. While riding his bicycle in Limay, west of Paris, he lost control going down a hill, slammed into a brick wall, and died instantly. It is possible that this was a strange form of suicide, as he was said to be suffering from depression at the time, but still, let this be a lesson to everyone that has ever scoffed at wearing a helmet!

Giacomo Puccini (1858–1924)

A cigar is just a cigar

Giacomo Antonio Domenico Michele Secondo Maria Puccini (how many names does a guy need?) is remembered as one of the greatest and most beloved Italian opera composers of all time. Inspired to write his own operas after a viewing of Verdi's *Aida*, he went on to create such works as *La Bohème, Madame Butterfly,* and *Tosca,* all of which are mainstays in the repertoire and still performed widely every year.

However, around the time of *Madame Butterfly* in 1904, things began to go downhill despite his success. In fact, the first performance in Milan might have been a bad omen. Madame Butterfly was spinning on stage, and this caused her kimono to billow up about her. Someone in the audience yelled, "Butterfly is pregnant," and this precipitated a whole round of remarks and catcalls for the duration of the opera, including barnyard animal sounds. By the end, the audience was laughing, not clapping. Puccini was mortified and forbade a second performance, returning his fee to the opera house. He modified the work and presented it again a few months later, to a much better reception.

This was not the first nor last of his misfortunes; he had nearly been killed in an automobile accident in 1903. In 1909 a strange incident occurred. His wife, Elvira, driven by unknown jealousies, accused their maid Doria Manfredi of having an affair with Puccini, but this was a false accusation. Fearful of the shame that such a scandal might bring, the maid committed suicide, drinking poison. Her family sued Elvira, won their case, and Puccini paid them damages to keep Elvira out of jail. Recent evidence shows that Puccini was indeed having an affair, but it was with Doria's cousin, Giulia. This liaison went on for some time, and she bore him a son, Alfredo, whom he supported in secret. Things got worse in 1912 with the death of Giulio Ricordi, Puccini's longtime editor and publisher.

In late 1923, he began to complain of a persistent sore throat. Puccini had been a heavy cigar smoker, and the diagnosis came back as throat cancer. His doctors recommended a new and experimental treatment option for him: radiation. Alas, the treatment failed, and he suffered a fatal heart attack as a result.

One story relates that when news of his death reached Rome, it was during a performance of *La Bohème*; another source says that this happened at the Met in New York. The opera was temporarily stopped, and the orchestra played Chopin's Funeral March in tribute, something Puccini would have no doubt appreciated. One report states that Mussolini paid tribute to him and declared that Puccini had asked him for membership in the Fascist Party. Puccini's request may or may not be true, but the party made him an honorary member, whether he requested it or not. He was not interested in politics, so it is doubtful that he changed his mind at the end of his life. Mussolini was clearly taking the opportunity to link his fascist movement with greater Italian culture, quite possibly tarnishing the composer's name in the process.

Gustav Mahler (1860–1911)

Tenth time's a charm, or not

The Austrian composer Mahler was known for his absolutely huge works—his dense symphonies, massive choirs, and the long running times in his compositions. He merits inclusion due to his alleged curious superstition about the numbering of his symphonies (trying to avoid a ninth symphony), which will be discussed in detail in the "Musical Superstitions" chapter in Part II. According to some sources, Mahler was very afraid of the consequences of writing a ninth symphony, and he may have been right.

Claude Debussy (1862–1918)

Wife-swapping

Debussy stands at the doorway between late Romantic and modern, as he experimented with many new ideas in musical construction and harmony, ideas that were considered cutting edge and even shocking at the time. His music was labeled "Impressionist," like the art, but he disliked this designation. He was inspired by the French literary movement known as Symbolism, which used metaphors, myths, and dreams to give subjects symbolic meaning. We have already witnessed his feud with Saint-Saëns over musical innovations. Debussy certainly reflected symbolic ideals in his music, particularly in his many fine works for piano.

His personal life practically defines the phrase "soap opera." A noted womanizer, he had lived with a woman named Gabrielle Dupont in artistic poverty for several years (from 1890, she had tried to support him), and then decided that he wanted to marry her best friend, Rosalie Texier, a fashion model, in 1899. A famous story relays that on the morning of their wedding, he had to give a piano lesson to earn enough money to pay for the wedding breakfast. Dupont was distraught at being dumped and attempted suicide with a gun, but failed.

Texier was sweet and practical, but not very artistically sophisticated, and this grew to irritate Debussy over time. So he did what any scandal-ridden musician would do and left her in 1904 for another woman, Emma Bardac, both the wife of a Parisian banker and the mother of one of Debussy's students. Bardac was quite different from Texier, being sophisticated, intellectual, and musically gifted.

Texier, like Dupont before her, tried to commit suicide with a pistol, shooting herself in the chest, but also failed. Debussy and Bardac (who was pregnant with his child at the time) fled to Eastbourne in England both to let the furor and scandal calm down and to avoid the legal issues. Bardac's family effectively disowned her, and many of Debussy's friends were scandalized and angry. The third time seemed to be a charm for Debussy, however. Both he and Bardac were able to divorce their respective spouses and thus return to some level of respectability; the two eventually married in 1908. Their daughter, Claude-Emma, was destined to be his only child, and he loved her dearly.

By 1916, Debussy was suffering from colon cancer and became one of the first to undergo an operation in an attempt to cure it. The procedure was unsuccessful, however, and he died in March 1918. At the time Paris was under attack from long-range German guns as a part of the Spring Offensive, a last-gasp German effort to win the war before the Americans deployed their many troops and resources; he died only eight months before the Allies won the war. The procession made its way to Père Lachaise Cemetery through abandoned streets to the sound of artillery shells. He was reburied a year later in Passy Cemetery, in sight of the Eiffel Tower. His daughter, Claude-Emma, lived for only another year, tragically dying in a diphtheria epidemic in 1919.

Enrique Granados (1867–1916)

Going down with the ship

Granados, from Catalonia in northern Spain, was a gifted pianist and teacher. Considered one of the last Romantics and a hugely important nationalist composer, he is recognized as one of Spain's most important musical figures.

Unfortunately, it was his fame that brought about his untimely end. He was invited to attend the premiere of his opera *Goyescas* at the Metropolitan Opera in New York in 1916. Granados was actually quite afraid of water, but he suppressed his fear and made his first journey by ship across the Atlantic along with his wife, Amparo. Once there, he met with acclaim and success, even having the opportunity to perform for President Woodrow Wilson at the White House. He also made sound recordings that still survive. Unfortunately, in being delayed by the recital and the recordings, he missed his ship back to Spain and so took a passenger ship, the *Sussex*, bound for Dieppe, France. This was a riskier endeavor, as World War I was raging in full force at the time.

The trip across the Atlantic was without incident, but in sailing across the English Channel, the ship was torpedoed by a German U-boat. Making his way to a lifeboat, he saw his wife flailing in the waters some distance away and jumped into the water to try to save her. Unfortunately, both drowned. In the end, Granados's thalassophobia proved to be justified.

Alexander Scriabin (1871/72–1915)

Color me confused

Scriabin was an odd one, to be sure. Known for writing very complex and difficult piano music, as well as having a fascination with occult and mystical writings and practices, he was also devoted to the idea of associations between colors and musical notes. The term for this is synaesthesia, a condition in which people associate one sense or cognitive pathway with another; it often involves colors. For example, one might "see" a particular color whenever a specific note or chord is heard, or each number or letter of the alphabet may have its own color in the person's mind.

Some doubt whether Scriabin was an actual synaesthete (how's that for a great word?). He seemed to assume that certain colors were fixed with certain notes, and that a listener should associate these with their assigned tones when hearing his music, presumably visualizing them. Interestingly, Rimsky-Korsakov seemed to agree with many of his color associations. The reality is that a synaesthete's experience of which color is associated with which note (or number, or letter, etc.) is highly individual.

In any case, Scriabin had grandiose plans to mount a work called *Mysterium* that was never realized. It would have been a full-on multimedia production, performed at the foot of the Himalayas in a half temple, in front of a large pool of water. The audience would sit at the opposite end of the pool in tiers arranged by "spiritual advancement"; the lesser-evolved would be seated near the back.

The spectacle would last for a week and involve not only music, but also color, scent, and movement; he was trying to include all the senses. He wanted an orchestra and a choir, visual effects (mists and special lighting), a large procession, and incense of various kinds. He would invite the whole world to attend, even animals and insects. After the performance, the world would end in a blissful state, the grandest finale of all. Scriabin was influenced by Eastern mysticism and theosophy, a popular European movement combining said mysticism with various occult practices that promised enlightenment and secret knowledge. He once wrote in one of his secret journals, "I am God."

Apparently, he wasn't. He died young and in a bizarre manner. He was invited to London in 1914 and, while there, developed an ulcer on his lip. Whether it came from a cut, a boil, or even an insect sting is not clear—maybe the insect was annoyed that *Mysterium* was never produced. In any case, the ulcer would not heal properly and ultimately became septicemic. He died in 1915 in Moscow at the age of forty-three.

7

The Modern Era

What a problematic term this is; just how does one describe something as "modern" these days? People in every era have rightly considered themselves "modern"—well, maybe not Attila the Hun. Then again, maybe he did too. The Inquisitor's apprentice in 1301 felt he was every bit as modern for his day (check out all the latest new torture devices) as the young, arty hipster sipping a cappuccino and using the latest social networking site that he was into before it was cool. As time marches on, what we can consider modern fades into the distance of the past, just as it always has and always will. So some clever types came up with the term "post-modern." We now live in the Post-Modern Age.

Except that this will fade in time, too. Then what will we have? The Post-Post-Modern Era? The end of history as we know it? The result of Scriabin's *Mysterium*? Again, we should just call it all the Later Middle Ages and be done with it; they'll thank us for it in the thirty-first century.

For purposes of this book, we will call everything from the twentieth century onward modern. Modern can represent everything we've come to know and love in our everyday world, from technology to culture, but also world wars, pollution, sleazy banks, mullets, and unisex polyester bell-bottom pants.

This final chapter of Part I covers composers whose main works appeared post-1900, or who at least produced a significant number of pieces after that date. However, as we shall see, living in this sophisticated "modern" world doesn't save one from a grisly fate.

Modern composers also have something of a tougher time of things in general, having to compete against so much posthumous greatness. Composer Arthur Honegger once quipped, "The public doesn't want new music; the main thing it demands of a composer is that he be dead."

With that in mind, as we move closer to our own age, we begin to encounter composers who have passed much more recently and are even still in the living memories of some. Here, the whole point of this book—presenting the grotesque in music history with a humorous twist—begins to get a bit shaky. Is it proper to present a gruesome story about someone who may have living children or grandchildren, especially in a humorous light? Not really. In the interests of good taste, we will tread a bit lightly here and generally leave the truly contemporary composers of our own time out of it all.

Composers in World War I (1914–1918)

The lost generation

The Great War (as it was then known) utterly changed the face of Europe, altering nations, leaving millions dead or injured, and shattering earlier popular ideas about war as a means to achieve nationalist glory. It left permanent scars across the continent and in Britain, and set the stage for an even more devastating war two decades later. A good number of composers in England, France, and Germany felt called to serve. Some did not return, and those that did had their lives changed forever.

Among the more tragic of the English was George Butterworth (1885–1916), once considered one of the most promising young composers of his generation. In addition to his musical gifts, he was a collector of English folk songs, a practice that had developed in the Edwardian years to help preserve traditional songs from being lost forever. He was also an avid folk dancer. Nevertheless, when the opportunity to serve in the military came in August 1914, he eagerly took it. He was killed by a sniper's bullet during the Battle of the Somme on August 5, 1916, and

The ancient Greek aulos, which could blow people away. (Public domain, Wikimedia Commons.)

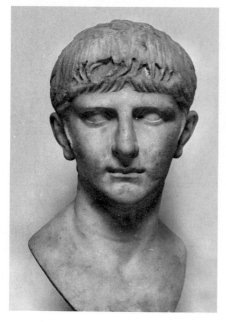

The young Emperor Nero, looking rather smug about his mediocre musical abilities. (Image courtesy of the University of Cologne and the German Archaeological Institute (DAI)/Arachne.)

The graves of Abelard and Héloïse, united at last in Père Lachaise Cemetery in Paris, though the poor man still has something missing. (Photograph by Tim Rayborn.)

Bertran de Born, condemned to carry his own head in hell, an afterlife worthy of a heavy metal song. Engraving by Gustave Doré. (Copyright free, Project Gutenberg.)

A wonderfully anachronistic depiction of the death of Richard the Lionheart, putting him back in the Holy Land and giving him the body of an underwear model. (Image courtesy of the Wellcome Library, London.)

Henry VIII and his fool, William Sommers. Neither looks particularly happy about being there. (Image courtesy of the British Library.)

John Bull, probably thinking about philandering and demolition. (Image courtesy of the Österreichische Nationalbibliothek.)

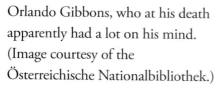

Orlando Gibbons, who at his death apparently had a lot on his mind. (Image courtesy of the Österreichische Nationalbibliothek.)

Jean-Baptiste Lully, looking impish and rebellious, but soon to be de-feeted. (Image courtesy of the Österreichische Nationalbibliothek.)

Henry Purcell, who has no idea of the chilly fate that awaits him. (Image courtesy of the Wellcome Library.)

EFFIGIES ANTONII VIVALDI

G. TARTINI

Né en 1692, Mort en 1770.

Gravé par Lambert d'après le Dessin Original
de E. Guérin appartenant à Mr. Cartier.

Antonio Vivaldi, with the smirk that launched a thousand speculations. (Image courtesy of the Österreichische Nationalbibliothek.)

Giuseppe Tartini, gazing in wonder at the devil's virtuosity? (Image courtesy of the Österreichische Nationalbibliothek.)

MODERN PROPENSITIES.

Frantisek Kotzwara, about to meet his unusual end. (Image courtesy of Google Books / the British Library.)

Wolfgang Amadeus Mozart as boy, looking confident. He was writing music when most of us were learning how to read. (Image courtesy of the Wellcome Library.)

Antonio Salieri, who doesn't look particularly diabolical or consumed by jealousy here. (Image courtesy of the Österreichische Nationalbibliothek.)

WELTSCHMERZ.

Romantic Weltschmerz, or writer's block . . . or just a hangover. (Public domain, archive.org.)

Hector Berlioz, whose bizarre love life would be rejected in a fictional story as being too unrealistic. (Image courtesy of the Österreichische Nationalbibliothek.)

The grave of Frederic Chopin in Père Lachaise Cemetery in Paris; he left his heart elsewhere. (Photograph by Tim Rayborn.)

Anton Bruckner. Numeromanic and corpse-obsessive, he lovingly cradled Beethoven's skull. (Public domain, archive.org.)

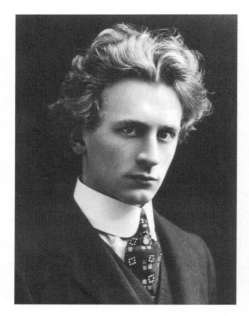

Percy Grainger, whose youthful good looks hid his obsession with much darker passions. (Image courtesy of the Lewis Foreman collection.)

Peter Warlock (Philip Heseltine): composer, music critic, black magician, and noted writer of dirty limericks. (Image courtesy of the Lewis Foreman collection.)

ORPHÉE.

Orpheus in a pastoral scene, sadly unaware of the terrible fate that awaits him. (Image courtesy of the Wellcome Library.)

Dionysus and his revelers, who are getting up to all sorts of debauched things. (Image courtesy of the Wellcome Library.)

The flagellants, whipping up some painful rhythms. (Public domain, Wikimedia Commons.)

Charivari from the Roman de Fauvel, wearing masks, baring butts, and scaring decent people. (Public domain, courtesy of the Bibliothèque nationale de France.)

Vlad Dracula, the grand-daddy of serial killers; he had a real stake in his country's future. (Public domain, archive.org.)

Barber surgeons and a patient who looks quite unhappy. Maybe she just needs a lute. (Image courtesy of the Wellcome Library.)

Robert Schumann. Did his spirit reach out from beyond to reveal the location of his long-lost violin concerto? (Image courtesy of the Österreichische Nationalbibliothek.)

Dead or asleep? Either way, the lady at the keyboard looks decidedly annoyed. (Image courtesy of the Wellcome Library.)

"Bloody" Mary Tudor. Was she the "quite contrary" lady in the nursery rhyme garden? Did she cut off three blind mice's tails, or something worse? (Image courtesy of the University of Leuven.)

THE ENRAGED MUSICIAN.

Loud street musicians, reminiscent of the Charivari. The "proper" musician in the window appears to be quite irritated. (Image courtesy of the Wellcome Library.)

Arnold Schoenberg, self-portrait, 1910. In addition to fearing the number 13, he seems to be missing an ear. (Wikimedia Commons, free license.)

mourned by many. Composer Ernest Moeran would later declare, "The death of Butterworth in 1915 [*sic*] was a tragedy, the nature of which no country with any pretensions to the preservation of culture and a respect for art can afford a recurrence."

Another promising young Englishman who lost his life was Ernest Farrar (1885–1918), a gifted composer and teacher from northern England. His service came quite late in the war; he was killed in the Battle of Épehy on September 18, 1918, less than two months before the armistice. His pupil, composer Gerald Finzi, later poignantly wrote in the 1950s, "then I was about fourteen and he was just over thirty. Now I am over fifty and he is still just over thirty."

The great English composer Ralph Vaughan Williams (1872–1958) desired to serve, but by 1914, he was already forty-two—too old for regular combat. He joined the Royal Army Medical Corps as an ambulance driver in France and had the terrible job of helping the wounded from the field and transporting them to makeshift hospitals. He survived the war, but it affected him deeply. His third symphony, the *Pastoral*, is in many ways his war requiem. Despite its name, it evokes the battlefields of northern France. He famously later stated, "it's not really Lambkins frisking at all as most people take for granted." The sound of artillery shells exploding nearby may have contributed to his increasing deafness late in his life.

For the French, Maurice Ravel (1875–1937) also felt called to protect his country from invasion. He wanted to join the new air force (developed in 1909) but was rejected due to a minor heart problem. Instead, he joined the Thirteenth Artillery Regiment in 1915, a potentially dangerous job that brought him under enemy fire. Fortunately, he escaped harm, though his health suffered from the terrible conditions of the battlefield.

During the war, Saint-Saëns (see the previous chapter) and others established the Ligue Nationale pour la Défense de la Musique Française, which advocated for a ban on performances of German music. Ravel, who had also taught Vaughan Williams a few years earlier, declined to join, believing that international contacts in the arts were still needed. He said:

It would be dangerous for French composers to ignore systematically the productions of their foreign colleagues, and thus form themselves into a sort of national coterie: our musical art, which is so rich at the present time, would soon degenerate, becoming isolated in banal formulas.

The Ligue was not happy with this response and, in a show of sour grapes, banned his music from its concert productions.

On the German side, composer and violinist Fritz Kreisler (1875–1962) was a notable recruit. As a violinist he had spent much time touring, including in England. Indeed Edward Elgar (of *Pomp and Circumstance* fame) composed his Violin Concerto for Kreisler, who performed it in London in 1910. With the outbreak of the war, however, he was recalled to duty and sent to Germany's eastern front. As a musician, he was keenly aware of the different types of sounds in battle and recorded his observations about them in his memoir:

My ear, accustomed to differentiate sounds of all kinds, had some time ago, while we still advanced, noted a remarkable discrepancy in the peculiar whine produced by the different shells in their rapid flight through the air as they passed over our heads, some sounding shrill, with a rising tendency, and the others rather dull, with a falling cadence.

As with the English and French, however, the hope of war glory soon faded:

Enthusiasm seemed suddenly to disappear before this terrible spectacle. Life that only a few hours before had glowed with enthusiasm and exultation, suddenly paled and sickened.

Kreisler was wounded by a bayonet while in battle with Russian troops and spent seven hours lying in a trench before he was discovered and rescued. He was later judged to be too seriously injured to return to battle and was released from further service. Eager to get back to music, he moved to New York, but encountered considerable anti-German sentiment. He lived again in Europe for a time before becoming an American citizen in 1943.

Richard Strauss (1864–1949)

Fallen in with the wrong crowd

Strauss (no relation to the waltz king, Johann Strauss) is most famous today for his 1896 piece *Also sprach Zarathustra* ("Thus Spoke Zarathustra"). You've heard it, or at least the first ninety seconds of it. It was used in the film *2001: A Space Odyssey* as the famous opening music. Oh, right, *that* piece! He also wrote a large quantity of other music over his long life.

The big point of controversy surrounding him was his affiliation with the Nazis—or not, and that's the bone of the contention. The question is just how much of his activity was him trying to survive in a very dangerous time, even remaining apolitical, and how much was a sincere belief in their goals? His behavior earned him the scorn of some of his colleagues, including the famed conductor Arturo Toscanini, who declared, "To Strauss the composer I take off my hat; to Strauss the man I put it back on again."

So, what actually happened?

In November 1933, Joseph Goebbels appointed Strauss to the post of president of the Reichsmusikkammer (the Nazi State Music Bureau), without consulting him or asking his consent. Goebbels saw him as useful but also considered him a "decadent neurotic" who would eventually have to be replaced. Strauss, for his part, thought of Goebbels as a "pipsqueak" who represented "untalented, lazy mediocrity."

Strauss kept the post, noting in his journal, "I accepted this honorary office because I hoped that I would be able to do some good and prevent worse misfortunes," but generally he wanted to remain outside of politics. Being "German" was not important to him, as he noted in a letter to his friend Stefan Zweig: "Do you suppose Mozart was consciously 'Aryan' when he composed? I recognise only two types of people: those who have talent and those who have none." Many saw his desire to remain separate from the issues of the day as naïve, then and now, and some have condemned him for not refusing the appointment. He was known to have befriended some important Nazis during his years in the post. Yes, he could have refused it to begin with, but did he really have a choice?

It seems that he was trying to use this position of influence to protect some of his Jewish friends, as well as Alice, his Jewish daughter-in-law, and her children from persecution. He does not seem to have supported Nazi anti-Semitism; he refused to call Hitler "der Führer" and he tried to help those close to him as much as he could. It's entirely possible that he was simply playing the game well, doing just enough to satisfy the Nazi authorities while keeping himself and his friends alive. But he ultimately seemed to alienate both the Nazis and their enemies in the process, the former at great risk to his life, the latter at risk to his reputation. It was a no-win situation.

He had to resign from the presidential post in 1935 because he refused to remove the name of his Jewish librettist, Stefan Zweig, from an opera program for his work *Die schweigsame Frau*. He had also written a private letter critical of the Nazis to Zweig, which the Gestapo intercepted. The opera was banned after only four performances.

He skillfully managed to avoid official persecution, but eventually some of his friends did suffer. In 1944, Alice and his son were arrested by the Gestapo. He was able to secure their release from prison, but they remained under house arrest until the end of the war.

Despite these dangers he made it through World War II, and was recognized by a music-loving American soldier in his house during the occupation, which spared him from harassment by American troops. However, he was investigated afterward on suspicion of Nazi collaboration. He was eventually cleared of any wrongdoing or complicity and was allowed to resume being a composer. Aware that his life was coming to an end and that his work was beginning to be seen as dated, he amusingly declared at rehearsals for the London Strauss Festival in 1947, "I may not be a first-rate composer, but I am a first-class second-rate composer!"

Erik Satie (1866–1925)

Mona Lisa's Moustache

Satie is one of the more colorful characters from the Impressionistic movement and could also be featured in the Romantic chapter, but many of his most important works were composed after 1900; he also certainly rejected various aspects of Romanticism in his music. He exerted a great influence on both Debussy and Maurice Ravel, the main representatives of Impressionistic music. Known for his immaculate, if flamboyant, dress sense, he would frequent the local cafés in his neighborhood, soaking up Parisian atmosphere on a daily basis. No one was ever permitted in his home, however, and after his death its contents were found to be surprising, even shocking, to those who knew him.

The son of a French man and a Scottish woman, Satie was born in Normandy, and after a brief time in Paris was sent there again following his mother's untimely death. His father eventually remarried a pianist, Eugénie Barnetche. She wanted to assist with his music training, but he didn't like her and resisted. She enrolled him in the Paris Conservatoire in 1879 but he made a poor impression, described by his first piano teacher, Émile Descombes, as the "laziest student in the Conservatoire" and by his intermediate piano teacher, Georges Mathias, as "worthless." He hated his time there and only stuck with it to avoid lengthy military service. In the end he was supposed to serve for one year, but he avoided that as well; he was invalided after deliberately infecting himself with bronchitis to get out of service in 1887.

Satie returned to focusing on composition and moved to Montmartre in Paris. For the last decade of the nineteenth century he was involved with the Rosicrucian Order, a self-styled secret society that most likely originated in the early seventeenth century. He was fascinated with the medieval, and the austere sounds of Gregorian chant moved him, influencing a good number of his works. Debussy referred to him as "a gentle medieval musician lost in this century." This quieter and more minimal sound went against the Wagnerian bombast that was the rage at the time. Satie was clearly an outsider.

He also indulged in jokes. His piece *Vexations*, for example, while only one page long, has written instructions on the score that it is to be repeated 840 times, a task which would make the piece twenty hours long. Critics and musicians dismissed it as a joke, though the experimental composer John Cage actually organized and oversaw a complete performance of it!

Other pieces included wonderfully silly titles, such as *Five Grins or Mona Lisa's Moustache*, *Veritable Flabby Preludes (for a Dog)*, *Three Pieces in the Shape of a Pear*, and *Sketches and Exasperations of a Big Boob Made of Wood*. He would scribble musical directions on some pieces—not the usual indicators, such as *andante* or *allegro*, but rather such whimsical instructions as "to be jealous of one's playmate who has a big head." The writer Jean Cocteau explained that Satie employed these ridiculous titles as a way of shielding himself from those "obsessed with the sublime," in other words, the snobby world of high-art critics and society that had so often disdained him. Satie collaborated with Cocteau on the 1917 avant-garde ballet *Parade* that also included costumes designed by Picasso—what a combination!

One of his writings, *A Day in the Life of a Musician*, outlines a mock daily routine through a number of whimsical entries. He notes that he is inspired between 10:23 and 11:47 a.m. precisely, takes lunch from 12:11 to 12:14, and feels more inspiration from 3:12 to 4:07 p.m. Dinner takes place between 7:16 and 7:20 p.m., and he only eats white foods: eggs, sugar, bones, fat, salt, coconut, rice, and certain kinds of fish, among other dishes. He sleeps with one eye open and has his temperature taken once an hour. He smokes on the advice of his doctor, for if he did not, someone else would do it for him.

While living and performing in Montmartre, Satie encountered Debussy, who was deeply impressed with and influenced by his works, though this would not be recognized until much later. Indeed, Ravel and Debussy grew famous while Satie long lived in obscurity, something that frustrated him greatly. Later, as he finally gained some acclaim, his relationship with Debussy became a bit strained.

At the end of 1898 he moved to the Paris suburb of Arcueil and remained there for the rest of his life. Amazingly, no outsider was to visit or even set foot in his flat there until after his death.

Throughout these years Satie, like so many others, indulged in heavy drinking, particularly absinthe. He died on July 1, 1925, of cirrhosis. After his death, his friends finally were able to enter his apartment, where they had never gone during his lifetime. What they found there was a bizarre scene. A complete mess confronted them, including many compositions previously unknown or thought to have been lost (often in piles behind his piano or even stuffed into the pockets of his coats), litter and rubbish strewn about (including some human excrement in one corner), and a general scene of chaos that was extreme, even for a rebellious alcoholic artist. Somehow he would leave this squalor behind every day—dressed immaculately in his velvet suits—and visit the cafés and bars of the neighborhood, dreaming up his humor-laden works and perhaps thumbing his nose at the artistic establishment, all while sipping fancy French coffee or his beloved absinthe.

Louis Vierne (1870–1937)

Organ failure

Vierne was born with a congenital cataract condition, leaving him nearly blind. Though his sight was partially restored after an operation when he was six years old, he was never able to see well. Regardless, he had a tremendous interest in music and developed considerable skill on keyboard instruments, most notably the organ. He was able to study at the Paris Conservatoire and eventually ended up as the principal organist at the famed Notre Dame Cathedral, a position he held from 1900 until his death. However, owing to political reasons and nepotism he was passed over more than once for the post of professor of organ at the Conservatoire, causing him much frustration. The loss of his brother and one son in World War I, a second son to tuberculosis, and a divorce from his wife left him seriously depressed and financially unstable, but he pressed on and won the admiration and backing of various wealthy patrons. His compositions for organ and other instruments are important; his organ music is a standard part of the repertoire.

Despite his hardships, his life ended exactly as he would have wanted. While giving his 1,750th organ recital at Notre Dame on June 2, 1937, he suffered a heart attack (he was a heavy smoker and took medications) just as he finished the main concert and was preparing an improvisation. He fell forward and then off the bench, his foot hitting the E note of the pedal. He had mentioned several times in the past that he wanted to die at this very organ and, amazingly, he got his wish.

Arnold Schoenberg (1874–1951)
Triskaidekaphobia

Schoenberg, loved or hated, is hugely important in the history of "modern" classical music, having created the twelve-tone system of atonal composition that seems like mathematical musical heaven to some and mathematical noise to others. He was an important music theorist and taught composition. Unlike Strauss, he wisely left Germany with the rise of the Nazis and ended up living in Los Angeles.

The reason for including him in this book is that he had a morbid, obsessive dread of the number thirteen throughout his whole life. This phobia is explored in more detail in the chapter on music superstitions in Part II.

Percy Grainger (1882–1961)
Where there's a whip, there's a way

Born in Melbourne, Grainger was a native of Australia but spent considerable time in Europe and later settled in America. As composers go, he was quite the innovator, and like several of his contemporaries, he was keenly interested in collecting and preserving English folk songs. Living in London from 1901 to 1914, Grainger hiked around Britain collecting such songs and was also the first to make wax cylinder recordings of many of them, ensuring greater accuracy in preserving them. This was a practice that the musical establishment was not completely convinced was necessary, but it marks him as an early ethnomusicologist. He arranged many of these tunes in settings for solo piano.

He was known for his boundless energy, sometimes walking from one concert venue to another while on tour (the tour bus hadn't yet been invented; trains were the norm). He even helped shovel coal in the boiler rooms of ships he traveled on. Can you imagine a modern pop band offering to do that?

Moving to America in 1914 at the onset of World War I, he eventually became a US citizen but continued to travel widely. He became a keen supporter of jazz and Duke Ellington, whom he considered to be one of the great composers of all time, along with Bach and Frederick Delius. In later years he even experimented with early forms of electronic and mechanical music and was known to enjoy the new rock-and-roll movies that were becoming popular. One suspects that he would have loved the explosion of new ideas in rock music in the '60s and '70s.

So what's the dark side of this tale? Well, Mr. Grainger had a bit of a fetish. He was heavily into S&M, especially flagellation. His practices also had a voyeuristic aspect to them, as he documented and photographed his activities with his wife; she seems to have tolerated it as a "wife's duty." He liked to be very thorough and specific, noting the date, time, and even the whip used in any given session. When he toured, he took whips with him for self-flagellation.

He was the son of odd parents. His mother suffered from syphilis and had a morbid fear of contaminating him with it; she withheld physical affection as a result. She whipped him regularly until he was sixteen and tried to limit and control his contact with others his own age, especially women; this latter behavior continued until he was nearly forty years old. She kept a disturbingly tight rein on Percy, bordering on obsession. As so often happened, her syphilis drove her insane, and she eventually committed suicide in 1922 by jumping out of a window from the eighteenth floor of an office building in New York City. The effect of her death on Grainger was devastating; his love of the whip was strongly connected to his love for her.

In the mid-1930s, he donated a sum of money to the University of Melbourne so that it could establish a museum dedicated to him. Humility clearly wasn't one of his strong points. In addition to the usual donations of music, instruments, letters, and manuscripts, he included various items from his unconventional hobby, including photographs of sessions, whips (more than eighty of them), and even a pair of bloodstained shorts (!) worn in one such session. Exactly what the university made of all this is unknown.

Among his other eccentricities:

- He wore wrinkled clothing; he considered ironing pointless for performances, since no one in the audience could see him up close anyway. Amusingly, he was arrested more than once for vagrancy due to his disheveled look.

- He liked to sleep under his piano.

- He was a vegetarian who disliked vegetables and preferred bread, milk, and fruit. He didn't like coffee, tea, or alcohol.

- He lived in the same house in New York for many years but apparently only mowed the lawn once during that time.

- He would hang items such as pens and pencils from his coat on pieces of string, rather than carry them in a briefcase.

He was an odd man who once declared, "I live for my lusts and I don't care if they kill me." It was abdominal cancer that eventually did kill him in early 1961 in New York. He was buried in a religious ceremony in Adelaide, Australia, against his wishes; he had been a lifelong atheist. Whether any whips went to the grave with him is not known, but he would no doubt have wanted them.

Anton Webern (1883–1945)

A shot in the dark II

The Austrian composer Webern is best known for working in the atonal style developed by Arnold Schoenberg; he was also a major proponent of the twelve-tone technique, a compositional form wherein all twelve notes of the western chromatic scale (i.e., all of the black and white keys of the piano in a single octave) are given equal treatment, so that a key or "center" to the music is not established. The result is not always pleasant to listen to, but the technique has intrigued musicians and composers for a century; it's quite a challenge to write a piece within these guidelines. General audiences mostly never really warmed to the idea, so you're not likely to ever see a twelve-tone song topping the Billboard charts. Many consider it to be nothing more than a mathematical exercise without much in the way of a pleasing aesthetic; others think it's just noise. English composer Ernest Moeran referred to it as "wrong note music." His fellow Englishman Vaughan Williams flatly stated in 1956 that it seemed to him "the most astonishing bit of mechanical pedantry which has ever been dignified by the name of art . . . apparently one must not use any succession of notes which sounds agreeable to the cultivated ear."

Webern ran afoul of the Nazis during World War II but managed to keep his wits and his head, and seemed at one point even to endorse Hitler; any Nazi sympathies that he had were probably more out of German patriotism than sympathy with their positions, and he certainly did not adopt anti-Semitic attitudes. In that time and place, one had to play the game of life very carefully. At the end of the war, when Germany and Austria were occupied by the Allied forces, he was at his daughter's home near Salzburg. On the night of September 15, he stepped outside to smoke a cigar, so as not to disturb his sleeping grandchildren; an Allies-imposed curfew was about to go into effect. US army soldier Pfc. Raymond Norwood Bell shot and killed him, believing him to be up to no good, possibly due to Webern's son-in-law having been arrested for black market activity. Bell was said to be so distraught with remorse over the shooting that he became an alcoholic and died in 1955.

Alban Berg (1885–1935)

Sheer foolishness

Berg was a member of the Second Viennese School that also included Schoenberg and Webern. He explored the new concepts of atonal music, and many now consider his output (difficult though it may be for first-time listeners to appreciate) to be among the richest and most important in contemporary music. Arguably the most popular of the School, he also incorporated tonal music into his works. One of these pieces, the oddly named *Five Songs on Picture Postcard Texts by Peter Altenberg*, caused quite a stir. Two of the songs were performed in Vienna in March 1913, conducted by Schoenberg. The music was so unsettling that it apparently induced a riot in the audience and the performance had to be stopped; the concert organizer was arrested. Of course, this reaction was a huge blow to the composer's ego. He was mortified and withdrew the pieces. They were not performed again until after his death.

He studied with Schoenberg for seven years, but unlike his teacher, who had a fear of the number thirteen, he had a fascination with the number twenty-three. He had apparently suffered his first asthma attack on July 23 (the year is uncertain) and saw this as significant. He may also have been interested in the work of Wilhelm Fliess, an otolaryngologist. That's quite a word! It refers to the study and treatment of disorders of the head and neck. We know them as ear, nose, and throat doctors, but their expertise extends much wider than that—well, only as wide as a given person's head. In any case, Fliess developed a theory that men and women went through regular sexual cycles, twenty-three days for men and twenty-eight for women, a precursor to the modern concept of biorhythms. Of course, Fliess also developed an extensive theory about the connection between the nose and the genitals, so maybe we can take his ideas with a grain of salt.

Regardless of the source of his musical symbolism, Berg was a fairly prolific composer, but as usual, had mixed financial success.

Again, this lack of money was to contribute to his untimely end. He was the victim of an insect sting on his back. The sting developed an abscess, and his wife, in an effort to save money, offered to remove it with a pair of scissors. Of course, this led to blood poisoning, and by the time he was admitted to a hospital it was too late. He died at the age of fifty on Christmas Eve. Do-it-yourself surgery is never recommended.

Wallingford Riegger (1885–1961)

Doggone it

Riegger was one of the first American composers to make use of the twelve-tone system, which is either good or bad depending on your point of view. He lived and studied in Germany on two separate occasions in the early part of the twentieth century, returning home when the United States entered World War I in 1917. After this, he spent much of his time composing and teaching at various institutions in New York State. His atonal works were admired by some, but one critic described a piece as sounding like "a dying cow emitting mournful groans."

In the 1950s, he was called before the House Un-American Activities Committee. They were investigating the infiltration of communist ideas into the musical world, and they may well have seen the twelve-tone system as a commie plot to undermine good old-fashioned tonal American music. Or they at least expected him to rat on those who were hiding their nefarious plans under the guise of some of the more suspicious types of "new music." Riegger had communist sympathies but surprisingly does not seem to have suffered much from the witch hunt.

In the annals of ridiculous and unnecessary deaths, his certainly takes an honored place. In 1961 he found himself entangled, literally, in the leashes of two dogs that were fighting. He tripped and fell to the hard ground. Though he received treatment, he died a short time later of complications from his injuries.

Sergei Prokofiev (1891–1953)

A good day to die?

Prokofiev led an interesting international life, having left the Soviet Union for America at the time of the Bolshevik Revolution (1918), feeling that his new music would not find favor under the strict Soviet policies being developed. Initially he went to San Francisco, then visited New York, and finally returned to Europe in the early 1920s. Touring through Europe extensively, he began to long for his homeland in the early 1930s. He returned by choice to the Soviet Union only to discover over time that its attitudes toward what kinds of art were acceptable were becoming much more rigid. He frequently found himself under suspicion, and his music was on occasion denounced as elitist and dangerous to the people. The Soviet government seemed to change its definition of what was acceptable and what wasn't as often as some change their underwear, so he probably never knew quite where he stood.

He also wasn't all that popular with his neighbors; once he was evicted from his apartment. The reason? A downstairs neighbor complained that he had played the same piano chord 218 times. Apparently, this person had nothing better to do than listen through the ceiling and keep a running count.

Prokofiev's estranged wife was convicted of espionage (most likely on trumped-up charges, as she was Spanish and there was a xenophobic attitude among the authorities) and sentenced to twenty years in Siberia, but Prokofiev himself managed to avoid a similar fate. However, he suffered several heart attacks and a bad fall, which led to declining health in his last years.

He died, probably of a cerebral hemorrhage, on March 5, 1953, coincidentally the same day as Josef Stalin, the man whose regime had caused him great amounts of hardship. Given that he lived near Red Square, the masses of "official" (i.e., obligatory) mourners that filled the place prevented the removal of his body for three days and dwarfed the tiny procession that carried his coffin to Novodevichy Cemetery. During the service, the organizers had to use paper flowers and potted plants, and a recording of funeral music from his ballet, *Romeo and Juliet*. This was because all the real flowers and actual musicians were reserved for Stalin's lavish state funeral, though some accounts say that many of the musicians secretly dedicated their performances to Prokofiev, while outwardly pretending to play for Stalin. Further, in a typical gesture of Soviet priorities, the leading music journal included notice of Prokofiev's death briefly on page 116. The first 115 pages were devoted to coverage of Stalin's death.

Still, he had the last laugh. He is regarded as one of the great twentieth-century Russian composers, and his music, including such wonderful works as *Peter and the Wolf*, is still loved.

Stalin? Well, he's not so popular anymore.

Peter Warlock (1894–1930)

It's a gas

Peter Warlock was the rather creative pen name of composer Philip Heseltine. He would alternate between his given name and his *nom de plume* depending on the circumstances; a fake name was a great way to pretend to be someone else and hide from the backlash of his often-harsh music criticisms. Warlock (as we'll call him here) was a part of the new movement of composers in early twentieth-century England. He was actively involved in writing about music and promoting the fellow composers of his day.

He was also deeply interested in music from Tudor times, which was then undergoing a revival in England, a "Renaissance" if you will—hey, it had to be said! He rediscovered the works of an obscure sixteenth-century English composer named Thomas Whythorne. This little-known fellow wrote what may be the earliest surviving autobiography in English, offering sage advice such as "He that wooeth a widow must not carry quick eels in his codpiece." There's something you'll never see in a fortune cookie! Warlock is now credited with being crucially important in bringing higher standards to musicology and to the way that early music was edited and prepared for modern editions.

He was also quite the limerick writer. No one was spared from his jests, as in this limerick, told of his friends, the singer John Goss and pianist/composer Hubert Foss:

> That scandalous pair Goss and Foss
> Once attempted to put it across
> A girl on a train
> But their efforts proved vain,
> So Foss tossed off Goss at King's Cross

And this was by no means the most scandalous one he wrote! He once typed out a series of them on a roll of toilet paper and then rolled it back up, as a joke.

As his pseudonym implies, Warlock had a keen interest in the occult and rubbed shoulders with various folks who shared his interest, including author Mary Butts, who had once spent time with the notorious Aleister Crowley at his home in Italy. There have been debates about how serious Warlock was in his devotion. We know that he spent a year in Dublin beginning in 1917 to avoid conscription into military service. While there, he may have suffered some psychological damage from too much dabbling in black magic and related things, but not everyone accepts this idea. His letters to a former teacher, Colin Taylor, dating from this time show that he was actively pursuing such interests. He writes:

> Since my voyages of discovery during the last six months have opened up for me such amazing and far-reaching vistas of hitherto undreamed-of possibilities, I thought you might find a new interest in life by following a similar track.

Later on, he warns:

> Please do not mention the books I have told you of to anyone else. This is important. When you have read them you will see that this kind of

book must not on any account fall into unfit hands. . . . There are far more dangerous books than obscene novels in existence.

In another letter, from 1918, he writes:

Please keep strictly to yourself anything I may have said in former letters about certain communications and predictions. These have developed into a very serious and important matter, of which I will tell you fully one day.

We don't know exactly what happened during that year, but his insistence on keeping silent about many details was in accordance with what practitioners of ritual magic believed. He once attended a séance in Dublin with his young wife but was met with resistance when an assistant to the ritual saw him and declared that he was "dogged by evil influences. Send him away." In 1918, Warlock claimed that he had received long messages of great importance from an unknown spiritual source, including some about music. At the same time he grew a goatee beard, saying that it made him more confident and was one of his "little magical energy-saving devices."

Some have speculated that his song "The bayly berith the bell away" may have been a reference to a black mass. The words are from a poem dating to the early sixteenth century at least, and may well simply describe bridal preparations:

The maydens came
When I was in my mother's bower,
I had all that I wolde.
The bayly berith the bell away,
The lily, the rose the rose I lay.
The silver is whit, red is the golde,
The robes they ley in fold.
The bayly berith the bell away,
The lily, the rose the rose I lay.

And through the glasse wyndow shines the sone.

How shuld I love, and I so young?

The bayly berith the bell away,

The lily, the lilly the rose I lay.

For the black mass interpretation, the ringing of the bell signifies the start of the black mass, the lily and rose are laid on the altar in blasphemous parody of a Christian ceremony, the colors red and white symbolize male and female, or perhaps purity and blood, the laying down of robes describes the removing of clothing for the ritual, and "how should I love" may describe the taking of a virgin on the altar. Admittedly this reading is a stretch, and many reject it, but it is the kind of work that Warlock would have been interested in, if he chose to read it this way.

Whatever his magical interests, he was also very fond of alcohol and spent some years in the mid-1920s sharing a home in the village of Eynsford, south of London, with his friend and fellow composer Ernest Moeran, living a life of excess and reported college fraternity levels of drinking. In addition, he suffered from depression (probably actually bipolar disorder) as he grew into adulthood. In the times when he was down he could do little for months, but in an up cycle he could compose a new song every day for a week.

He made many enemies in his life with his sharp wit and acidic tone. He once told prominent music critic and author Percy Scholes to do something creative to himself with a "well-greased pair of bellows." Scholes threatened a lawsuit in response.

Warlock was eventually found dead from gas poisoning in his Chelsea flat in London in December 1930. The official investigation kept the matter open. Suicide is suspected, of course, given his bouts of black moods. Investigators observed that his cat had been put out of the room into a yard, so maybe he wanted to save its life and only take his own. It's also possible that it was simply a tragic accident, though most today accept the suicide explanation, since he was depressed and had little money and no prospects.

There is a third possibility, which is (of course!) that he was murdered. He had named Dutch composer Bernard van Dieren as his heir, and Warlock's son, Nigel Heseltine, would later accuse van Dieren of murdering his father. This is doubtful, however, and no charges were ever brought. While suicide is the most likely explanation, the mystery of Warlock's death remains unresolved.

Sins and Omissions

*Y*ou may have noticed a few big names missing from Part I. Richard Wagner is absent, but he deserves a whole book to himself; in fact, there are several of them. Likewise with Stravinsky—the riot caused by the premiere of his ballet *The Rite of Spring* is legendary. Recent discoveries also suggest that Johann Sebastian Bach's life both in youth and in old age was far from pleasant, though we did cover him a bit in the Baroque chapter. If your favorite composer wasn't among those profiled, that might actually be a good thing; they escaped the clutches of various horrible fates, or at least led pretty good lives until the end.

One important point: you may also have noticed the depressing lack of female composers in the preceding chapters. On the one hand, that's good news for them; they didn't seem to have such horrific things happen to them! On the other, what it once again shows is the systemic exclusion of women from acknowledgment and credit in so much of artistic life (and other areas) throughout history, a worldwide problem. The women who lived in these times certainly wrote and played music. Vast numbers of them also sang and danced, often in the face of strenuous objections from religious authorities or disapproving fathers and husbands.

Unfortunately, far fewer achieved the fame and status of men until more recent years. The number of well-known female Western composers is terribly small compared to their male counterparts, despite the fact that they wrote many fine works over the centuries. From Hildegard of Bingen to Barbara Strozzi, from Fanny Mendelssohn to Clara Schumann, women have made important contributions to music across its whole history.

Likewise, this section featured composers of Western classical music, and so focused almost exclusively on Europeans, with a few American and Australian exceptions. There is literally a whole world of wonderful music out there, but in the interest of brevity, it's just not possible to wander very far into it.

In Part II, we will venture into some non-classical genres, such as folk, rock, and jazz, while further exploring plenty of classical music oddities.

Part II

A Dark and Weird Musical Miscellany

1

Odd Musical Origins

When did we start making music? This is one of those questions thrown around on a regular basis, with all sorts of theories from the fields of anthropology, psychology, archaeology, and many other –ologies. Music-like sounds are certainly produced by other members of the animal kingdom, whether the chirping of birds or the haunting and mournful songs of the great whales. Do these constitute *music* in the way that we think of it? Or are they forms of vocal communication, and so more like languages? If we go back far enough in our own species' family tree, is there even a difference between speaking and singing?

There are many books on these kinds of questions, and it would be difficult to summarize them here. So instead, let's start off Part II by looking at a few of the theories, findings, and speculations about music in prehistory, as well as the bloody origins of music in some myths. From vocal fish to cavemen choirs to gods with anger issues, the distant musical past is a stranger place than we might imagine.

Biological origins: singing fish

Most of us use our voices every day, sometimes all day, with the exception of the mute and those who have taken vows of silence. Our incredible capacity to make sounds with our vocal cords, those vibrating membranes, is something most of us take for granted. Just about everyone has temporarily lost their voice at one time or another, whether from sickness or yelling too much at a concert, or wherever, and we all know how frustrating it is. It's even more remarkable that these vibrations can be made into different pitches and types of sounds, and we associate meanings with them when they are combined. But the strangest thing of all is that we may have acquired this physiological feature from fish all those many millions of years ago.

Cornell University professor Andrew Bass (yes, that is his real name, and I'm sure that he's quite sick of the jokes) has found fascinating evidence in a species of fish, the midshipman, that produces sounds for various purposes. Males make grunts and noises—a kind of humming—during mating season (of course), while females make grunting sounds at other times—probably due to their annoyance with the horny male fish. People have reported hearing low-level humming sounds coming from the water during the fish's attempts to get it on.

Professor Bass and his team analyzed how the connection between the midshipman's vocal muscles developed, linking this process to neurons between its brain and its spinal cord. In "higher forms of life," including (allegedly) us, there are very similar neural pathways. What does that mean? Basically that this adaptation was useful to prehistoric fish very early on and remained with succeeding generations over eons, spreading to countless other life forms. In other words, we owe our ability to make sounds of all kinds to it. We also got our ears from these primeval ocean-dwellers, because they obviously had to be able to hear the sounds they were making.

So now we know that fish are still vocalizing up a storm under the waves, just as they've done for millions of years. It's time to give them the recognition they deserve for getting it all started. How about a tribute concert featuring "Aquarium" from Saint-Saëns's *Carnival of the Animals*, Satie's *The Dreamy Fish*, and a rousing performance of Schubert's *Trout Quintet*? The sea's the limit!

Biological origins: cavemen choirs

Though our knowledge about our ancestors and hominid cousins increases with each year, many questions remain, and of course there are still some silly misconceptions. The very term "caveman" is so loaded with incorrect images and ideas that it's useless. Generally when we're talking about our immediate forebears, we are speaking of Cro-Magnons and our extinct cousins, Neanderthals. We don't know if these folks made music, though researchers have found some intriguing clues in recent years.

Most people are aware of the amazing cave art in southern France and Spain; the network of tunnels at Lascaux in France is the most famous and spectacular example. Made by our direct ancestors (Homo sapiens sapiens) during the Upper Paleolithic Age roughly fifty thousand to twelve thousand years ago, these paintings deep inside caverns often depict remarkably lifelike animals, hunting scenes, and other imagery.

Iegor Reznikoff of the University of Paris X in Nanterre specializes in very old music. He has discovered that in many of the caves, the areas with the most paintings also offer the best acoustics. Since the shape of these caverns would not have changed much, if at all, since those times, it stands to reason that the markings were made in these locations deliberately, and that sound accompanied whatever rituals were conducted there.

Further, given the incredible difficulty in navigating the tunnels in darkness, these people probably used echolocation, relying on the reflection of sound to determine where they were. Vocals would make the most sense, though bone flutes and whistles have been found in some caves, suggesting that they may have been used for this purpose and maybe also for various rituals. Studies of several of the tunnels in a number of caverns have revealed that wall markings were placed at exactly the points where sound would carry the farthest and be heard best. The sound of sustained notes at various pitches would have traveled well through the caves, which indicates that they may have used primitive melodies, whether sung or played. Did they sing songs as part of hunting rituals and initiations in those dark caves, lit only by flickering fire? We don't know for sure, but given how universal singing and chanting are throughout the world, there is reason to believe that our direct ancestors did the same.

Steve Mithen, a professor of archaeology at the University of Reading in England, has recently made a case that melodies were not merely the

invention of our close ancestors, nor some useless evolutionary byprod-
uct, but rather were wired into us from the time that we first started
walking upright. Over millions of years, the larynx in proto-humans
descended farther down as the neck got longer, allowing them to produce longer, more sustained sounds in greater varieties than chimpan-
zees or other apes could.

Tones and vocalizations were essential to early hominids for expressing
primitive emotions, engaging in mating rituals, connecting to their young,
and a multitude of other functions, and probably actually predated language. These sounds were very useful for surviving the harsh conditions
that our ancestors encountered wherever they ended up, which is why we
still use them in our complex languages—being able to yell loudly while
being chased by a hungry lion definitely had some advantages, even if we
don't have to do that very often these days. Mithen is not without his
detractors, but if he is right, we have been musical creatures for a very long
time. Perhaps the term "early music," as used to refer to music from about
1000 to 1750, is no longer the most accurate label.

Mythic origins: the Egyptian music goddess with a violent past

Before there were disciplines like archeology or science, our ancestors
had to devise their own explanations of how the world was made, how
they came to be, and how everything began: from music to sex, from
agriculture to wombats. In ancient Egypt, Hathor was the goddess of
love, fertility, beauty, motherhood, dance, and music. She was enor-
mously popular, especially revered by women, and her worship extended
beyond Egypt and Nubia into present-day Libya, Somalia, and Ethiopia.
As a patron of dancers, Hathor was associated with percussion instruments—especially the sistrum, a kind of metal rattle—and her priests
were frequently artists and musicians of various kinds.

Egyptian gods and goddesses often had associations with each other
or had different names and identities during different periods. Hathor
once was said to be the Eye of Ra, a feminine counterpart to the sun god

that acted as his protector and was known for violence. Indeed, one myth relates that when Ra ruled early Egypt as its pharaoh, his enemies plotted against him. He sent his protector in the form of the lion-headed goddess Sekhmet to deal with them, and with those mortals who had forgotten him and spread evil. But Sekhmet was bloodthirsty and she unleashed wholesale slaughter, killing people by the thousands and destroying cities. After the other gods objected, Ra implored her to cease, fearful that she would murder everyone on Earth, but she was overcome with blood lust and continued her rampage.

In order to stop her, Ra had large quantities of beer dyed red and poured over the land. Sekhmet eagerly drank this beer, thinking it to be blood. In time, she consumed so much that she became intoxicated and fell into a drunken sleep. When she awoke, she had calmed and transformed into the gentle Hathor, thereafter the loving patron of music, artistry, and joy. The greatest threat to humanity had become its greatest benefactor. Both Hathor and Sekhmet were worshipped in ceremonies that included copious amounts of beer and wine to remember the goddess's bloody history, and probably in acknowledgment of entertainers' fondness for large amounts of alcohol.

Mythic origins: the god who made a lyre from a turtle

The Greco-Roman heritage is particularly important to us not only for its myriad beliefs, but also, as far as Western music is concerned, for its discoveries and theoretical writings. The Greek myths and their Roman counterparts are embedded in our consciousness in ways we don't often consider. The names of the planets in our solar system immediately come to mind. A few months of the year have mythic connections: January, the month of the god Janus; February, the month of a purification feast; March, the month of the god Mars; and June, the month of the goddess Juno. One day of the week, Saturday, is named for the old titan Saturn.

Almost everyone has heard of the Greek god Hermes, known as Mercury in Roman mythology. We might remember him as the messenger of the gods, with wings on his helmet and little wings on his sandals, and no concern for silly mortal things like lift, gravity, and aero-dynamics. His reputation for swiftness even contributed to the naming of a metal after him, since it is quick and unpredictable in its liquid state.

In the myths, Hermes is the son of Zeus and Maia, one of the daughters of the titan Atlas, the one who held up the world; how Atlas managed to father children while constantly engaged in this task is another question entirely. Zeus found a way to have a secret rendezvous with Maia in a mountain, and the result was little Hermes, whom she wrapped in a blanket. Already being inclined to move quickly, he soon crawled away toward the cave entrance. Once there, he saw a turtle happily chewing on grass. Hermes was amused by this creature and decided to bring it back with him, but he wasn't looking for a pet. The poor animal had a grisly fate in store for it. Taking a knife, he stabbed the turtle repeatedly until it was—cue dramatic movie music—dead. Using the shell, he attached two stalks of reed, covered the front in animal hide (presumably from some other poor victim), and attached seven strings made of sheep gut. Incidentally, this was the material used in the making of strings for lutes, violins, harps, and similar instruments well into the nineteenth century; it is still used in modern times for re-creations of historical instruments. Hey, if it was good enough for a god . . .

And so, Hermes invented the lyre. The lyres played by the Greeks were frequently constructed in a similar way (minus the infant god bit), so this tale would have made sense to those musicians who heard it. However, the ancient hymn that tells the story also records that Hermes wasn't very talented, and that his first attempts at making music failed. He tried improvising and singing about the other gods and their deeds. How he knew of them as an infant we don't know, but he killed a turtle and made a lyre, so we just have to go with it. After several attempts, he laid the instrument aside in his cradle and went off (quickly, we presume) in search of other adventures. You may be wondering just where his mother was during all of this. She comes into play shortly, so there's no need to worry about her lax parenting skills.

At dusk, Hermes found a herd of cattle that belonged to Apollo, who was also a son of Zeus but by another titan's daughter, Leto; so they were half-brothers. This did not stop Hermes from making more mischief, however, and he stole the herd. Apollo was not amused. Hermes fled back to his cave only to discover that his mother had bolted and chained the entrance, apparently to keep him in and away from causing trouble; that obviously didn't work so well. Hermes, in an act that would make every teenager who has ever come home later than promised green with envy, turned into a mist and simply floated through the keyhole. He then curled up in his cradle and pretended to be asleep with his new lyre. Maia wasn't fooled, though, and demanded to know what he'd been up to. Hermes was defiant that he would win them a place among the gods with his thieving skills.

Then Apollo came calling and demanded to know where his cattle were, already aware by his gift of prophecy that the infant had stolen them but apparently unable to use that same skill to locate them. Maybe he just wanted to shame the little godling. The argument became heated, and it was decided that Zeus must settle their dispute. Their father ruled that they had to settle their differences and told Hermes to show Apollo the location of his herd. Maybe Hermes thought he could charm them both, so he brought out his lyre and started playing. Apollo was intrigued and wanted to give it a shot. Hermes offered it to him freely, as a gift— probably because he wasn't a very good musician, anyway—and to bury the hatchet, Apollo let him keep the cattle herd.

Apollo showed great skill with the lyre and thus became known as the god of music, poetry, and prophecy. There are two hymns dedicated to him (the Delphic hymns) that actually survive with music, dated from about 128 BCE. They are the longest-surviving pieces of music from the Classical world and offer a fascinating insight into the nature of composition and music making from the time. They are complex, in a meter of five beats, and have very unusual, almost modern-sounding melodies.

Apollo's musical skills were challenged more than once. The goat god Pan boldly asserted his musical superiority due to his skill on the pipes (whence comes the name "panpipes"), but in a contest between the two, Pan lost badly. Apollo was so angered by the insolence of Pan's only sup- porter, Midas, that he turned his ears into a donkey's; talk about a way of dealing with your critics! A satyr, Marsyas, also challenged Apollo, thinking his musical skills to be better. The Muses judged the contest, and Marsyas lost, of course. In response, Apollo flayed the poor creature alive for being so conceited as to challenge him. He then nailed his skin to a tree as a warning to others who might think themselves musically superior. Apparently, Apollo was pretty touchy about his "god of music" role and had a lot of pent-up aggression he wasn't dealing with. Perhaps it went back to that issue with the stolen cattle.

2

Magic in Music

Music holds great power over its listeners and performers. The mysteries of musical notes in a series or in harmony, and the effects that they have on us, have not been solved by science, religion, or philosophy. Music stirs the emotions, inciting love, anger, passion, calm, hope, and any other sensation you can imagine and feel. We've all experienced the amazing effect that a song can have on us when we're in a particular state. It might instantly remind us of childhood or a lost love, or inspire us, or anger us, or make us horny. Everyone has their favorite songs and their favorite types of music; these are as unique as each individual.

The odd and mysterious thing is how a piece of music might mean the world to one person and elicit no response at all from another. The same song might make one person happy and another sad. We bring our own experiences and emotional baggage to the mix, of course; maybe you just broke up with someone and heard a particular song on the radio when it happened, while another person had their first kiss to that same song. But even allowing for different experiences, the stark difference in reactions is a strange phenomenon. This is one reason why arguments over favorite music can become so heated. An attack on one's preferred music feels very much like an attack on oneself.

Probably for as long as we've been human, we've been aware of this mystery, and how music can be used for good or bad. The presence of music in religious and magical rituals is pretty much universal and may well derive from the same sources as superstition. Somewhere, sometime ago, someone made a sound or sang some notes and saw a result. Maybe the clouds parted. Maybe a friend in pain felt a little better. Maybe the primitive musician felt transformed.

However it happened, music has become inseparable from religion and magic, whether in folk rituals, shamanism, or High Mass. Here are some fascinating stories from different cultures about the use of music in magical, ritual, and religious contexts. From Celtic bards raising boils on an enemy's face to the danger of being seduced by fairy tunes and lost to the world, music has been viewed as powerful and dangerous, and many have attempted to control it, from Plato to the Soviets.

It is difficult for a modern listener to comprehend how powerful the ancient art of singing and storytelling would have been. In the days before TV, movie theaters, Internet, and even widespread literacy, it must have been a mesmerizing experience to gather around a fire and hear a master performer relate tales of the origins of the world or the exploits of great heroes and gods in story and song. The aforementioned prehistoric cave paintings and sounds associated with them may well be an ancient form of this kind of storytelling ritual. Indeed, many of these old tales are mythic, containing legends of valor and heroism, as well as moral lessons and warnings of the dreadful fates of those who transgressed the laws of the gods. This chapter will look at different cultures' perceptions about the magical qualities of music and its effects on the mundane world.

The myths of Orpheus

The story of Orpheus has been immortalized in poetry and music, notably in the operas of Monteverdi (*L'Orfeo* from 1607) and Gluck (*Orfeo ed Euridice* from 1762). In fact, dozens of operas have been written with Orphic themes since 1600, including works by Telemann, Haydn, Offenbach, Darius Milhaud, and Philip Glass, among many others.

Orpheus was a supreme musician and poet said to be able to charm all things with his magical songs, even the rocks and trees. His lyre was a gift from Apollo, and his mother, the muse Calliope, taught him to sing.

He aided the hero Jason and his Argonauts by playing better and louder music than the sirens, who desired to lure sailors to their deaths. They sang so beautifully that they caused ships to divert toward their voices, crashing into rocks; talk about disrespecting your fans. With Orpheus on board, Jason and his crew successfully resisted the sirens' call to doom.

The most famous story (dating from the time of Virgil) told of the death of his beloved wife, Eurydice; it is a model of tragedy. On their wedding day, she was accosted by a lecherous satyr. In her efforts to escape, she stumbled onto a nest of vipers, was bitten on the heel, and died. Orpheus was heartbroken and sang sad tributes to her that made even the gods weep. He was able to travel to the Underworld, where his song was so sweet that it moved Hades and Persephone to allow Eurydice to return to the mortal world, on condition that he walk in front of her and not look back until they were both again in their own realm. Orpheus mistakenly looked back to her when he had safely returned to our world but she had not yet. She vanished, and they were separated forever.

Later, he was ripped to shreds by a group of Maenads, followers of Dionysus (we will investigate them later in this chapter). Different stories give different reasons for this. One account says that he gave up devotion to all gods save Apollo, and the Maenads killed him for dishonoring their master. Another relates that after Eurydice's death, he swore off all other women (favoring only young men instead), and some female followers of Dionysus killed him in revenge for being spurned. Even in death, he could not be silenced. His head continued to sing and his lyre made music; both floated down a river to the Mediterranean—that must have been quite something to see and hear! The sea carried them far away to the island of Lesbos, where its people placed his head in a shrine. The muses collected his lyre and carried it to the heavens, giving it a place among the stars—a fitting end to the tragic life of mythology's greatest musician.

A boil on your nose: the power of the Celtic bards

Modern sensibilities and some well-meaning New Agers have tended to romanticize the peoples known as "Celtic" who once inhabited large parts of Europe. Later, the term described the inhabitants of Gaul (ancient France), northern Spain, the British Isles, and Ireland. In response, the more scholarly minded have tried to point out the harsh realities of the age, showing that while the Celts may not have been as savage as the Romans portrayed them, they certainly had their dark side; they had a liking for taking the heads of their enemies as trophies, for example.

There is also a trend among some modern scholars to hypothesize that the "Celt" is largely a modern invention (dating to the eighteenth century), and that the ancient peoples to whom we have given that name really had no unified cultural identity at all. Others view this perspective as too extreme, and the answer—as always—probably lies somewhere in between. For the purposes of this book, we'll assume that there were Celts who had some kind of a shared identity—and linguistic commonalities— even if these were more limited to local tribes and communities.

Within Celtic social structure there were various degrees of authority, presided over by the Druids. Huge amounts of ink have been spilled theorizing about these venerable people. Some of these ideas are very good, while others are complete rubbish. This is due to the unfortunate fact that the Druids left no writings about themselves; we only have what the Greeks and Romans said about them. But we do know that a very important part of the Druidic system was the class known as the bards. A Druid began his or her profession by training as a bard, and over many years of study and preparation progressed to the status of Druid.

Ancient Celtic culture was essentially non-literate (though a script, called Ogham, was invented later) and relied on oral traditions to keep its memories alive; bards were crucial to this process. There are several nuances of the term, and it could mean different things in different places (in Ireland and Wales, for example). Eventually, the Irish bards were "downgraded" to being mere entertainers.

Bards were keepers of the lore of a community—myths and legends, histories, genealogies—and as such, had to commit huge amounts of information, especially poetry and songs, to memory. This was a laborious process that took years to accomplish and was always ongoing. They were also expected to compose new works of praise to their lords and patrons.

Bards held magic in their words, and this power could both heal and harm. Their poems and songs could make the fortune of their patron or take it away. The anger of a bard was not something one wanted to rouse, for he might compose a satire (*glam dicen* in Gaelic) about the guilty party. This was not just a mocking poem, a Celtic Don Rickles kind of thing—"I tell ya, that chieftain is so obese, he needs to come into the hall twice just to get all the way in!" The stakes were much higher. It was said that a bard's words and songs could raise boils on an enemy's face, or cause serious illnesses, even death. The bard was not just reciting a poem condemning an enemy, but rather creating a kind of magic spell that would have real-world effects.

As such, bards had quite a bit of freedom of speech and artistic expression, almost unheard of in the ancient world; no one wanted to piss them off! Bards had a kind of diplomatic immunity and could expect hospitality wherever they traveled. Killing a bard was a complete no-no, as it could bring a curse and bad luck on the one who dared to do it, as well as on his whole tribe. Even if a lord was not superstitious about the magical effects of their work, he could still have his reputation ruined by an onslaught of invective, which in those days was just about as unwelcome a fate as death. A superior bard could also undo and displace his lesser colleagues. The poem "Journey to Deganwy," attributed to the sixth-century Welsh bard Taliesin, includes the following lines:

> I will enter the hall
> My song I will sing,
> My verse I will proclaim
> And the king's bards I will cast down.
> In the presence of the Chief
> Demands I will make
> And chains I will break

Taliesin's most famous poem, "Primary Chief Bard," tells of the importance of bardic culture and how it has existed since the beginning of time. Using a first-person narrative, he declares:

Primary chief poet I am to Elffin
And my native country is the region of the summer stars
John the Divine called me Merlin
But all future kings shall call me Taliesin . . .

I was with my king in the heavens
When Lucifer fell into the deepest hell
I carried the banner before Alexander
I know the names of the stars
From the north to the south . . .

I was in Africa before the building of Rome
I came here to the remnant of Troy . . .

I was instructor to the whole universe
I shall be until the judgement on the face of the earth . . .

There is not a marvel in the world
Which I cannot reveal.

The Christian overlay in this poem may be a later addition. Indeed, pagan bardic power gradually waned with the coming of Christianity, and bards began to be downgraded to the status of storytellers and court poets since the Christian Church wanted to hog the mystical duties for itself. Despite this decline, the prestige of bards was long preserved in Celtic tradition. Undoubtedly there was still a little apprehension about crossing them, even if the new religion no longer imbued them with power. As late as the thirteenth century, the Welsh poet Phylip Brydydd boldly told his patron, "I made fame for thee," a clear example of just how important a poet still was to the leader's reputation. Phylip may also have been implying that with his words, he could take that fame away.

The importance of music and poetry in Celtic cultures (real and imagined) never completely waned despite English attempts to suppress it from the sixteenth to the eighteenth centuries. A Celtic artistic revival began in the eighteenth and nineteenth centuries, though it was heavily romanticized and even subject to outright forgery. This revival continues today, with countless Celtic music festivals, Irish pub sessions, mega-hit Riverdance-type shows, and dozens of other examples. The Celts of today have drawn on their unique musical, magical, and poetic traditions and enriched the world. As an old Gaelic proverb says: *Thig crioch air an saoghal, ach mairidh gaol is ceòl*—"The world will pass away, but love and music will endure."

Fairy music and its dangers

First of all, when we talk about fairies (often spelled "faeries" and also known as the fey) in the Irish and British context, we're not thinking of Tinker Bell and the gossamer-winged tiny beauties of Victorian imagination. The fey of ancient times (and well into the Middle Ages) were primal powers, fearsome and dangerous, but sometimes helpful if appeased. They could look just like a normal human, or take any of hundreds of other shapes and forms. In ancient times they were like gods and known as the Sidhe (pronounced "shee"). With the onset of Christianity they were condemned as demons. In the minds of many, they were perhaps downgraded from gods to nature spirits, but they lost none of their power to strike awe and even terror into the hearts of the common folk who feared what might happen if their supernatural neighbors were disturbed or angered. This belief persisted well into the nineteenth century in some rural areas of Ireland and Britain.

Fairy lore is immense in scope and would require a massive tome (or three) to do it justice. But there are many interesting accounts about fairy music and its effects on mortal listeners, not always pleasant in outcome. In these tales—many told by those who claimed to have heard it—the music is described as otherworldly, enchanting, haunting, and intoxicating. It often leaves the human listener with an unbearable longing. One example illustrates this clearly:

A man once entered a small house in County Clare, and there he saw a young woman sitting by the fire, singing a sad and melancholy song. It didn't have words or even a melody that repeated. Curious, he asked her about what she was singing. She replied that once she had heard an enchanted fairy harp and it had affected her permanently. She said that anyone who heard it forgot love and hate and could hear no other sound except that harp. If the spell were ever broken, the unfortunate mortal would die. Well, that's one way to ensure you stay in the top ten.

A similar tale was told about fairy food; it was widely believed that if a mortal tasted it, he or she could never go back to eating human food again and would prefer to wither away and die. Thus, the common people warned their children never to try fairy delicacies if they were offered, and never to listen for long to fairy music if they thought they heard it. Those who ignored such advice and risked hearing this music could be made to dance against their will beyond exhaustion, or else be lulled into eternal sleep, even death, by the sounds that no mortal was meant to hear.

On the Isle of Man there is a long folk tradition of interaction with fairies, and in the nineteenth century many claimed to have heard their music firsthand. One elderly man recounted how, on two separate occasions, he heard fairy music coming from the vicinity of an old abbey; in each case he had listened for nearly an hour, but he seemed to escape any negative effects from his eavesdropping. There are many similar accounts, including from a few musicians who overheard fey tunes, memorized them, and then played them later on their fiddles and harps. Whether they suffered any consequences from this is unknown, but at least one man claimed to have been struck blind by the little people after seeing them dancing one night. They were so offended by his presence and presumption that they swore he would never look upon them, or anything else, again.

These activities were not limited to Britain, as stories of dangerous "little people" and their music can be found in many places around the world. A 1596 Elizabethan book, *Of Ghostes and Spirites, Walking by Night*, which is a translation of a work by Swiss theologian Ludwig Lavater, briefly describes mysterious music from various parts of the known world:

> Olaus Magnus in his third booke and eleuenth Chapter *De Gentibus Septentrionalibus*, writeth, that euen in these our dayes, in many places in the North partes [Scandinavia], there are certaine monsters or spirites, which

taking on them some shape or figure, use (chiefly in the night season) to daunce, after the sounde of all maner of instruments of musicke: whom the inhabitants call companies, or dances of Elves, or Fairies. Somewhat also is to bee reade touching this matter in Saxo Grammaticus, in his historie of Denmarke. Such like things are those which Pomponius Mela reporteth in his third booke of the description of Aethiopia, that in Mauritania beyonde the Mount Atlas, many times in the night season are séene great lightes, and that tinkling of Cymballs, and noyses of Pipes are also heard, and when it is daylight no man appeareth.

There is an unsettling account of possible fairy music in America that dates from 1812. In Vermont on a July morning, fourteen-year-old Elizabeth McCallum set out on horseback to visit family friends who lived some miles away; the journey required her to ride through a thick forest. Upon arriving at their home, she excitedly told her hosts that she had heard the most amazing and beautiful music deep in the woods that seemed to block out everything else. She described the exact spot where she had heard it. The family listened with interest, knowing her to be trustworthy and not prone to flights of fancy.

After lunch, she was eager to return home and tell her parents about what she had heard, but she never arrived. As night descended, her worried family sent out a search party and found her horse, alive and well. But Elizabeth was discovered dead in the same spot where she had reportedly heard the unearthly music. She showed no signs of injury or attack, and the cause of death was not determined. Perhaps she suffered a stroke or some other brain problem, and the music had been a symptom. But why would she have died in the exact spot where she had first heard it? Only the forest knows.

In dealing with the fey, the message was clear: proceed at your own risk!

Bacchanalian rites in ancient Greece

Well, that got your attention. Now you're thinking: excessive amounts of alcohol, bountiful food, pretty dancing women in skimpy clothing or less, or muscled men in mini togas hand-feeding you grapes. That will shake you out of your complacency and remind you why you're actually reading this book: for the salacious bits and the dark stories! Parties! Orgies! Drinking! It's ancient Greek spring break! So, what exactly were these decadent rites, and were they as naughty as we believe (and secretly hope)? Let's find out.

In ancient Greece, the god Dionysus (also known as Bacchus) was associated with vegetation and the cycles of the seasons, including how plants "die" in winter and are reborn in spring; the god symbolized that process, as did several other deities in the cultures surrounding the Mediterranean. The dying-and-resurrecting god motif is very old, certainly dating back to ancient Egyptian times. The cult of worship around Dionysus may have begun on the island of Crete before 1,000 BCE, probably inspired by even older fertility and life-cycle myths. It was absorbed into the larger culture of Greece after that, certainly within the next five hundred years; things moved much more slowly back then.

Eventually it became a complex religion with rites and ceremonies, initiations and rituals. These often involved veneration of nature and natural cycles and included generous amounts of wine. Euripides's *Bacchae*, written in the fifth century BCE, contains perhaps the best-known descriptions of Dionysian worship, but these scenes are almost certainly embellished for dramatic effect. Nevertheless, lurid tales of the cult's activities circulated widely.

It was said that the worshippers' goal was to induce trancelike states (called *bakcheia*, hence "Bacchus") and even divine madness and ecstasy through the use of wine, music, drumming, and dance. This would eliminate inhibitions and social mores and return the revelers to a more primal and natural state of being. Whatever happened at this point was up to the worshipper: singing, dancing, laughter, gluttony, drunkenness, free sexual activity, even primal screaming, animalistic behavior, and violence. Indeed, Dionysus was also known as "the Liberator" (*eleutherios*) because he freed one from the artificial bonds of everyday life. Musicians were on hand to play the aulos and drums to help usher the participant into this state. It was believed that the goddess Athena invented the aulos but threw it away when she realized how ridiculous she looked while playing it, which made it a perfect instrument for revelry and making a fool of oneself.

Not surprisingly, these celebrations caught on with ordinary citizens, especially women, who generally did not have a high social status. It gave them a sense of empowerment, the chance to be free in defiance of almost constant oppressive social constraints, and to have a direct relationship to their god. Also not surprisingly, some authorities were not happy about this freedom. However in cities like Athens, Dionysian theatrical dramas were staged at certain times of the year, especially winter and spring, to celebrate the god's death and rebirth respectively.

Concerned about the stories that were circulating and seeing Bacchic rites as a political threat because they were free of government control, the Roman senate issued a decree in 186 BCE that limited the cult's size and scope, seeking to reform it into a state-approved religion; it also ordered the death penalty for those that disobeyed. This harsh new law was not completely successful and illicit worship continued, especially in southern Italy. Anyway, who were mortals to decree that a god's will should not be done? In fact, Dionysus was an acceptable god to the Roman authorities; it was just the ways of worshipping him that were questioned. The new legislation was worded so as not to offend him by outlawing his worship completely.

Salacious rumors naturally followed the cult wherever it went, and people were always eager for titillating stories; tabloid journalism has been around as long as civilization. Some of the women initiates, known as *maenads*, were said to run screaming and dancing through the forest, naked except for the grapes and vines they draped about themselves— get your minds back on topic. They were, so the stories say, mad with divine drunkenness, attacking and eating live animals, some said even humans. Eating the animals alive and drinking their blood was a way of inviting the essence and power of Dionysus into their bodies, a form of divine possession; it's also pretty gross. Poor Orpheus, as we saw earlier, was torn asunder by these wild ladies, according to one account. These stories are almost certainly exaggerated, if not completely made up; the actual rituals were generally far more sedate.

Related to the Dionysian cult (and often depicted as being in the god's retinue of revelers) was the presence of Pan, the goat-footed god famous for playing his syrinx, or panpipes. Syrinx in fact was the name of one of the nymphs he was chasing in his lustful pursuits; he had a never-ending appetite for them! In order to escape him, she asked for help from the water nymphs, who transformed her into a clump of reeds. Not happy at being denied his prize, Pan nevertheless fashioned a set of pipes from these reeds, which he played as he roamed the countryside.

The music—said to be haunting, even unsettling—could arouse whatever feelings the god intended. Indeed, our word "panic" derives from the effects of Pan's music on his mortal listeners. He could induce wildness and ecstatic behavior in his followers, just like Dionysus, and his wanton sexuality (among other attributes) would later lead to his demonization by the Christian Church. The goat god became the devil, and later depictions of the Prince of Darkness often resembled the mischievous piping faun of the ancient Greek woodlands.

Music and magic in the chilly north

In Scandinavia and Finland, Russia and the far north, the magical properties of songs have long been known, praised, and feared—though when you consider how long the winters are up there, there really wasn't that much else to do! From ancient times, music and singing were thought to have great power and were used by shamans for ceremonial and ritual purposes.

The Saami (Lapland) people of northern Sweden and Norway have a singing tradition known as joik (pronounced "yoik" and often spelled that way) that is highly personal to each singer. Somewhat resembling Native American chants and likely deriving from ancient shamanic practices (a Saami shaman is called a noaidi), perhaps with roots in Siberia, it seeks to bring the essence of its topic into the song itself. In other words, one does not joik *about* a bear, one *joiks* the bear; the bear is depicted in the song, a magical way of viewing the interaction of sound and essence. This can be done by imitating natural sounds and using onomatopoeia, practices that may originate with Siberian shamans. It can have words, but doesn't need to.

There are joiks for people, for animals, and for the land itself. Each person develops their own personal joiks, just as they have a name. The idea of joiking an animal or the land probably has its origins in ancient, even prehistoric, practices. Joik cannot be thought of in terms of western musical theory; it is not thematic, and it doesn't have a specific beginning or ending point. There is little "stylistic" difference in a joik for a person and one for the land or a wolf. This lack of distinction springs from the belief that all things are of the same essence.

The Christian missionaries to Saami lands naturally viewed joik as devil worship and thus banned it because of its pagan associations. They forcibly prohibited it when they could, into the early twentieth century. Nevertheless, the tradition survived and, having undergone a major revival in the past few decades, is now widely available on recordings.

Northern traditions of magic in song can also be found in Viking culture across several centuries of the early Middle Ages. Now, the Vikings are usually thought of as unkempt barbarians who spent their lives raiding, raping, and pillaging coastal villages and defenseless monastic communities, and while that's true to a point, they also were traders, farmers, explorers, and magnificent storytellers. In fact, the unruly rabble who did the raiding, raping, and pillaging were sometimes the younger sons—who inherited nothing and had to seek their fortunes elsewhere—or troublesome reprobates that communities were happy to ship off (literally) to other areas and have them out of their long, braided hair.

Though there was a class of professional poets known as *skalds* that probably recited rather than sang their poetry, it is likely that certain epics and myths were sung and chanted, relaying ancient stories of gods and giants, dragons, and elves. Many of these myths were extremely dark and violent, reflecting the harsh culture in which they originated. Indeed, the original story of the ring of the Nibelung (*Niflung* in Old Norse) was well known in northern mead halls. It was from these tales of a cursed and coveted ring that Wagner would draw inspiration for his four colossal operas and J. R. R. Tolkien would form ideas for his own stories of an evil ring that brings ruin—desired by many, but truly possessed by only one.

The collection known as the *Edda* contains many accounts of gods and heroes that would have enthralled audiences on those long, cold winter nights. One, *Völuspá*, predicts that even the gods of the Vikings will eventually fight a final battle, known as Ragnarok, the "doom of the gods." They will be killed, and the earth will be destroyed. Talk about depressing! There is hope though, for out of that destruction will come a new age, with even mightier gods and a new earth to replace the old. This may have been a Christianizing of an older set of myths—the Eddic poems weren't written down until Iceland had become Christian—but regardless, the tale warns that evil will remain. You just never seem to get rid of it.

There are several descriptions of the Vikings' music making, generally from biased outside sources, but still enlightening and entertaining. The Arab merchant Ibrahim Ibn Ahmad Al-Tartushi traveled to Haithabu (Hedeby, near the modern Danish–German border) around the year 950. He heard some of the locals singing and remarked: "I have never heard any more awful singing then the singing of the people in Schleswig. It is a groan that comes out of their throats, similar to the bark of the dogs but even more like a wild animal."

A fascinating story comes from the Danish theologian and historian Saxo Grammaticus (*ca.* 1150–*ca.* 1250). He noted an unusual performance by a lyre player for King Eric I of Denmark (*ca.* 1060–1103) and his court. Eric was a Christian, but he retained musicians in his hall in the ancient pagan custom. The story, here retold by philosopher and music theorist Marin Mersenne (1588–1648), notes that the lyre player boasted of his ability to arouse any emotion he wished in a listener, and he proved it in the following manner:

> First, the musician poured into his hearers a certain sadness by means of grave sound; then by a better accompaniment, he changed the sadness to joy, so that they all but danced for merriment. Then in sharper

modes of intensity he excited a certain indignation, and when it became strong the king and those around him were observed to rage. Presently the musician gave the signal . . . that they should enter and hold fast the raging king . . . but such was the strength of the man, that he killed certain of them with his fist.

Eventually the music-induced madness left the king, and in his remorse he paid compensation to the men's families—I'm sure that made everything just fine.

Now this tale was probably a fabrication of Saxo's to warn against the repeated intrusion of pagan customs into newly Christian territories, or it might be an embellished retelling of a drunken evening that got out of hand. It was also probably a useful way for Saxo to set up the story of the king's pilgrimage to Constantinople; he obviously had something for which to atone. But underneath it is the fascinating account of a link between music and emotions, and the idea that a skilled player can manipulate and draw out certain feelings in the listeners, as if by magic.

Composers and magic

Many composers have immersed themselves in the study of magic, occultism, and esoteric practices. Secret societies were all the rage in Europe from the later eighteenth to the early twentieth centuries, including groups such as the Masons, the Illuminati, and the Rosicrucians. Composers were among the many kinds of intellectuals drawn to such groups for their unconventional ideas and the promise of hidden knowledge. This is a vast topic, but a few examples should illustrate the point.

We have already seen several cases: Mozart was a Freemason, and masonic ideas imbued works such as *The Magic Flute*. Satie was at one time active in the Parisian branch of the Rosicrucians, and Scriabin was deeply involved in esoteric philosophies and their relationship to music. Peter Warlock was attracted to the teachings of Aleister Crowley and seems to have dabbled in black magic while living in Ireland.

Beethoven was also interested in Freemasonry, along with Indian philosophy. He came to believe that "God is immaterial and transcends every conception," a Hindu concept. He immersed himself so thoroughly in composing some works that he was oblivious to the world while writing. During these times, he felt that he was approaching the Godhead—becoming one with it—through music.

Wagner's operas were known for their rich mythological content, and his own philosophies resembled those of the Theosophists, the fashionable esoteric movement led by Madame Blavatsky in the later nineteenth century. Wagner came to believe that "imagination creates reality" and hoped that his music would induce trancelike states in the audience. His use of Norse and Arthurian magical imagery in his operas was hugely effective and influential on the generation of composers after him.

Debussy apparently hobnobbed in occult circles in Paris, and at least one other composer, Cyril Scott, proclaimed that Debussy was channeling the music of Atlantis for the modern age. It is difficult to pinpoint what Debussy's activities were, which is probably exactly what he wanted. However, in an 1893 letter to Chausson he called for music to be sequestered away from the masses and given its rightful place among esoteric subjects:

> Music really ought to have been a hermetical science, enshrined in texts so hard and laborious to decipher as to discourage the herd of people who treat it as casually as they do a handkerchief! I'd go further and, instead of spreading music among the populace, I propose the foundation of a "Society of Musical Esotericism."

This is a remarkable attitude from one who eventually wrote more than 140 pieces, taught piano, and was in demand as a conductor. Perhaps related to the idea of keeping music as a hidden art, he wished to separate his own music from concrete interpretations, saying, "Let us at all costs preserve this magic peculiar to music, since of all the arts it is most susceptible to magic." One wonders if he meant "magic" in both a poetic and a literal sense.

3

Plague and Penitence: the Rather Awful Fourteenth Century

Modern-day people often hold some very pointed views and prejudices about the Middle Ages. The term frequently takes on a derogatory tone, such as when we call someone's old-fashioned or offensive views "medieval." There are so many assumptions about the time period that simply aren't true, but that's another whole discussion. Unfortunately, the calamities and disasters of the fourteenth century in Europe tend to play right into those misconceptions.

Up until the early 1300s, things had been reasonably good across Europe. Perhaps not what *we* would think of as good, but the weather had been stable for some time and food supplies were fairly reliable, and as a result, the population was growing, as were towns and cities. Yes there were also wars, crusades, the Inquisition, and other assorted atrocities, but civilization in Western Europe seemed to be on a winning track, with the growth of universities and commerce, the proliferation of new music and poetry in everyday languages, advances in art and architecture, and other signs of flourishing culture.

So what happened? It may have started with the weather, or rather shifts in climate, in the first decade of the 1300s. This instability led to a reversal of the warmer pattern and therefore more unpredictable weather. By 1315, storms had become more severe, and crops failed across the continent. This was probably the starting point to what became known to modern climatologists as the Little Ice Age, a period of colder weather that persisted on and off until the mid-nineteenth century.

In addition to storm damage, there were also food shortages and full-on famines. Large populations were suddenly faced with problems over which they had no control—and neither did the Church, royalty, or anyone else. Prayers went unanswered, and things became increasingly bleak. It wasn't a meltdown of civilization and a descent into anarchy; it just meant that life, which was already tough for the lower classes, got that much tougher. Of course, this led to political instability and (literal) saber-rattling. The biggest of these conflicts erupted into what became known as the Hundred Years' War between England and France. It really lasted from 1337 to 1453, which is actually 116 years, but that doesn't sound as catchy. Obviously it wasn't a full-on battle that entire time, but rather a series of smaller wars and skirmishes over territorial disputes and who owed whom what homage and how much.

While this head butting raged, Europe was hit by a much bigger, or rather smaller, problem: rats carrying fleas (some now say gerbils—yes, gerbils) that harbored a particularly nasty bacterium, *Yersinia pestis*, also known as bubonic plague. The plague itself seems to have originated in China (at least this particular strain, now thankfully believed to be extinct) and migrated across Asia via trade routes. Once ships reached ports in Italy, southern France, and elsewhere in 1347– 1348, the rats jumped ship and went off to their new vacation homes, bringing a nasty surprise with them.

Later historians gave the outbreak the charming name of the Black Death; at the time it was often just called the "Great Mortality." Its deadly effectiveness was probably exacerbated by a population that was weakened because of the food shortages, poor sanitation, and weather changes, as well as war. Death came swiftly and mercilessly. Lodewijk Heyligen, a musician and cantor of the St. Donatian's Cathedral in Bruges in 1348, described the symptoms and noted that there seemed to be a type of plague that attacked the lungs (now known as pneumonic plague). He wrote that sixty-two thousand had already died in the area of Avignon in southern France, with eleven thousand of them buried in one place.

At this time, of course, no one had any clue as to the real cause. Explanations ran the gamut (itself a musical term, interestingly)—from foul air to the wrath of God to the poisoning of well water by Jews— with all the ugly and tragic persecutions that went along with these ignorant beliefs.

The plague eventually subsided by the mid-1350s, but the devastation it wrought changed Europe forever. Some have argued that the social breakdown it caused brought about the rise of the middle class and even helped contribute to the Renaissance, the Reformation, and the weakening of the Catholic Church's absolute power.

Why is all of this important for us, other than being ridiculously gruesome? Well, the arts changed pretty dramatically as well, especially painting and music. In fact, both began the long trek to the Renaissance style. This was the century of Petrarch and Boccaccio, Chaucer and Langland, the great French composer Guillaume de Machaut, and artists such as Giotto (who died before the horrors of the plague) and his pupils (who lived through it). Turbulent times invariably lead to innovation, and for all of the horror of the mid-century, it upset the established order so completely that change was forced on everyone. This chapter looks at music in that terrible time, from flagellants whipping themselves in eerie processions while singing penitential hymns, to harsh criticisms of church and state in popular music, to the strange sounds of the *ars subtilior*, an avant-garde French musical movement from the end of the century that produced songs unlike any heard before or since.

The flagellants and their gruesome spectacles

The flagellants were part of a movement that began in the thirteenth century as a show of piety among common people. Such things are often termed "popular movements," though the modern reader probably will have a hard time figuring out why this one was ever popular. Self-flagellation, or whipping, had been a common act of penitence in Christian practice for centuries; it was particularly endorsed by an Italian cardinal named Peter Damian in the eleventh century. But the flagellants elevated it (or brought it down, depending on your view) to a whole new level. Traveling through towns and making a public spectacle, they would sing dark hymns and whip themselves using scourges, rather like the cat o' nine tails. Each of these tails had a knot in it, and sharp nails were sometimes set into these knots. The flagellants' bloodstained clothing and cries of pain were a part of the whole gruesome spectacle.

First appearing in Italy, the practice was somewhat spontaneous and did not have Church backing. It was eventually condemned and banned by the pope in 1261 because participants were making heretical claims, like the idea that participating in one of these masochistic processions was a valid way for sins to be forgiven. This was an absolute no-no, since the Church had an exclusive claim to that right. In any event, the movement didn't die out completely but migrated north over the Alps into Germany, where similar conflicts with authority occurred.

Some of the wind eventually was taken from its sails until—you guessed it—the arrival of the Black Death. From that time on, the flagellants became a major movement across Europe. Believing that the plague was a divine punishment for their sins, they were determined to be as openly and painfully penitent as they could. Dressed in white, they would travel from town to town and set up camps nearby. Their displays took a variety of forms. In one example, it was said that they began their rituals with the reading of a letter from an angel authorizing their actions. The singing of hymns followed, while they fell to their knees and whipped themselves in rhythm to the music.

This grim spectacle was beheld and feared by many, with masters in charge who demanded obedience from the followers. Surprisingly, quite a few rushed to join the movement, which took on the trappings of a religious brotherhood. Many must have felt that the only way to appease an angry God was through this act of self-torture. In the absence of any proper medical knowledge to stop the plague from spreading, it had to be worth a try. The irony, of course, is that by traveling widely, many flagellants invariably became infected with the plague and spread it farther. Indeed, at some point they went from being welcomed in towns and cities to being feared instead.

Although Church officials initially permitted limited processions as a legitimate expression of an appeal to God to end the plague, they grew concerned as the movement got out of control and started spouting all sorts of dangerous ideas. In an attempt to reassert that control, in 1349 Pope Clement VI officially condemned the flagellants in a papal bull (a proclamation, not a large male bovine).

This time he wasn't messing around. The flagellants were condemned as heretics, and in the next couple of decades more than a few were burned at the stake, usually the leaders, who could say some pretty outlandish things. For example, Flemish and German flagellants claimed that the Holy Roman Emperor Frederick II (who had been an enemy of the pope and had died way back in 1250) was going to be resurrected. One actually claimed to *be* Frederick and said he had come to prepare the world for the impending Judgment Day. The Inquisition intervened in 1369, and he, like his goals, went up in flames in his own personal last judgment. The Church intensified its work, burning hundreds of flagellants and members of similar groups by the early fifteenth century in the hopes of stopping the movement completely. It lingered on into the Renaissance, however, arising whenever there were tough times—which, of course, was often.

A key component of this movement was the singing of hymns, and the flagellation itself was a kind of grotesque accompanying percussion. It makes sense from a musical point of view: large numbers of people singing the same tune do much better if there is a definite rhythm that holds the piece together. The sound of scourges hitting flesh provided an effective, if horrid, way to keep them on track.

Interestingly, some of these songs survive. In Germany the participants were known as *Geissler*—simply the German word for flagellant—and their songs as *Geisslerlieder*. A chronicler named Hugo von Reutlingen wrote down the words and music to six of these songs in about 1349. The music is simple enough and easy to memorize. Some melodies may have been drawn from existing popular songs, while others may have been folk hymns. The words were often in vernacular languages rather than in Latin, because they were songs of the common people. The texts were penitential in nature and spoke of praying for deliverance or resisting the devil. One declares:

> Now approaches the deluge of evil.
> Let us flee from burning Hell.
> Lucifer is an evil companion.
> Whomever he seizes, he smears with pitch.
> Therefore we want to shun him.

These were certainly not memorable art songs, and they had no place in courtly society or the realm of medieval church music. That they survive at all is remarkable given the controversial nature of the flagellants and the general turmoil of the time. They provide an interesting window into the tortured minds of those faced with a horror beyond comprehension, those who knew of nothing else they could do but try to appease the wrathful deity who had sent such an awful punishment for their many sins.

Kyries: lovely music for awful occasions

Most listeners of classical music are aware of musical settings of the standard texts for the Catholic mass. These sections are the Kyrie, Gloria, Credo, Sanctus, and Agnus Dei—together known as the Ordinary because they are repeated each day—with additional texts and music for a given saint's feast or other celebration.

The Kyrie is a simple Greek text repeating the words, "Lord have mercy, Christ have mercy, Lord have mercy." The remaining four sections are in Latin. The Gloria is a hymn proclaiming the glory of God; the Credo is the testimony of Christian faith, also known as the Nicene Creed, formulated in the fourth century; the Sanctus is another hymn glorifying God; and the Agnus Dei is an invocation of Christ: "Lamb of God, you who take away the sins of the world, have mercy on us."

Most of the great composers seem to have tried their hands at composing mass music at one time or another: Bach's B-Minor Mass, Mozart's

Requiem, and Beethoven's *Missa Solemnis* are three magnificent examples. Settings of the Ordinary have a long history. Originally anonymous compositions, from the fourteenth century onward these sections started being set to music by specific composers—beginning with Guillaume de Machaut, the greatest composer of his age. By the Renaissance, these mass settings were often soaring, beautiful works of complex melodic lines interweaving with each other and producing exquisite results. Exceptional examples can be found among the works of Josquin des Prez, Victoria, Palestrina, and many others.

We like to think of the Kyrie as a sweet, often inspiring piece. With its gentle prayer asking for the Lord and Christ to have mercy, it seems to embody the Christian message, exalt forgiveness, and serve as a logical opening for the rest of the mass. But this was not always the case. Medieval Kyries could be vigorous, even aggressive. Based in the Gregorian chant tradition, they sought to glorify God and, just as importantly, to remind everyone who was in charge.

Intended to inspire bravery and whip up warlike feelings, Kyries were sung by armies going into battle often as a prayer for strength before slaughtering the enemy. The crusaders most certainly would have heard them sung by priests and probably taken part in the singing themselves. Before the final assault to retake Jerusalem from the Muslims during the First Crusade in July 1099, the crusaders marched barefoot around the city walls (ouch!) singing psalms, celebrating mass, and hearing the blowing of trumpets, probably self-consciously recalling Joshua and the battle of Jericho. Although mocked by the inhabitants, the music helped to inspire the crusaders' sense of divine mission. They recaptured Jerusalem on July 15 and proceeded to butcher most of the inhabitants. Amidst the carnage a mass was celebrated at the Holy Sepulcher, and there was much singing in thanks for the slaughter, while blood ran in the streets.

Kyries were also sung for executions, particularly those of heretics such as the flagellants. The most common method of killing was burning, a horrid death. The Church itself was not permitted to carry out executions, so they used a technicality to get around this restriction. The Inquisition would try and ultimately find the defendant guilty and then turn over the condemned to secular authorities (kings, princes, nobility, etc.) who would carry out the sentence. But the Church officials and other clergy usually attended the burning, of course, and a Kyrie chant may have been used as a prayer asking for God to forgive the sins of the heretic.

The condemned were most often given the chance to recant and embrace the faith before the sentence was carried out. Some did, though this did not free them; they faced a life in prison, which would undoubtedly be a short one given the wretched conditions of most medieval dungeons. If they held on to their beliefs and refused to give in, as many surprisingly did, the Kyrie chanted by monks would be the last music they would hear in this life.

During the fourteenth century Kyries were also likely sung by the flagellants as part of their penitential pleas, as well as by other groups of sufferers eager to try anything that might stave off the epidemic; their pleas mostly went unanswered.

The Fawn-Colored Beast: anti-establishment satire

The *Roman de Fauvel* ("The Romance of Fauvel") is a strange and magnificent work of satirical music and poetry dating from early fourteenth-century France. It condemns corruption in authority, whether in the Church or the state. It was produced over a period of years, and in a way inaugurated the new musical style that was developing, the *ars nova* (more on that later in this chapter). A hugely important collection, it is a long poem interspersed with more than 150 pieces of music, both monophonic (for a solo singer) and polyphonic (in parts). The music came from contemporary and older sources, spanning over one hundred years of French musical creativity. Indeed it is the most important musical manuscript surviving from the time. Though it was written before the onset of the calamities that pummeled the rest of the century, it already reflected existing troubles in politics and religion.

The political situation in France at the time was, frankly, pretty horrible. The first twenty years of the century witnessed a number of conflicts. King Philip IV was known as the Fair, which may have referred to his complexion or it may have been ironic. He was harsh, greedy, and had an ongoing feud with Pope Boniface VIII (himself no prize), even going so far as to have said pope arrested. For much of the second half of the fourteenth century there was more than one pope and, to put it mildly, they and their respective followers didn't get along very well.

Philip aggressively suppressed the Knights Templar, executed their leaders, and confiscated their wealth. He expelled the Jews from France in a heartless move, and two of his daughters-in-law were involved in a scandal that rocked the establishment. Indeed, their accused lovers were tortured, flayed (that means had their skin removed, and yes, that was a common enough torture then), and executed. Fate seemed to have had the last laugh, as Philip died in a hunting accident in November 1314. This was only months after Jacques de Molay, the last Master of the Templars, cursed both Philip and Pope Clement V as he was about to be burned at the stake.

Needless to say, certain French courtiers and other bigwigs were pretty tired of the scandals and the violence that only seemed to be getting worse. *Fauvel* was a reaction to all of these troubles. It called out abuses of power by various other nobles—along with clergy, friars, and anyone else living large and behaving badly—especially those who rose in social station too quickly and took power that was not rightly theirs.

So, why would such a critical work be called a "romance"? Well, the word as used in medieval literature did not mean what it does today. While love could certainly feature in the tale, a romance was primarily a type of narrative characterized by a hero or knight, his quest, his love for a lady, allegorical and symbolic characters (who often imparted moral lessons), and the idealization of chivalry, among other topics.

Fauvel makes fun of the romance genre. The main character in this work is represented as a horse or a donkey. His name is an acrostic for the vices that were certainly present in the court and elsewhere: *Flatterie* (Flattery), *Avarice* (Greed), *Vilenie* (Guile), *Variété* (Inconstancy), *Envie* (Envy), and *Lâcheté* (Cowardice). The letters "u" and "v" are interchangeable in Latin and other Romance languages. In an additional play on words, the word *fauvel* can also mean "veiled lie."

Fauvel has ambition and pride. He does not want to remain in his lowly stable forever, so he schemes up a way to get moved into his master's room in the great house. Once there, he has it converted to suit his equine tastes, and instead of driving him out, nobles and clergy are now coming to him with praise and service, giving in to corruption. The Latin song *Floret fex favellea* declares:

> Fauvel's dregs are flourishing;
> The world is changing
> The curia [Church administrators] becomes like iron
> And Fauvel is exalted
> Today every poor person is the object of contempt . . .
> The multitude congratulates
> The adored animal

Fauvel ascends to power, and his courtiers include such allegorical lowlifes as Envy, Sloth, Deceit, and Perjury, represented as characters. The message relayed here is easy enough to see; it is a commentary on the awful state of affairs in the French government and church at the time. Indeed, those that oppose this corruption oppose Fauvel, as the French song *Porchier mieus* makes clear:

> I would rather be a swineherd
> Than curry Fauvel
> I would rather let myself be flayed.
> I have no interest in his money
> And I do not prize his gold.

The Lady Fortune, one of these allegorical characters, favors Fauvel for the moment, and so he prospers. She is most often represented in medieval art with the Wheel of Fortune, which was a popular symbolic image throughout the Middle Ages; sometimes you're on top, and sometimes it's crushing you. The piece *O varium* observes:

O fickle, ever-changing Fortune . . .

You cause uncertainty,

However, perversely raising the poor man

Up out of the dung

And lifting Fauvel to the sky

Knowing that Lady Fortune only favors him temporarily, Fauvel desires to marry her to secure a safe fate. She naturally resists but offers instead the figure of Vainglory as a bride more suited to him. The wedding is grand, and Fauvel invites many more allegorical figures, such as Fornication, Adultery, and Hypocrisy. A group of Virtues attends as well—Goodness, Repentance, Humility, and many others—and fights the Vices in a mock tournament the following day.

Fauvel and his bride retire to the bedchamber, while outside revelers celebrate by making noise and singing dirty little songs and snippets of tunes, featuring such charming lyrics as "Lady if your oven is hot," "Your beautiful mouth will kiss my ass," and "Thirty-four moldy farts."

At the tournament the next day, the Vices are defeated one after another. Lady Fortune predicts that Fauvel will one day fall, but not before doing considerable damage to the land. Fauvel and Vainglory will produce many children, little Fauvels that will run rampant and scatter vice and corruption everywhere. The poem ends by noting that many fear the damage and ruin that Fauvel and his offspring are spreading throughout France, but the author is confident that it will end one day. The poem's final lines have a sentiment that musicians would appreciate: "Now I need a drink of wine. God! Let me have it!"

Although this strange masterpiece of words and music was quite controversial at the time for daring to ridicule the court and Church, it survived and was written down in a beautifully illustrated manuscript. We don't quite know how it was intended to be performed, or even whether it was performed. It may have been done as a kind of early opera, with a narrator reading the main poem and pausing for the vocal pieces to be sung as interludes; instruments were probably also used.

Maybe different readers recited the voices for different characters. Given its length, it would have needed to be performed over the course of several evenings, perhaps as after-dinner entertainment.

The *Roman de Fauvel* represents a growing awareness of institutional corruption and the attempts to speak out against it, though obviously within limits; it was written under the patronage of certain nobles to attack other nobles. It was not a revolutionary work in the sense of trying to overthrow the established order, but its authors had no problems holding up certain authorities to ridicule and explicitly hoping for better times to come. Unfortunately, as we've already seen, the fourteenth century would inflict a lot of terrible suffering before things would improve.

The Fumeurs: avant-garde artists or medieval stoners?

Fourteenth-century music from Europe is known for sounding a bit strange to unfamiliar listeners. The period has been dubbed *ars nova* ("new art"). The name was drawn from the title of a 1322 book long attributed to a music theorist named Philippe de Vitry, though there has been recent debate over his authorship and how much, if at all, he was involved. Philippe did contribute a number of excellent pieces to the *Roman de Fauvel,* so he is important as a composer, at least. In any case, the name *ars nova* has stuck, and it refers to the many significant changes that began to take place in French and Italian music between the later thirteenth and early fourteenth centuries. Why did these changes happen? There are many reasons, but one important cause was the development of new, more precise methods of music notation that allowed for complex rhythms to be indicated clearly. Also, many new experiments began with the use of chromatic notes (those would be the black keys on a piano). The results led to the creation of a new music that sounds familiar but also rather strange, because the melodies and harmonies don't quite go where we would expect. In order to really appreciate it, you simply have to hear some for yourself. Do an Internet search on composers such as Guillaume de Machaut or Francesco Landini, sit back, and take in the strange and wonderful sounds.

This music, odd though it may seem, was the prelude to Renaissance music and the more "modern" sounds that we are used to. It represents the dusk of one era and the dawn of another. The style lasted until the 1370s, when something even stranger replaced it. As sometimes occurs in artistic movements, they reach their logical conclusions and then go to extremes before burning themselves out and being discarded for simpler approaches. The *ars nova* did exactly that, tipping into a thirty- or forty-year period in France where things just got plain weird. This new form has come to be known as the *ars subtilior* ("the more subtle art"). Using notational systems that were ever more accurate in recording rhythms (including differently colored musical notes to represent different rhythmic values), composers were able to create exceedingly complex music: three-part vocal pieces, for example, where each line was in a different rhythm or time signature. And the harmonies took the *ars nova* sensibilities to the extreme. It's some of the most difficult and complex music in Western history until the twentieth century, and it actually inspired some of the works of twentieth-century composers when it was rediscovered.

Contained in manuscripts such as the *Chantilly Codex* from the late fourteenth century, the music is often beautifully notated, some of it in artistic forms such as in the shape of a heart or a circle. While the topics of most of these songs hadn't changed much from those of the last few centuries (such as the pain of love or social commentary), there were a handful of poems that seemed to be about something quite unusual, quite unusual indeed. Let's have a look at the words to *Fumeux fume*, by a composer named Solage (and that's pretty much all we know about him):

A smoker smokes through smoke
A smoky speculation.
Is, between puffs, his thought:
A smoker smokes through smoke.

For smoking suits him very well
As long as he keeps his intention.

A smoker smokes through smoke
A smoky speculation.

What? This strange text about "smoking" is one of a number that have similar content. It seems to be about a mysterious group known as the *fumeurs* who are mentioned in the poetry of Eustache Deschamps (1346–1406). Deschamps was an incredibly prolific poet and diplomatic messenger to King Charles V of France; he wrote eleven volumes' worth of material. The songs that mention the *fumeurs* all have texts by Deschamps. But what was he talking about?

Once again, there have been many theories. The idea of anyone "smoking" anything in those times seems unlikely, since tobacco, a New World herb, was not introduced to Europe until the sixteenth century. The more exotic and amusing explanation was that there was a "society of smokers," young poets who had gotten a hold of and were inhaling opium or hashish and then praising its effects in their works. The problem with this theory is that those substances were usually ingested rather than smoked. On the other hand, the idea of inhaling smoke could hardly be unknown, given that fire was the only source of heat and light, and there have been some archeological finds of medieval objects similar to pipes that have traces of burnt drugs in them. It may be that such substances had some limited use as medicines in a few places that were able to obtain them from the Middle East.

Further, the music of Solage's *Fumeux fume* is just so weird that many have suggested that it might perhaps have been composed under the influence of something a little stronger than French wine. Written for three male voices in a low vocal register, it features very odd harmonies and passages that are extreme even by the standards of the *ars nova* and the *ars subtilior*. Look up the composer and this song online and see if you can find a recording of it. It's one of the weirdest things that you will ever hear. It certainly could be medieval music under the influence of a controlled substance. So, was Solage stoned? Was there a medieval summer of love in 1367?

Well, another theory is that the *fumeurs* were trying to have a fifth humor added to the existing four. In medieval and Renaissance medicine, the humors were the four temperaments of human personality and behavior. Belief in them went back at least as far as Hippocrates in ancient Greece. These were the fluids in the human body that had to be in balance. If they were not, then illness could result; medical treatments were designed to restore these balances. The *fumeurs* may have been trying to add smoke as a new humor; smoke is ephemeral, momentary, and capricious—rather like artists themselves. This idea makes sense, though unlike the other humors, smoke is foreign to the human body unless it is inhaled, which brings us right back to that question! Another translation for the word is "fuming," and perhaps it refers to attempts to release the other humors from the body. Finally, there may not have been a group at all. Deschamps may have been merely satirical (he was known to do that quite often) and meant nothing in particular.

So, while the actual smoking of something seems unlikely, we just don't know. Whether drug-inspired or not, the music of the *ars subtilior* is strange and alien to the modern listener. It represents a very brief period that burned itself out (no pun intended; well, maybe a little) quickly and in so doing gave way to new, simpler styles that would evolve over the fifteenth century into the glorious and much-loved music of the Renaissance.

4

Blood and Guts

As we've seen with composers, there was more than a little violence dis-
rupting the lives of some of the great masters. From Gesualdo's murders to Liszt's mutilated and bloated corpse, there are bloody tales aplenty
behind the makers of the world's great music. Violence has, unfortunately,
always been a part of human nature, and scholars, philosophers, theologi-
ans, and anthropologists have kicked around (small pun intended) every
idea imaginable as to what makes us do what we do. Did we inherit these
tendencies from ape ancestors? Did the devil make us do it? How can some
people commit such despicable acts, while others aspire to such noble ones?
How can the same people do both? These are problems that can't be solved
in one book. If you were hoping for that, you might be disappointed.

Instead, in this chapter we will look at some shocking instances of
violence, murder, bloodletting, and reverence for the dead bordering on
morbid obsession. Here we will discover the history behind a sinister fairy
tale, encounter the real-life Dracula, meet musicians hired to sing for a
corpse, and learn something that might make you reconsider your next
hair appointment.

The malevolent Pied Piper of Hamelin

You may wonder why there is a children's fairy tale in a more or less
grown-up book about doom and gloom in the music world. Is this an

attempt at family-friendly respectability amid all the gruesomeness? Not at all.

In fact, if you've read some fairy tales in their original forms, like the Grimm stories, you'll find that they are quite—well, grim. There are none of those happy Hollywood endings where everyone sings and the lovers are reunited amid cute animals, celebrating options for two sequels and a toy line. Quite often, the original stories are more like this: *A sweet little boy with the face of an angel wandered into the forest, got lost, met an evil old troll who flung him in a cooking pot and ate him. The end.*

If you're wondering where the happy ending and the group sing-along are, there are none. The moral of such a tale was often quite different from a modern story. People in those times lived much closer to the edge of death than most of us in the Western world today—with our comfy homes and access to modern medicine and clean resources—would like to think about, or probably can even imagine. Infant mortality was high, diseases had no cures, and a small wound could easily become infected and deadly. Life might indeed be nasty, brutish, and short, as Hobbes would say (the philosopher, not the tiger), and such tales served instructional purposes. In the above example it would be "don't go into the forest alone." The innocence of childhood that we love and treasure now is more of a Victorian invention; prior to then, children were often treated as miniature adults and were expected to behave accordingly. The wisdom of such an approach is debatable, but the fact is worth noting. Some have theorized recently that many of the Grimm stories were not intended for children at all, but were adult versions of popular tales.

With that in mind, let's get back to the story at hand: the Pied Piper of Hamelin. It is a familiar one. In 1284 a swarm of rats descended on the hapless residents of Hamelin, a town in northern Germany. In those days rats were frequent but unwelcome visitors, so the townsfolk offered a reward to anyone who could rid them of their rodent problem. Enter a colorfully dressed piper, whose music lured the rats away and into a river where they drowned. For whatever reason (bureaucratic issues?)

the town officials didn't pay him, so the piper had his revenge, playing his pipe again and luring all of the town's children up a hill called Koppen, which swallowed them up. Neither they nor the piper were ever seen again.

The story calls to mind some of the fairy music tales (see the chapter "Magic in Music"), suggesting that the piper may have been one of the fey (fairies) luring mortals to their doom. Certain types of fey, such as goblins, were believed to take the form of rats, so this tale might be a reflection of a long-lost folk tale.

However, there may be more real history to the whole affair. Modern Hamelin still has a street called Bungelosen Straße, wherein the children were said to have run when following the piper's deadly tune. Interestingly, it is against the law to play music there.

In the 1980s, two researchers discovered some interesting facts while researching the story behind the folk tale. The theory they developed was that in the late thirteenth century, there were a number of migrations toward Eastern Germanic territories (mostly in modern Poland) to settle new lands. Count Nicholas von Spiegelberg, a nobleman connected with the area, looked for potential colonists among the young. Apparently he convinced a number of teenagers to join him (probably against their parents' wishes), and they set out on a ship. It was wrecked in July 1284 and sank near the coastal town of Kopahn (also in modern Poland), killing most of the people on board. The name of the town is obviously very similar to the hill of Koppen. That this happened in the same year as the tale may well be more than coincidence.

This would seem to offer an explanation for a group of young people leaving the town *en masse*, following one man and later disappearing. So what of the rats? Well, there were rat removal techniques that involved the playing of a high-pitched whistle, mostly in England but also on the continent. Perhaps there was a terrible rat infestation around that time. Perhaps von Spiegelberg had some hand in helping to remove the rodents, offering piping rat removers in exchange for letting a certain number of young people go with him to establish a new colony.

We'll never know all the details, but this story illustrates how even the most outlandish folk tales and myths can have their origins in facts and real events. Trying to convince an exterminator that you have an infestation of goblins, however, may be a bit more difficult.

The historical Dracula

Dracula, the stuff of nightmares! Bram Stoker's late nineteenth-century classic has thrilled generations and inspired countless imitators, from Anne Rice's controversial works to *Buffy the Vampire Slayer* to Stephenie Meyer's recent *Twilight* series. Vampires are big business, and every year new films, books, comics, music, and games are released on the theme, some still focusing on the old Transylvanian count himself.

Vampire legends seem intertwined with the Balkans, almost a part of the landscape. But who or what inspired the legendary Dracula, a name now synonymous with evil? In fact, there was a real, living man behind Stoker's creation. Let's begin the search with a fifteenth-century German poet and musician named Michel Beheim.

The son of a weaver, Beheim was born in 1416 in the German state of Württemberg (Germany at the time was a collection of smaller states rather than one unified nation). He was a soldier of fortune who studied music and became a *Meistersinger*. These "master singers" were lyric poets and musicians whose tradition had grown out of the earlier German *Minnesang* ("love song") tradition. The *Meistersingers* flourished from the fourteenth to the sixteenth century and kept alive the medieval practice of solo singing long after it had been replaced by other forms in France, Italy, and Spain. These professional singers belonged to guilds—like members of other trades—and were ranked according to position, standing, and length of membership.

Beheim showed a talent for writing historical epics and ballads. He was in the employ of a number of wealthy patrons, including King Ladislas V of Hungary and eventually Holy Roman Emperor Frederick

III. During this time, he composed epics recounting recent events, such as ongoing crusades against the Ottoman Turks who were pushing ever farther into Eastern Europe after taking the Byzantine city of Constantinople in 1453 (today's Istanbul in Turkey). This event had shocked the Western world and caused many nations to call for new efforts to push back the Turkish military onslaught. Indeed, some Balkan leaders were prepared to do whatever it took to achieve this, as Beheim was about to discover.

In 1462 Beheim accompanied Frederick III to Wiener Neustadt, a town south of Vienna. There he met a monk, Brother Jacob, who had fled from the region of Wallachia in modern-day southern Romania. In various discussions and interviews in the spring and summer of 1463, Beheim learned an appalling story about a cruel and vicious tyrant who had ruled Wallachia with an iron fist, terrorizing and brutalizing his subjects. His name was Vlad Dracula, also known as Ţepeş, or "the Impaler."

Beheim must have listened in revulsion and hastily scribbled down the gory details, already imagining in his mind an epic poem that would hold his audience spellbound. By late 1463 he had produced the work, the *Story of a Bloodthirsty Madman Called Dracula of Wallachia*. The poem was a hit, recited (and probably sung) to the emperor that winter; nothing like mass murder to add a little Christmas cheer! The emperor apparently liked it greatly and requested a repeat performance on a number of occasions over the next few years. Through Beheim's work, the Austrian and German courts began to get a picture of the monster that lived not far from their borders.

So what had Brother Jacob told Beheim that was so shocking? Why did the story of Vlad disseminate and pass into legend? Well, it was aided by the new printing press, which published the lurid details in what was the first mass-market circulation of a horror story. And the details were simply so shocking—even by fifteenth-century standards—that soon everyone was talking about it. Who could resist a song that opened with these lines?

Here begins a very cruel and frightening story,
About a wild, bloodthirsty madman named Dracula of Wallachia,
Of how he impaled people on wooden stakes,
And boiled their heads in kettles and skinned them alive,
And hacked them to pieces, like cabbage.
Many other horrible things are written in this poem,
Of the dreadful land that he ruled.

Vlad's complex biography is a mixture of known historical fact, folk legend, and political propaganda. Sorting through this mess is a challenge, but a picture of the man has emerged over the past few decades. Vlad III (1431–1476) was the ruler of the province of Wallachia, a state independent from the Hungarian territories to the north, which included the more famous Transylvania. His father, Vlad II, had been known as Dracul, meaning "dragon" in old Romanian. Vlad III adopted the title Dracula, or "son of the dragon." One of Dracula's chief preoccupations was fending off the very real and ever-present threat of a Turkish invasion. He was also fixated on restoring what he saw as morality and honesty to a nation that had grown lax and permissive. He set about achieving these goals in several terrible ways.

His nickname, the Impaler, was very appropriate. Vlad's favorite method of torture and execution was to impale his victims on long wooden stakes, leaving the bodies on public display to serve as a warning; they could take hours or even days to die in unimaginable agony. This was not some periodic bit of sadism in which he indulged; it was a wholesale obsession. It is possible that tens of thousands perished under his harsh rule, most by impalement and some in equally repulsive ways. Beheim writes of a group of merchants who didn't obey his trade laws:

He impaled some, and others he assembled in a huge cauldron,
With holes in the lid, so that they could peer out.
He ordered that boiling water be poured over them,
And boiled them alive.

Of course, not all of his courtiers approved, and Dracula had a response for them:

> When, at one of his executions,
> A certain noble could no longer stand the stench,
> And held his nose in revulsion,
> Dracula had the man seized and had a longer stake prepared.
> Presenting it, he said, "you may live up there,
> Where the stench cannot reach you."

Dracula did not invent impalement; the Turks and others had used it, and perhaps he saw it as a way of answering them. But he perfected it to an art form, if such a thing can be said.

Detesting foreigners "polluting" his land, he was especially harsh toward Germans and Roma (gypsies) as well as criminals, the homeless, and outcasts of any kind. Not unlike Hitler, he had a vision of a "pure" homeland wherein only desirable people would live.

Hearing all of this, Beheim worked the details into his poem, sparing his audiences none of what Jacob had reported to him. He noted how Dracula had contempt even for ambassadors, who should have been given immunity. Once, he was receiving Italian envoys. Other versions say that it was Turkish ambassadors; perhaps it was both on different occasions. Beheim records the meeting:

> They [the envoys] removed their hats.
> Under their hats, each of them wore a skullcap
> That they did not take off.
> Dracula asked them why they did not remove them.
> "This is our custom," they replied,
> "We are not obliged to remove our caps under any circumstances,
> Even in an audience with the sultan or Holy Roman Emperor."
> Dracula said "in all fairness, I want to recognize and strengthen your customs"...

Then, this tyrant took some large iron nails,
And planted them in a circle in the skullcaps of each ambassador.
"Believe me," he said, as his servants nailed the skullcaps to the envoys'
heads,
"This is how I will strengthen your customs!"

In the summer of 1462 (the year Beheim met Jacob), the Ottoman sultan brought an army to Wallachia, easily three times the size of Vlad's. For all of his cruelty, Vlad was not foolhardy or stupid. Knowing his forces could not defeat a much larger, better-equipped army in an outright battle, he had to resort to guerrilla tactics in the form of nighttime raids to try to even the odds a bit. He followed a "scorched earth" policy of burning crops and villages so that the Turkish forces would find no food or water. He even committed a kind of early biological warfare by sending afflicted individuals (with tuberculosis, leprosy, plague, and other diseases) into the midst of the enemy army dressed as Turks. If the sick survived both their illnesses and their mission, Vlad promised he would reward them handsomely. These tactics did have an effect, and Turkish morale began to wear down.

But it was his most brazen act of defiance that not only blackened his reputation forever, but also actually succeeded in driving back the Turkish army—something that no other Balkan leader had been able to do. In spite of the setbacks, the sultan was poised to attack Wallachia's capital city, Tîrgoviște. In response, Vlad played his last card, probably because he knew that the city could not withstand a siege.

Arriving at a point about sixty miles north of their destination, the Turkish army encountered a scene of horror unlike any they had ever seen:

The Turks saw, in a half-circle a mile wide,
Thousands of stakes holding the bodies of 20,000
Turkish soldiers captured in battles.
It is said that birds of prey made their nests in the skulls of some,
So long had they lain bare to the elements.

What a desolate spectacle this was for the Turks,
And for the sultan himself.
So overwhelmed by disbelief in what he saw,
He said that he could not take this land away from a man
Who could do such terrible things,
And that surely a man who had accomplished this
Was worthy of greater things.

Given the heat of the summer, the stench of rotting flesh and decay must have been unbearable. This ghastly scene was enough for the Ottoman troops and even the sultan, who at last conceded defeat and ordered the army to retreat. Ultimately he must have decided that, at least for the time being, Wallachia was not worth the price he would have to pay to take it.

Vlad had triumphed and halted the advancement of the mighty Ottoman Empire, but his victory was short-lived. Not long after this event Vlad fell from power and ended up as a prisoner in Hungary for several years. His own people had clearly had enough; what he demanded of them for their freedom was simply too much. He briefly returned to power again in 1476, but was soon killed in another Turkish attack. Beheim mused:

It is conceivable that the devil himself
Would not want Dracula.

Dracula's story passed into legend and became fodder for various propaganda machines. Beheim reported these stories as they were told to him by Jacob, but just how accurate are they? Undoubtedly, Vlad was a monster; there are a number of independent reports that confirm several of his atrocities, but we have to use some caution before believing everything that was said, no matter how horrifyingly fascinating it sounds. The Holy Roman Emperor and the Hungarian kings had long-standing political rivalries with Wallachia and it was in every way to their advantage to portray Prince Vlad as a kind of Antichrist. As a sycophant to Frederick III, Beheim would have wanted to please his emperor; most historians are convinced he embellished his poem quite a bit, making the horrible parts even more horrific. Estimates that Vlad killed one hundred thousand people, for example, are probably far too high. Likewise, the stories of his cannibalism and blood drinking are both probably untrue.

It would be foolish and wrong to try to excuse his actions by saying that he was a product of his times, but the terrible tortures he is said to have committed already existed and were practiced in other countries; he merely refined them and ordered their use on a greater scale. His unorthodox warfare techniques did stop the Turkish juggernaut, at least for a few decades. As a result, many Romanians now view him as a national hero. It's certainly not the case that he got a bad rap, but the evils that he did commit were at least partly amplified by those looking to sell books or please their patrons.

Whether he was a psychopath, a tyrant, or just an extreme patriot, the chilling words of a German musician ensured that the Son of the Dragon and his legend lived on to disturb and frighten many later listeners and readers.

Joan the Mad and singers for her husband's corpse

Queen Juana I of Castile (1479–1555) is often known as Joan the Mad, though historians have debated whether or not she was truly mad. It's quite possible that she was declared insane for political reasons, as there were those who had much to gain from this label. What is certain, though, is that she was a temperamental and passionate woman deeply in love with her husband, Philip the Handsome of Austria (1478–1506); what a great name! For her, it was a love bordering on obsession that continued well after his untimely death.

Born in 1479, Joan was the second daughter of King Ferdinand II of Aragon and Queen Isabella I of Castile. The marriage of these two united Spain, and their military efforts drove the Moors from the south of the country forever. In 1492 Granada fell, the last stronghold of Moorish resistance. They were also the monarchs who supported Columbus's first journey, and their daughter, Katherine of Aragon, was to marry that accomplished musician, King Henry VIII of England. Joan herself was said to be gifted in music, playing the harpsichord and lute and having a fondness for dancing.

By the age of sixteen she was betrothed to Philip, the son of Emperor Maximilian of Germany. They met in 1496 and fell in love (or lust, given Philip's epithet) immediately. It was said that they found the nearest priest to marry them on the spot so they could be off to the bedroom. A "proper" church wedding was conducted the following day, just to make things nice and official. While Joan was hopelessly infatuated with her husband, Philip was used to drinking, eating, and philandering; he had no intention of changing his ways, regardless of his attraction to Joan. She was just another bonus in what must have been a pretty darned good life. For him, the marriage had been political, but for Joan, it was a love match, and she became very jealous and angry as he continued his wanton ways. She was irritable and moody, and her anger about his infidelities caused him to avoid her for days at a time. She remained in love with him despite this, and was determined to see him reformed into the ideal husband that she wanted him to be.

Over the next several years, a number of incidents seemed to push Joan closer to the edge. As her instability increased and she became more suspicious of Philip's activities, his trip to Spain caused nearly irreparable family problems. Philip had no taste for the austere and conservative Spanish court and wanted to be away from it. He left, but Joan was forced to stay behind, a decision she raged against incessantly.

By the time of her return to Flanders in 1504, Philip had taken a mistress. Joan consulted her servants for love potions and spells to try to bind him back to her. He discovered this and dismissed them. Eventually the two were reconciled. Later that year, Joan was proclaimed Queen of Castile. Wary of this and fearing his own loss of royal power, Ferdinand set in motion a series of events to try to deprive Joan of her right to rule.

However, in September of that year Philip took ill with a fever. Within days he was dead, at only twenty-eight. Joan, pregnant at the time, was inconsolable. She refused to have his corpse removed, staying beside it and caressing it. She wore only black from then on, and her mental health seemed to gradually deteriorate.

She intended that he be buried in the south of Spain, a journey that would take some time given her condition. In the meantime, the body was interred temporarily at the monastery of Burgos. Rumors began to spread that each night Joan would open the coffin and gaze at her husband's remains, overcome with grief. In fact, she did open the coffin more than once to ensure that the body was still there. She is said to have begun kissing the corpse's feet when it was unwrapped, and she had to be forcibly removed from its presence.

Eventually she set out on the journey. She had the coffin escorted by an armed guard and insisted that women not be allowed near it; she must have feared Philip's philandering ways even beyond the grave. The retinue traveled only at night and would not stop at nunneries; Joan apparently thought that nuns were particularly susceptible to a dead man's charms. During this time, she engaged some of Philip's musicians and composers in a macabre ritual. Philip had a following of musicians in his employ. Most of them had departed back to Flanders and France upon his death, but Gilles Reingot and Pierre de La Rue remained in her service. La Rue is known these days for his fine songs and sacred music (masses and motets). Joan was quite fond of him, raising him in rank to her *premier chapelain*, the head of the chapel; she also paid him twice what the other singers received. This generous salary was probably enough of an incentive to remain with the increasingly eccentric queen. He journeyed with her and the coffin through Spain, and each night the chapel choir would sing a Requiem Mass to the corpse. Whether or not it was visible is not recorded, though legend says that Joan wanted to view the ever-decaying body on a regular basis, so perhaps she frequently forced the singers to gaze upon the grisly sight while they chanted and sang for Philip's soul.

To put a stop to this whole business, her father Ferdinand eventually shut Joan away in the town of Tordesillas, in central Spain. He dismissed her singers, and Reingot and La Rue went back to Flanders. By 1508 La Rue was in Brussels, and he stayed there and in the vicinity until 1514; apparently, hoofing it around Spain singing to a dead body had somewhat soured his taste for travel.

Was Joan truly mad? She may have been schizophrenic, or perhaps she suffered from paranoid delusions. Inbreeding among the royal families and the resulting unspecified mental illness has also been offered as an explanation for her bizarre behavior. On the other hand, Ferdinand had a lot to gain, in terms of power, by declaring her insane and ruling in her stead.

Both La Rue and Reingot remained with her long after they were required to. They could easily have found comparable employment elsewhere (as they eventually did). But they seemed quite content to say prayers and sing masses to a corpse to humor their patron.

La Marseillaise and the French Revolution

The *Marseillaise* is the rousing national anthem of France, associated with the country almost as strongly as the Eiffel Tower and baguettes. Created during the time of the French Revolution and an impending war with Austria, the song has a curious history. In 1792 the revolution was in full swing, and Austria had declared war on France for imprisoning Marie Antoinette, who was Austrian by birth. In the town of Strasbourg on the German border, the mayor, P. F. Dietrich, sent out the call for a new anthem to raise the morale of the French troops and give them heart and enthusiasm for the fighting ahead.

A captain of engineers, Claude Joseph Rouget de Lisle (1760–1836), responded with the song that became world famous, writing the words in one night. He borrowed music from a work written by Italian composer Giovanni Battista Viotti in 1784 and called it the "War Song for the Army of the Rhine." The troops took to the tune immediately, and it became so popular that when some volunteer soldiers from Marseilles took it with them to Paris, it was attributed to them and dubbed *La Marseillaise*. Indeed, it was declared the French national anthem on July

14, 1795 (the date now known as Bastille Day). However, when the revolution ended and Napoleon took power, he banned the song because it had the ability to stir up strong feelings and had come to be associated with loutish behavior, riots, and disorder. It was rather like a late eighteenth-century European football fans' chant. It was made legal in 1830 and then banned once again by Napoleon III. It was only finally restored permanently as the anthem in 1879, long after revolutions and wars had faded in immediate importance.

Ironically, the mayor who had commissioned the work to inspire patriotic fervor and revolutionary spirit was ultimately sent to the guillotine because of his aristocratic background. He became the victim of his own success. De Lisle himself was imprisoned in 1793; no one was safe from suspicion or the terror of the blade. He was eventually freed and went on to write other songs, but nothing ever came close to the fame he had achieved with his anthem. He lived until 1836 and died in poverty, which, of course, is a common fate for many creators of lasting works of art.

Blood-letting and a haircut

We think of barbershop quartets as groups of men singing close harmonies, adorned with impressive moustaches, turn-of-the-century clothing, and straw hats, though there are women's groups, too. There is something "county fair in the American heartland" and nostalgic about them that may suggest cheesiness to some, in spite of the obvious talent required to harmonize so well.

How did the genre acquire its name? There are actually two different histories, one considerably bloodier than the other. In sixteenth-century England, barbers were not just those who trimmed hair and whiskers; they had multiple roles. They were often associated with surgeons, and the two belonged to the same guild, the Company of Barber-Surgeons, which had merged in 1540. If that makes you uncomfortable, it should. They offered such services as bleeding (believed to restore health and balance), leeches, the binding of wounds, and tooth extraction. Indeed, the familiar barber's pole, with its red and white stripes, originated in this time, the white representing bandages and the red symbolizing blood. Just remember that the next time you go in for a trim.

So what is the musical connection? Those who went to the barber often found that there were instruments provided for making music while they waited. This practice actually seems like a good idea, offering patients a means of calming themselves before submitting to whatever curative torture they were seeking. Barbershops provided lutes, citterns (a kind of early mandolin), and virginals (a small harpsichord), and encouraged the singing of popular tunes. The music provided cheer and quite possibly drowned out the patients' screams. Writers such as William Shakespeare and Ben Jonson referred to barber music, and the composer Thomas Morley noted that one popular pavane (a slow dance) was sometimes called the "Gregory Walker" after a well-known hairdresser and musician, though he further implied that barber's music is hardly worthy of serious consideration.

What connects this English cultural oddity with modern barbershop music? An error of historical interpretation. The vocal harmonies that we know today had their origins in poor, working class populations, especially in African American communities. The barbershop served as a kind of social center, where informal singing and harmonizing of popular songs began at the end of the nineteenth century.

With the invention of the phonograph and the desire for recordings, barbershop repertoire caught the attention of the new recording businesses because the groups were small and literally could all fit in front of the recording horn (the precursor of the microphone). But it wasn't the men from the barbershops who were being recorded. There was probably a racist assumption that white singers would be more appealing and marketable than black, so new groups were formed to meet the demand, and the genre was solidified.

Some confusion about the origin of the term arose later. Music historian Percy Scholes made an error in the 1930s when reading about the practice of making music in Elizabethan barbershops. He assumed that this meant that the modern barbershop quartet had come from England and was a contemporary survival of an old practice, when in fact the two were separate art forms. His *Oxford Companion to Music* notes, for example, "Possibly, however, these terms [barbershop quartet and music] are a mere survival of an English expression now obsolete in the land of its origin—'Barber's Music'—for any kind of extemporized noisy tune-making." As a result, he created an erroneous association between them, assuming that the vocal groups were Elizabethan in origin, perpetuated in his reference book. Barbershop music continues to this day and has both its admirers and detractors, though thankfully, leeches, teeth-pulling, and the opening of veins are no longer involved.

5

The Dead Speak

Belief in spirits, ghosts, and the afterlife seems to be an essential component of human culture. One would be hard-pressed to find any group of people in the world that didn't hold to some kind of belief in disembodied spirits at one time or another. Some theorize that we are hardwired for metaphysical yearnings and belief in an afterlife. Such ideas could have been useful as a survival mechanism of some kind back in the day—well, *way* back in the day. Countless debates rage about how valid any of it is, and they will almost certainly never end.

The musical world, as you've probably already guessed, has its share of hauntings, contact with the dead, and mysterious ghostly manifestations. What follows is only a sampling of the hundreds, if not thousands, of stories. Skeptics will scoff and believers will believe, but here are some unsettling stories that might make you wonder what's really out there, beyond our everyday perceptions.

They just decomposed

Born in 1916 to an electrician and a caterer, Rosemary Brown was, to outward appearances, an ordinary enough person. The London resident was the mother of two, a widow, and not someone who sought attention. But Rosemary seemed to have an extraordinary gift. Throughout her life, starting in her early childhood years, she claimed that the spirits of many of the great composers communicated with her and often dictated new compositions.

The first composer to appear to her was Franz Liszt, when she was seven years old. She didn't know who he was until she saw his portrait ten years later, but described him as a man with long white hair wearing a black robe. This was exactly how he would have looked in old age, since he ended his life as a priest. He told her that one day he would give her music. It seems that her mother and grandmother considered themselves psychic, so perhaps she wasn't too surprised to be contacted by a spirit.

In any case, she set this visitation aside, married, and raised a family. It wasn't until 1964 that the visits began in earnest. She suffered an accident at the school kitchen where she worked and decided to take up playing the piano again during her recovery, having quit more than once in the past. It was then that Liszt returned to her, and it was he, she said, who brought in other composers to communicate with her. For more than twenty years, she would receive numerous communications from a galaxy of classical music stars, each giving her their "new" pieces to present to the world. The thing is, Rosemary's musical talent was limited, and she had little knowledge of theory or composition. She could not improvise or play from memory. She freely admitted to the inability to play many of the pieces dictated to her, simply because they were too technically demanding.

The works that she received and transcribed included a lengthy sonata and twelve songs by Schubert, piano works by Chopin, Beethoven's tenth and eleventh symphonies (!), plus new sonatas by him. Other composers included Bach, Rachmaninoff, Brahms, Grieg, Debussy, Schumann, and later the newly departed Stravinsky, who apparently wanted to continue right on with his work and wasn't going to let a little thing like death get in his way.

Each of these luminaries had a preferred method of relaying their works. Chopin and Liszt liked to guide her hands on the keyboard, and she could write down a few notes at a time. Beethoven and Bach liked to dictate the notes to her, but she wasn't as fond of this method because she could not hear how the pieces would sound. She said that Chopin had watched television with her and was appalled by what he saw. She claimed that Beethoven, incidentally, was no longer deaf and didn't have his "crabby look," though he was once very annoyed when they were interrupted by someone at the door. Schubert liked to sing his works to her, but, she noted, "he hasn't a very good voice."

So what did people make of all of this? It's a fantastic story, to say the least. Needless to say, the skeptics were up in arms and the press had a field day, though usually they poked fun at her in a good-natured way. How about composers, conductors, and musicologists? Surprisingly, she was met with some rather enthusiastic support for the pieces she produced. Hephzibah Menuhin, sister of Yehudi and an accomplished concert pianist, found the pieces to be impressive, noting that Rosemary was sincere and that the works she had produced were "absolutely in the style of these composers." British composer Richard Rodney Bennett became a noted advocate. He said that he had been stuck in one of his own compositions, but that Debussy, via Rosemary, had offered a solution that had worked. In an interview for *Time* magazine he stated, "If she is a fake, she is a brilliant one, and must have had years of training. . . . Some of the music is awful, but some is marvelous. I couldn't have faked the Beethoven."

Others were less impressed. André Previn, the conductor of the London Symphony Orchestra at the time, remarked that if these were genuine, they should have remained on the shelf. Leonard Bernstein said that he could "buy" one of the Rachmaninoff pieces, but the rest didn't impress him much. Alan Rich, music critic for the *New York* magazine, felt that they were simply subpar reworkings of existing pieces, though what he heard was only a recording of the simpler compositions.

On the other hand, Peter Katin, a well-known pianist and respected interpreter of Chopin, recorded some of Chopin's dictated works and was impressed. In 1969 the BBC asked Rosemary to sit at a piano and contact Liszt to present her with a short piece, which he did. She was unable to play it because of its technical precision, but when a Liszt expert examined it later, he noted that it was indeed very much in his style. When a recording was made of some of the pieces in 1970, she asked noted musicologist Sir Donald Tovey to write notes for the record. He was happy to oblige, suggesting that:

> In communicating through music and conversation, an organized group of musicians who have departed from your world, are attempting to establish a precept for humanity, i.e. that physical death is a transition from one state of consciousness to another wherein one retains one's individuality.

The thing is, Tovey had died in 1940, but she claimed to be in regular contact with him.

So, what was really going on? Honestly, we just don't know. Various psychologists and musicians examined Rosemary, and none of them came away with the impression that she was faking, cheating, or otherwise trying to commit fraud. Some suggested that she had latent musical abilities of which she wasn't even aware, or that maybe she had more talent when she was younger but blocked it out due to some trauma. Others suggested that she had a hidden accomplice, one who was very much alive. The fact remains that some of the pieces were excellent and others were mediocre, which is probably exactly what we would expect from any composer's output. In the mid-1980s, the ghostly visitations ceased, and her health began to decline. She died in 2001, the mystery of her musical revelations still unsolved.

Schumann's violin concerto, brought back from the dead

The 1930s witnessed another remarkable case of a composer reaching out from beyond, one of those who would give new works to Rosemary. We have already seen what a troubled life Robert Schumann lived. As he was increasingly beset by hallucinations in his later years, his grasp on reality became more and more tenuous. Despite this, he continued to compose music. In the autumn of 1853 he wrote his only violin concerto. He intended for it to be played by the great violinist Joseph

Joachim, a master with whom he had collaborated in the past. There was a problem, though: Joachim was aware that Schumann's mind was going. Seeing the piece as a product of the composer's increasing madness—especially after Schumann's attempted suicide—he was not at all inclined to perform it. Joachim found the music to be morbid and did not want it performed. He wrote in a letter that it contained "a certain exhaustion, which attempts to wring out the last resources of spiritual energy."

So he stashed it away and never had it published, not even in Schumann's complete works published by Brahms and Schumann's widow, Clara. Joachim may have thought that it would tarnish the composer's reputation and convinced them to omit it, owing to the composer's mental state when he wrote it. Interestingly, Brahms did later publish a piece titled "Schumann's last musical thought," which was a theme on which Brahms was composing variations. Schumann, believing one of his many delusions, had claimed that this melody had been dictated to him by the spirits of Mendelssohn and Schubert, when in fact Schumann had written it for the slow movement of the violin concerto itself. His mind was already well on its way to going, and he didn't even recognize music from his own previous work.

After Schumann's death, Joachim retained the concerto manuscript and later gave it to the Prussian State Library in Berlin. In his will (he died in 1907), Joachim requested that the piece remain there and not be performed or published until a hundred years after Schumann's death, which would be 1956. That's where the matter should have rested, but then things got weird.

In March 1933, Swedish ambassador Baron Erik Kule Palmstierna held a spiritualist séance in London. These gatherings were hugely popular in later Victorian times and still retained some of their allure and mystique among the curious well into the twentieth century. In attendance were Joachim's grandnieces, Jelly d'Arányi and Adila Fachiri, who were sisters and both violinists themselves. The medium conducting the séance revealed that a spirit voice claiming to be Schumann was asking for Jelly to locate and bring to light one of his unpublished works. Jelly

214 ~๑ *Beethoven's Skull*

later claimed that she had no knowledge of any of his works that were hidden from the general public.

Schumann also asked her to perform the piece. As if to answer their next question about where it was located, another message came through in a later session, claiming to be from Joachim's spirit; he told them to ask Baron Palmstierna to go to the Hochschule Museum in Berlin. This turned up nothing, but a new tip led the baron to the Prussian State Library where he found the manuscript. This incident is remarkable because up until this time very few even knew that the piece existed, though one account does mention that the first movement may already have been performed a few years earlier. How this information came to light has never been explained. Perhaps Schumann's spirit did indeed reach out to them, though Joachim also being on hand to point them in the right direction is probably a little too good to be true.

In any case, nothing came of it immediately. Four years later, however, violinist Yehudi Menuhin received a copy of the score from a music publisher in Mainz, asking for his opinion. Somehow they'd gotten word of its existence and obtained a copy, obviously in violation of Joachim's instructions in his will. Menuhin was impressed and wanted to offer a world premiere in 1937. The problem was that Jelly d'Arányi then came forward and claimed the right to the first performance, based on the information she had received at the séances!

As you can imagine, this claim didn't hold much legal water, despite the remarkable revelations that the séances seem to have produced. Menuhin fared no better in his efforts. The copyright resided in Germany, and Hitler's Nazi government was in no mood to allow Menuhin, a Jew, to be the first to premiere a lost work by a major German composer. A German violinist named Georg Kulenkampff gave the first performance in Berlin in November 1937; a recording followed soon after. Menuhin was able to perform it at Carnegie Hall in December, and d'Arányi gave her performance in London, also in December, so ultimately everyone was happy (we hope).

The piece came to light at last, but there is still no logical explanation for what happened at those séances.

Haunted concert halls and opera houses: where the dead keep giving encores

There is probably no human settlement on Earth where someone hasn't reported a ghostly encounter at some point. Every kind of building imaginable and most natural areas have been tagged as homes for ghosts, and the music world is certainly no exception. The casual researcher can discover huge numbers of haunted theaters that have doubled for both plays and musical productions. It would be impossible to list more than a few, so here are a handful of interesting ones, with many more waiting to be explored. Set your skepticism aside for a bit and read on, if you dare.

Twin City Opera House, McConnelsville, Ohio

This theater, which hosts everything from movies to concerts, opened in 1892. Its first show was a production of *The Mikado* by Gilbert and Sullivan. Over the years it has been beset by paranormal activity, and its website even encourages visits from would-be ghost hunters. The incidents range from the benign to the truly frightening. There are at least fourteen different ghosts who roam the building, among them the spirit of Everett Miller. Miller was an usher at the theater for thirty years and it seems he has no intention of leaving any time soon. He is frequently seen and has been contacted by those who do such investigations. There is Red Wine Robert, a stagehand at the turn of the twentieth century who allegedly has been captured on tape saying, "I've got red wine." Lucky ghost! There is the spirit of John Leezer, who was stabbed to death in the ballroom at the beginning of the twentieth century; who knew that a dance floor could be so dangerous? There is also the mysterious lady in a white Victorian dress—sometimes seen walking across the stage—but her identity is unknown.

By far the most unsettling, however, is the black amorphous shadow that has been encountered many times deep in the basement, near old blocked-up tunnels that run under the town. This entity, if that's what it is, seems to radiate malice and does not like being approached. Numerous people have observed it, and it has been photographed; the photos usually show dark areas or splotches in one corner or another. Frightened witnesses have reported hearing it growling and even warning them to "get out." Drastic drops in temperature have been felt in its presence (a common indicator of ghostly incursions), and witnesses have felt sick around it. Why this particular building would attract such a thing, or any of the spirits observed here, is not known, but the theater continues and thrives, in part because of its haunted reputation.

Rhoads Opera House, Boyertown, Pennsylvania

This theater no longer exists, but it was once the scene of a terrible tragedy. The term "opera house" as used in America at the time was frequently something of a misnomer. More often than not, such places showed plays and vaudeville—some of which were unsuitable for children and those of a "delicate" nature—but they used the name "opera house" to make themselves seem more respectable, especially in small, conservative, and religious communities. The Rhoads Opera House was such a place, and on the fateful night of January 13, 1908, it was showing a play about the Scottish Reformation, a subject that would have appealed to the local Protestant community. Hundreds turned out to watch a dramatization of the Scots sticking it to the Catholic Church.

During the course of the evening, a stereopticon—a device used for showing slide photographs—seems to have thrown a bit of a fit, crackling and sparking. This unnerved those in the audience who didn't know what was happening, and a number made their way toward the stage to get a better look. In the commotion that followed, someone kicked over a kerosene footlight that ignited a nearby barrel of oil, sending the stage up in flames. The crowds panicked and rushed to flee the theater, but this was in the days before proper fire codes, and the doors opened inward rather than outward. Over 170 people died from smoke inhalation and flames, and the building was reduced to ruins.

In the aftermath of what became a national scandal, new fire safety codes were drawn up for all future buildings in the state, and these eventually set the standard for the rest of the country. This was of no help to the dead, and no comfort to their families and loved ones.

Shortly after the accident, eerie things began to be reported in and around the shell of the building. Levelheaded people told of hearing agonized screams and moans coming from the ruin; were these sounds the cries of the victims? One elderly man was convinced that the ghost of his wife had asked him to come to the building to be with her, so he tried to squat there but was eventually removed. Others nearby reported that their homes had since become haunted, perhaps due to the restless spirits that were still lingering about the area. The opera house was not rebuilt and today the site is covered with shops and apartments. There have been periodic reports of ghostly screams of pain, heard both in the area and at the local cemetery where many were buried. Perhaps an event so horrific has somehow imprinted itself at the site, like a terrible recording set on repeat.

Metropolitan Opera House, New York

Unlike the previous two examples, this one has more humor than horror. Located at Broadway and 39th Street, the opera house was home to many of the great singers and productions in the first half of the twentieth century. The legendary Enrico Caruso was a regular performer (and yet is said to haunt the Brady Theater in Tulsa, Oklahoma), Arturo Toscanini conducted there, and Puccini premiered his opera *The Girl of the Golden West* at this theater. One soprano, Frances Alda, took up residence as an apparition for a time in the 1950s and 1960s. Born in New Zealand, she became a star in the opera world, performing at the great houses in Europe and America. She died in Venice in 1952 at the age of seventy-three but apparently wasn't content to stay there.

Shortly after her death, people reported seeing her back in New York at the Met. Patrons would say they had witnessed an aged woman, gaudily dressed, sitting at the end of their row, or even next to them, muttering to herself or making critical comments about a given evening's particular production. She is said to have clicked her tongue and tapped her program, or waved her hands about, often in displeasure at the sopranos' performances. The interesting thing is that she would never return after the first act. The manager and the ushers became used to hearing patrons complain about this woman—whose description matched Frances—and promised to take care of the matter. After eventually realizing that it was her ghost, they didn't bother to follow up, knowing that she wouldn't return for the rest of the performance. This strange phenomenon went on until 1966, when the Met moved its company to the more modern Lincoln Center. Frances didn't move with the company, however, and her critical hauntings ceased. The old building was demolished, so perhaps she's at peace at last, or maybe she's still stirring up trouble somewhere else.

Her Majesty's Theater, London

The current building dates from the late 1890s, though there has been a theater on the site since 1705. The modern theater has been hosting Andrew Lloyd Webber's musical *The Phantom of the Opera* since 1986. Curiously, there is one audience member that keeps returning. The spirit of a certain Shakespearian actor with the wonderful name of Herbert Beerbohm Tree has been spotted numerous times since the 1970s at various locations, including stairs, wardrobe, and backstage. One actor playing the role of the Phantom noted that he once felt a strange presence standing behind him in his dressing room but saw nothing. Patrons have reported that doors to box seats open by themselves, and that the temperature drops unexpectedly. Tree was a manager for the theater at the turn of the twentieth century, but why he should choose to return in modern times is unknown.

Place de l'Opéra, Paris

Speaking of *The Phantom of the Opera*, the Place, completed in 1875, was the inspiration for and the setting of Gaston Leroux's 1910 novel, which inspired movies such as the classic Lon Chaney silent film from

1925 and Lloyd Webber's musical. Leroux noted in a famous quote about Erik, his phantom:

> The Opera ghost really existed. He was not, as was long believed, a creature of the imagination of the artists, the superstition of the managers, or a product of the absurd and impressionable brains of the young ladies of the ballet, their mothers, the box-keepers, the cloakroom attendants or the concierge. Yes, he existed in flesh and blood, although he assumed the complete appearance of a real phantom; that is to say, of a spectral shade.

Based on this comment, some believe that the Place itself is haunted (though the management dismisses this notion), and there are some strange stories from the vicinity if not the venue itself. Locals describe one ghost as that of an elderly woman who roams the streets near the opera house. Legend says that she committed suicide when her husband abandoned her for a much younger woman, and that now her spirit wanders eternally, never able to find peace or happiness.

How many more theaters and concert halls out there have similar tales to tell?

Music from beyond

The flautist in Emmitsburg Cemetery

In the town of Emmitsburg, Maryland, some say that a ghostly annual tradition makes itself known at Christmas. The story begins in the early nineteenth century, when German musician and composer Casper Dielman came to America. He enjoyed success in his career, including composing inaugural music for American presidents and directing orchestras in major cities like New York and Baltimore. Taking up a place at Mount Saint Mary's College, he settled into a life of teaching. He had hoped that his son Larry might follow in his musical footsteps, but the latter, while showing some musical talent, was never the prodigy his father had hoped for, instead becoming a grocer and preferring the banjo—as one does.

After some personal tragedies, Larry reconsidered his rejection of his father's music. First Larry's wife abandoned him, and he became sad, lonely, and withdrawn. Then his father passed away in the 1880s, and Larry, having rediscovered the flute Casper had once given him, became determined to learn to play it. At Christmas he went to his father's grave and played as a tribute, attracting the attention of the locals. The ritual became an annual tradition, with townspeople following Larry, Pied Piper–style, to the grave. This continued until 1922, the last year that Larry made his pilgrimage. He was found unconscious in the snow, died the next spring, and was buried next to his father. So it ended, apparently.

However, as late as the 1970s some locals swore that they continued to hear the ghostly music of the flute coming from the cemetery each year at Christmas. One recalled vividly hearing sleigh bells, the sounds of people, and above it all, a flute that made dogs howl. Did Larry continue his annual tribute to his father to atone for disappointing him?

The musical ghost of Monaghan Hall

This grand building in Spokane, Washington, is a part of Gonzaga University, Bing Crosby's alma mater (though he has nothing to do with this story). Originally the private home of wealthy nineteenth-century businessman James Monaghan, the building is now used by the university's music department. It has been the source of a number of chilling stories, especially in the 1970s. Some experienced the familiar ghostly activity of footsteps, locked doors found open, power outages, and shapes appearing in the upstairs windows when viewed from outside. Rumors circulated of terrible things happening there, such as a student committing suicide by hanging. Monaghan himself does not seem to be the cause of the hauntings, though there were whispers of photos of his coffin in the presence of upside-down crucifixes; one of the photos was said to be impossible to burn. This is classic horror story fare, but no evidence has been found to prove it.

Various people experienced far creepier encounters in the house, such as growling sounds from the basement or the feeling of being choked by icy cold hands. There is also a story from a live-in caretaker who believed that something was subtly encouraging him to hang himself, perhaps the ghost of the student who had met that unfortunate fate.

Whatever haunts the hall, it seems to have musical talent. A cleaning lady once reported that in November 1974, she had to return to the building one night, having forgotten an item. She found the front door unlocked and heard organ music, a simple melody repeated over and over. The door to the organ room was locked, and when she opened it, she saw that the room was empty but that *the keys were playing by themselves.* Not long after, a music professor heard phantom flute music wafting through the halls but could find no source. One day, he was absentmindedly tapping out a melody on a piano when the cleaner confronted him and told him that he was playing the tune she had heard on the organ. He then realized that it was the same song he had heard the ghostly flute playing.

Additional stories circulated that an exorcism, or at least holy rites, was performed in the building and that things quieted down afterward—or maybe not. A burning smell was noticed without a source, a heavy blackboard on wheels apparently moved of its own accord, and various other ghostly things continued, but no one was hurt, and the phenomena seemed to ease up over the years. Is there an angry musical ghost in the hall? If nothing else, it makes a grand story to tell each new crop of incoming freshmen at the beginning of the academic year.

The ghostly piano of Gardner Lake

A curious legend has grown up about Gardner Lake in Connecticut. During a fierce winter in the 1890s, the owners of a certain home near the water had what they thought was a brilliant idea. They wanted to move the house to the other side of the lake and thought that the frozen February weather would give them a perfect opportunity. So in a splendidly stupid undertaking, the house and all of its contents were moved to the shore, lifted up onto sled-like structures, and slid out onto the ice.

From there, horses were supposed to pull it for an easy trip over to their desired new location.

Except, of course, that's not what happened at all. Once out on the ice, the movers soon realized that the home was far too heavy for mere frozen water to bear. It got bogged down, began to tilt, and the ice underneath it began to crack. Most of the family's belongings were hastily retrieved, but the house itself was doomed. Tourists came from far and wide to view with amusement the home that was now slowly sinking. Reports say that it actually remained afloat for some time, even after the ice melted, but eventually gravity took its toll and the whole thing descended into the depths, finding a watery grave at the bottom of the lake.

An oddball story, to be sure, but what makes it mysterious is that over the years, many people—particularly those in boats out on the lake—have reported hearing a faint, ghostly piano. The source of the music is difficult to determine but seems to be coming from the water itself. It turns out that a piano was one of the casualties of the sinking; it went down with the house and could not be saved. No one seems to have died in this misadventure, so why a watery ghost would be playing a submerged piano remains a mystery, but many insist that they have heard it. Maybe it's the musical fish we met at the beginning of Part II.

The ghost of Chopin at the "Honky Chateau"

Chopin has had quite an afterlife, it seems, what with being buried mostly in Paris and partly in Warsaw, while also finding time to dictate new music to an unassuming English woman. Another account says that he may have spent some postmortem time at the "Honky Chateau," more formally known as Château d'Hérouville, in the Oise Valley north of Paris. Chopin may have resided here, while still alive, with George Sand.

After years of neglect, the manor house was remade into Strawberry Studios in 1962 and became a place where rock and pop bands recorded some of their most legendary works; the list of stars includes Elton John (from whom the studio gained its nickname), Iggy Pop, Fleetwood Mac,

Jethro Tull, the Bee Gees, and the late David Bowie, among others. During a stay in 1973, Bowie and his producers felt strongly that Chopin and Sand were still there, and when taking a tour of the building Bowie refused to sleep in the master bedroom, being completely unnerved by it; a portion of the room seemed darker and colder than the rest. One of the producers took the bedroom instead and was woken up at night by someone shaking his shoulder, but saw no one. Perhaps Bowie was right? The studio closed its doors in 1985, but efforts are now under way to restore it again, with or without Chopin's approval.

A spectral soprano in Handel's house?

The London home where George Frederic Handel lived for thirty-six years until his death seems to have been host to a bit of supernatural activity. The house was occupied for generations after his death; at one point Jimi Hendrix resided next door for a short time. During renovations in 2001, in preparation for opening it as a restored eighteenth-century home and museum dedicated to Handel, one of the trust fund-raisers had a hair-raising experience while on the premises.

He described how, while measuring for curtains, he felt the air become "thick" and saw a shape resembling a woman hovering near him. He described it as being like an after-image on one's retinas from looking at the sun for too long, but felt that it was not menacing. Others noticed a lingering smell of perfume in the composer's old bedroom. It turns out that Hendrix also claimed to have seen a ghost in his next-door flat during his stay, and after all, what are walls to a ghost?

The identity of this apparition was a mystery, as Handel was not known to have entertained women in his home. But people assumed that it was someone from Handel's time, and the candidates were narrowed down to either Faustina Bordoni or Francesca Cuzzoni, two sopranos who vied for roles in his operas. Perhaps one or the other was not at rest, still waiting for the composer's next work?

In any case, a priest was called to perform an exorcism, because the trust could not decide whether having a ghost in their newly opened museum was a benefit or something that might literally scare some potential visitors away. Also, since many valuable historical items were going on display, they didn't want to risk a supernatural vandal causing any harm, apparently confusing a ghost with a poltergeist. In any case, the house seems silent now, so perhaps the restless Baroque soprano has sung her last aria?

6

Nursery Rhymes: the Good, the Bad, and the Downright Awful

Our collection of nursery rhymes is beloved. The very name suggests simple poems that are suitable for the youngest of children. Many grew up with their parents singing these songs and reciting these rhymes; they are used to comfort tiny babies and send them off to sleep or to entertain toddlers with colorful, silly stories. They seem about as far away from the strange and the gruesome as it gets.

So, why might many of them have absolutely appalling backstories? The answer lies partially in the fact that some may have been cryptic political commentaries and satires, while others were perhaps moral fables to keep wayward children in line, like some of the equally dark Grimm's fairy tales. Over time, the original meanings became garbled or forgotten, and what we are left with is the often-surreal imagery and what sounds to us like nonsense; rather like Internet comments and discussions. What better way to disguise an agenda, a political attack, or some other statement you'd rather keep hidden?

It's important to note that there are scholars who reject all of the following interpretations on the basis that there isn't enough evidence to make a definitive case for them. Modern folks, they argue, are reading too much into simple silly rhymes and looking for meanings that were never there. They might be right, but where's the fun in that? In any case, here are some of the darker examples.

Three Blind Mice

A version of this poem and its tune appeared in a book of rounds put together by the Jacobean composer Thomas Ravenscroft in 1609. A round is a canonic song, like "Row, row, row your boat," where one singer begins the melody, and at the second line, a new singer begins the tune at the top, and so on, revealing hidden harmonies in an otherwise simple one-melody song. This particular story might refer not to mice being chased by a farmer's angry wife, but rather to three unfortunate folks who took part in a conspiracy against Mary I, Queen of England, and met a bad end. As Henry VIII's eldest daughter, she was a devout Catholic. After the death of Henry and then his very Protestant son and heir, Edward VI, she set about doing everything she could to restore Catholicism to England, including burning Protestants at the stake. Nearly three hundred perished in this manner between 1553 and her death in 1558, earning her the unpleasant nickname of Bloody Mary. The round in Ravenscroft's collection could have been a bit of political propaganda. He may have written the words and melody himself. "Cutting off their tails" may have been a metaphor for the persecution, or perhaps even a reference to a grisly form of torture before the victims were burned.

Mary, Mary, Quite Contrary

This rhyme may also refer to Bloody Mary. We can easily see how she could be considered "quite contrary," and the garden may refer to her lack of heirs, her attempt to impose the Catholic faith again on England, or even the graveyard of her victims. The "pretty maids all in a row" may refer to her miscarriages, buried in the ground. The lack of any living children is what allowed her sister Elizabeth to ascend to the throne after Mary's death. Others have speculated that this poem refers to Mary, Queen of Scots, or it could refer to Catholicism itself and its veneration of the Virgin Mary. The cockleshells have been described as everything from the shell badges worn by pilgrims after completing their journey to the shrine of Saint James in Spain (Santiago de Compostela) to genital-torture devices used by Mary I's inquisitors—there's a lovely thought. The rhyme does not seem to appear before the eighteenth century, though, so all of these speculations may be wrong, or the rhyme could have been some other political commentary.

Jack and Jill

Everyone knows this strange and violent little rhyme. Two children go up a hill to fetch water and Jack falls, breaking his head, or his neck, or something. Not to be left out, Jill takes a tumble after he does. There have been many attempts to source the meaning of the story, but the evidence is inconclusive. We do know that "Jack" was a kind of Everyman character in English drama. Indeed, Shakespeare even mentions a Jack and Jill in both *A Midsummer Night's Dream* and *Love's Labour's Lost*, where they appear as archetypal young lovers. So the nursery rhyme may be nothing more than another scene starring a pair of stock characters.

There are two more interesting interpretations, however. The first is that the rhyme refers to an attempt by King Charles I to regulate taxes on drink sizes. A "jack" is a half-pint and a "gill" is a quarter-pint. Charles attempted to reduce the volume but keep the tax the same, which was obviously unpopular and was vetoed by Parliament, hence "Jack fell down" and "Jill came tumbling after." Of course, after the Civil War the king's own crown was "broken." Another fanciful story says that the rhyme refers to the executions of Louis XIV and Marie Antoinette. Jack's crown (head) was broken, and Jill's head came tumbling after. This delightfully gruesome interpretation would be perfect were it not for the fact that the rhyme's publication preceded their executions by nearly thirty years.

London Bridge Is Falling Down

This ever-popular tune seems to date from the nineteenth century, but the poem can be traced to the seventeenth and may even refer to something far older—medieval, in fact. There are bridge songs from other countries, including the traditional German rhyme *Die Magdeburger Brück*, the traditional Danish *Knippelsbro Går Op og Ned*, the fifteenth-century French *Sur le Pont d'Avignon*, and the fourteenth-century Italian *Le porte*, any of which may have influenced the London poem.

As for the meaning of the rhyme, one theory suggests that it was a reference to the destruction of an early version of London Bridge by Olaf II Haraldsson of Norway during a Viking raid in about 1014. There are references to this event in Viking poetry, but not in any Anglo-Saxon sources, so some scholars doubt that it happened; the Vikings may have just been bragging. On the other hand, the English may have been hugely embarrassed about losing their bridge to a bunch of Northmen.

Another interpretation suggests that the rhyme refers to a superstitious belief that the bridge was held up by human sacrifices, possibly those of children. This idea was advanced by a folklorist named Alice Gomme in the late nineteenth century, but there is neither cultural nor archeological evidence to back it up.

Yet another theory states that the song simply refers to the deterioration of the bridge over many centuries. London Bridge in the Middle Ages was a wonder—with a good number of houses and shops standing on it—but over time, of course, these started to fall apart and were further damaged by a fire in 1633. However, the bridge acted as a firebreak in the great fire of 1666, thus helping to spare the south bank of the city.

Ring around the Rosy

This rhyme has a special place in the speculations about dark origins of nursery rhymes. It has long been claimed that this light-hearted song and dance actually referred to the dreadful scourge of the bubonic plague, specifically the 1665 outbreak in London and surrounding areas, or perhaps to the original Black Death in the fourteenth century. The argument goes that the "rosy ring" refers to the rash and bubos that appeared on the victims. The posies indicate the belief that the plague was carried by bad smells and could be prevented by the armor of fresh scents. Ashes could refer to the burning of the bodies, though an alternate line reads, "A-tishoo! A-tishoo!" that is said to symbolize the sneezing of the afflicted. Finally, "we all fall down" means, of course, the victims soon die—lovely.

All of this seems wonderfully sinister and plausible at first, but most modern folklorists reject this reading of the song for a number of reasons. The plague interpretation did not appear until after World War II. In fact, the rhyme was only first printed in 1881 and may not have existed for too long before that. Further, the alleged symptoms being described are not particularly close to what plague victims actually experienced.

A more likely explanation has to do with nineteenth-century bans on dancing in certain strict Protestant communities in England and the United States. Some teenagers and children were able to circumvent the ban by creating rhyme "games" involving circle or ring dances with no musical accompaniment. Despite the wonderfully gross images that it evokes, this rhyme likely comes out of that tradition and has no deeper meaning.

Georgie Porgie

This seemingly innocent little rhyme was known in the mid-nineteenth century, but there is a theory linking it to a very sensitive political issue from several centuries earlier concerning George Villiers, First Duke of Buckingham (1592–1628). As a young man, George was brought to the attention of King James I, who took a great liking to him. Rumors of the king's sexual liaisons with handsome young men were already whispered away from polite conversation, and George seems to be the perfect candidate for such an arrangement. The exact nature of their relationship is unknown, but George did indeed become a royal favorite, was well rewarded, and for a time had the support of various courtiers. He played the game well.

He declared an admiration for Anne of Austria (1601–1666), queen consort of King Louis XIII of France, which caused a bit of a scandal, though we don't know if they were conducting an actual affair (Alexandre Dumas portrayed them as lovers in *The Three Musketeers*).

Though he had good looks and charm, he was also rude, crass, and a loudmouth who screwed up a number of diplomatic military missions. Only his favored status with the king kept him from the harm that some wished on him, or at least from being ostracized and ruined. Eventually the resentment of fellow courtiers and men under his command caught up with him, which may be what is referred to in the lines "When the boys came out to play, Georgie Porgie ran away." In August 1628, while he was preparing for another military venture, he was stabbed by one John Felton, a soldier from an earlier campaign who was angry at being passed over for a promotion. George allegedly rose to chase after him, but died of his injuries. Felton was later hanged, though quite a few were glad that the vain Duke of Buckingham was gone, and poems circulated proclaiming Felton a hero.

Sing a Song of Sixpence

The earliest mention of this rhyme dates from the eighteenth century. The reference to blackbirds in a pie may refer to a medieval practice for putting live creatures, and even musicians (!), into large pies to have them later burst out for the amusement of noble diners. Indeed, at a grand banquet from the year 1454, a troupe of no fewer than twenty-eight musicians emerged from a piecrust to entertain the guests with their songs.

Known as the Feast of the Pheasant, the banquet was hosted by Duke Philip the Good of Burgundy (1396–1467). Other entertainments included jousting, plays, and a live elephant. All of this was done as part of Philip's very public gesture—and that of some of the lesser nobles in attendance—to take up arms in a new crusade against the Ottoman Turks, who had taken the city of Constantinople the year before, much to the shock and horror of the West. Despite his declaration to fight the Turks, nothing ultimately came of his proposed crusade except crumbs in the musicians' instruments.

In any case, blackbirds or pigeons flying out of a pie for medieval courtly amusement certainly happened from time to time, and not just at such lavish feasts. These pies were not meant to be eaten, by the way, in case you are revolted by the thought of bird feathers and germs all over the food—or even worse, musician germs.

The title of the rhyme seems to have been drawn from a long tradition of paying musicians a meager amount for a song; nothing ever changes. Shakespeare writes in *Twelfth Night*, act II, scene III: "Come on; there is sixpence for you: let's have a song."

The only problem with the whole bird theory is that there is an earlier version of the rhyme, printed in 1744, with only one verse, the second half of which reads, "Four and twenty Naughty Boys, Baked in a Pye." This is quite different and conjures up some rather unpleasant mental images. So which came first? Was there a "bird version" already circulating based on medieval and Tudor extravagance? Or were the "naughty boys" the originals, changed to blackbirds a few decades later because cannibalism was rather unacceptable? In either case, the modern "exotic dancer" bursting out of the birthday cake is probably a descendant of this strange tradition.

7

Musical Curses, Bad Luck, and Superstitions

Belief in curses extends back throughout our known history and has been used to explain all kinds of bad luck. Curses can be spoken, or put on objects as a means of protection from harm or interference by outsiders, or perhaps they come about by unknown methods. We have all heard the stories of the "mummy's curse" that was said to have been placed on King Tut's tomb by sorcerers, though these rumors probably actually date from the time of the tomb's excavation. The story would have been meant to discourage grave robbers and treasure-seekers. Indeed, a number of accidents, maladies, and deaths did befall those involved in excavating Tutankhamen's tomb. These misfortunes are usually put down to coincidence or even the power of psychology. If one believes in a curse, one can be harmed by it. Others involved in the excavation experienced no problems at all, so we can take comfort in that.

Many sources have been blamed for curses, including black magicians, witches, necromancers, and the like. In some cultures in past centuries, it was even possible to visit one of these individuals and, for a price, have a curse put on an enemy. Plato noted in the *Republic* that such individuals would, for a fee, bring harm to anyone, good or evil. King James I of England had a paranoid fear of black magic and believed that witches were conspiring against not only his reign, but all that was good; he fully believed in their power to curse. Shakespeare was aware of this fear, which partially influenced his inclusion of the three witches in *Macbeth*.

Superstitious behaviors and beliefs are also as old as humanity, at least as old as we've been able to think and understand. They probably arose through people engaging in some action and seeing a result, whether positive or negative. Confusing correlation with causation, it was easy to associate a given action with a given outcome, no matter how unrelated they actually were. In our haughty modernity we like to scoff at these behaviors, dismissing them as outdated, primitive beliefs to which *we* as sophisticated modern folks would never succumb. After all, we have cell phones, high-speed Internet connections, and laser surgery. How could we ever fall for something so stupid?

Well, think about it the next time you decide to step around a ladder because you don't want to walk under it, or you sing a good-luck song and wear your lucky cap to "help" your favorite sports team win that playoff game, or you feel just a twinge of dread when something goes wrong on Friday the 13th. How many of your friends complain about mechanical and communication failures during a Mercury Retrograde? We've all done these things; don't deny it.

We still have our superstitions; they may well be hardwired into our simian brains. Some of them have become more complex or better rationalized, but in the end, we are very interested in trying to influence the world around us and will often resort to irrational and even very silly things in our attempts to do so.

Music—which stirs the emotions and embraces mysticism, spiritual belief, and personal expression—seems a natural place for superstitions to arise. The heightened state of feeling induced by music can encourage strong beliefs of all kinds. Indeed, many major composers held deeply superstitious beliefs right into modern times, and a number of personal rules, traditions, and regulations about performing and playing have arisen over the centuries. We will look at a sampling of these, from the amusing to the stupid, including a few that will make you wonder if there isn't a little something more to the whole thing than irrational belief.

The curse of "Gloomy Sunday"

The idea of a work of art being cursed or bringing bad luck is well established in theatrical circles, where Shakespeare's *Macbeth* is a popular example. The play is so surrounded with superstition that one must never even say its title on stage (i.e, during rehearsals), but instead must refer to it only as "The Scottish Play." This practice might amuse those who would dismiss the whole thing as silly, but many actors still insist on following the tradition.

Examples of musical curses are not as well known, but there is at least one song that has earned the reputation of bringing very bad luck not only to those who sing it, but also, and especially, to those who hear it. There are numerous urban legends about it, some contradictory, most unproven. Written in 1932 or 1933 by a Hungarian composer named Resző Seress and lyricist László Jávor, the tune is called "Gloomy Sunday." One account says it was written shortly after Seress's fiancée called off their engagement, another that he was concerned about the state of the world, which was in the grip of the Depression. The words told the story of a man whose beloved had died, and how he was considering suicide to be reunited with her; cheery stuff.

At first, some publishers rejected the opportunity to publish the sheet music, feeling it was just too . . . gloomy. But it was eventually published, and that's when things got interesting. It is rumored that a string of suicides occurred over the next few years, all involving people who had heard the song. In 1933 a young man asked a band in a Budapest café to play it. After it was over, he went home and shot himself. If this story is true, he was probably planning on killing himself to begin with and just wanted a suitably depressing soundtrack for making his exit. It seems that by 1936 the song was connected to a wave of suicides in Hungary, and certain regions banned it. The story was taken seriously enough that *Time* magazine reported on it in March of that year.

Billie Holiday (who struggled with her own drug and alcohol problems) made an English-language recording of the song in 1941, and another example of its influence comes from London. A young woman was playing the song over and over on a gramophone. Hearing this, her neighbors knocked on her door, but she didn't answer. Eventually they broke the door open to find her lying on the floor, dead from a drug overdose. Did the song make her do it?

The suicides didn't stop there. One urban legend claims that over two hundred people have killed themselves listening to this song. Unfortunately, this astonishingly high number cannot be proven or dismissed. Various accounts claim that the situation was worrying enough to convince authorities to take action, but these claims have proven difficult to confirm. It is said that the Hungarian government discouraged the playing of the song, and several radio stations in the United States refused to play it, though there was no outright ban. The BBC considered similar actions in the 1940s, and one source states that the lyrics were deemed to be too upsetting for its audience, so only instrumental versions were broadcast. Maybe they feared a curse, but more likely they were worried that stories of the song causing suicides might actually encourage some listeners to take their own lives. One report says that the BBC did not lift this unofficial ban until 2002, but another says that it was played at least a few times in the 1980s. Again, stories conflict and the most fanciful tale usually wins out.

In any case, fear of the song lessened over time, but its composer was destined to suffer a tragic fate of his own. In 1968 he killed himself by jumping off a building in Budapest. Beyond this fact, the legends once again take over, with one story saying that he noted beforehand that he had never been able to write another hit song. In an unverifiable twist, the woman who had rejected him and inspired the song was reportedly found dead some time earlier, having killed herself by poisoning. Next to her was a piece of paper on which she had written "Gloomy Sunday." Another version says it was the sheet music for the tune. Did the cursed song doom them both?

Tchaikovsky's cursed symphony?

A newspaper story from early 1950 related that the conductor of the Nottingham Orchestra in England was cancelling all future performances of Tchaikovsky's *Pathétique* Symphony, because each time it was performed one of the orchestra members would die. In response, Johannes Norrby, the director of the Stockholm Concert Association, defiantly included the symphony in one of his own concerts to debunk the superstition. He confidently told reporters that the symphony "does not murder musicians." It was performed that night without a problem, and the concert program moved on to Shostakovich's Sixth Symphony. During this piece, clarinetist Ludwig Warschewski, who had played with the Stockholm Symphony Orchestra for thirty years, collapsed and died on stage. Several doctors who were in the audience rushed to attend to him, but he could not be saved. See what happens when you tempt fate?

The Babe's piano

Though it's no longer an issue, since the Boston Red Sox have currently won three World Series since 2004, there was a persistent belief among some die-hard fans that there was a musical component to the "Curse of the Bambino." The bad luck was brought about when Babe Ruth was traded from the Red Sox to the New York Yankees at the end of 1919, as a result of which the Sox didn't win a World Series for eighty-six years.

While still playing with the Red Sox, Babe had rented a cabin in Sudbury, about twenty miles west of Boston near a body of water called Willis Pond. Versions of the story differ, but one says that during a certain winter night entertaining friends with his wife, Babe opened the doors to temporarily move his piano outside, not only to freshen up the room a bit but also to give them more space. Then disaster struck. In a scene straight out of a slapstick comedy, the piano slid out onto the ice of the pond and got stuck there. As the ice melted some time later, the piano simply sank to the bottom of the pond and lies there still. Another version of the story is that the whole party moved outside, piano and all, and then it got stuck in the ice. Locals believe it, and many elderly residents could recall Babe throwing some wild parties in those days.

Some of the superstitious sports fans—and honestly, most are pretty superstitious—came to believe that this unfortunate event was a bad omen. Ruth was traded soon after, beginning eight decades of baseball agony for Boston fans. For some time, these fans believed that if the piano could actually be raised from the pond, the curse would be lifted. A number of divers actually attempted to do this over the years, but they always had trouble locating it, prompting others to say that the story was just an urban legend.

It's a moot point now, of course. But Babe's cursed piano may yet lie at the bottom of the pond. If so, who knows what may happen if it's ever retrieved?

The 27 Club

Only the good die young. Well, the good, and rock and rollers, and jazz musicians. The origin of the term "27 Club" is obscure, but there is a curious coincidence among some popular performers of the last century: they lived fast, partied hard, and died at the young age of twenty-seven.

In an effort to shed light on the phenomenon, statisticians at Queensland University of Technology in Australia studied British artists who had number-one albums in the UK between 1956 and 2007, but found only three who died at that age. The researchers concluded in the *British Medical Journal*, "The study indicates that the 27 club has been created by a combination of chance and cherry picking." However, they admitted that the number of fatalities might be greater in other countries. They did find that musicians who are more famous face as much as three times the risk as their less popular counterparts of dying young (in their twenties and thirties), due to poor lifestyle choices.

Whatever their conclusions, there are at least fifty "members" of this club, with new ones being added every few years. Here are some of the more famous examples:

Robert Leroy Johnson (May 8, 1911–August 16, 1938): an important blues guitarist and singer, credited by many later rock and roll musicians as a defining figure in the blues genre. Details of his life are not well known, but he died after consuming whiskey that may have been poisoned. One story tells that he was flirting with a married woman at an event and her jealous husband laced the drink with strychnine. Whatever the cause of his death, he had another legend attached to him: that he sold his soul to the devil at a crossroads to obtain his musical talent. He used to practice in a cemetery where it was quiet, which probably gave fuel to such Faustian rumors.

Brian Jones (February 28, 1942–July 3, 1969): a founder and guitarist of the Rolling Stones. He drowned in a swimming pool, but drugs and alcohol probably played a role. Rumors persist that he was murdered, as it was said that various items were stolen from his home.

Jimi Hendrix (November 27, 1942–September 18, 1970): a pioneering rock guitarist who influenced a generation after him and is still regarded as one of the most important guitarists ever. He overdosed on sleeping pills and choked on his own vomit.

Janis Joplin (January 19, 1943–October 4, 1970): a popular solo singer-songwriter and a major star at the first Woodstock Festival. She died of a heroin overdose, possibly from a variety that was more potent than normal.

Jim Morrison (December 8, 1943–July 3, 1971): lead singer of the Doors. Officially he died of heart failure, but it may well have been a heroin overdose complicated by asthma. Many controversies linger over the exact nature of his death, with some claiming that he faked the whole thing. His grave in Paris's Père Lachaise Cemetery is still a site of pilgrimage for his fans.

Ronald "Pigpen" McKernan (September 8, 1945–March 8, 1973): a founding member of the Grateful Dead, he suffered from congenital biliary cirrhosis, an autoimmune disease of the liver. He died of a gastrointestinal hemorrhage.

Kurt Cobain (February 20, 1967–*ca.* April 5, 1994): the lead singer for the platinum-selling Seattle-based grunge band Nirvana, he shot himself in the head with a shotgun, though there have been a number of conspiracy theories stating that he was murdered. There were also claims that Cobain had expressed interest in joining the 27 Club. His death made the idea of the club better known in the popular imagination.

Amy Winehouse (September 14, 1983–July 23, 2011): the very popular jazz and R&B vocalist who won five Grammy awards in a single ceremony. She struggled with substance abuse and mental issues, as well as run-ins with the law, and was found dead by her bodyguard. Alcohol poisoning was determined to be the cause of death.

Superstitions about the ninth symphony

One of the stranger fears appearing in the nineteenth and twentieth centuries was a belief held by some prominent composers, among others, that a composer could only write nine symphonies. If he tried to write more, he would die soon after completing his ninth. Gustav Mahler (so said his wife, Alma) and Arnold Schoenberg both believed this. This superstition seems to have stemmed from the fact that Beethoven wrote only nine symphonies, as did Schubert (though the numbering of them during Mahler's time was different) and Bruckner, who perhaps intentionally composed his ninth symphony in D minor, the same key as his beloved Beethoven's ninth. The Czech composer Antonín Dvořák stopped writing symphonies after his famous *New World* Symphony. It was his ninth, though he considered it to be his eighth, since the score for his first symphony was lost and not rediscovered until after his death. Also, his ninth was originally numbered and published as his fifth, since three other early symphonies were not published in his lifetime. Got that?

The story goes that Mahler was so convinced of some kind of nine-symphony curse that he titled what would have been his ninth symphony *Das Lied von der Erde* ("The Song of the Earth"), in the belief that he could beat the system by not assigning it a number. Then he went ahead and composed a "ninth" symphony. Confident that he had cheated death, he began work on a tenth, but he died before he could complete it. However, scholars have recently questioned whether Mahler believed in any curse at all, suggesting that his widow may have invented the whole story.

In any case, Arnold Schoenberg—whose obsession with the number thirteen we will explore later in this chapter—wrote about this belief, essentially saying that writing a ninth symphony was the limit. The universe or some higher power did not yet permit a composer to go beyond nine symphonies, perhaps because humanity had not yet evolved enough.

This seems like irrational nonsense. You may be thinking that it makes for a good story and an interesting coincidence, but—putting on your scholarly hat—look at Mozart, who wrote over forty symphonies, with many others attributed to him, and Haydn, whose symphonies number over a hundred. This is true, but they lived before Beethoven, and some would declare that the curse began with him. This is probably due to the belief that Beethoven was the greatest symphonic composer of all, so he may be expected to have set the limits.

Okay, you say, we're still not buying any of it. Think of modern composers like Dmitri Shostakovich (fifteen symphonies), Heitor Villa-Lobos and Darius Milhaud (twelve symphonies each), and Alan Hovhaness (at least sixty-seven, forty-three of which were written after the age of sixty!). There, that proves it.

Yes, it does prove something. But there were other composers who did indeed die after completing their ninth, such as Alfred Schnittke. Composer William C. White said of Schnittke's ninth, "I think this is music of someone who is already dead. . . . [it] sounds like the exploratory wanderings of a ghost during his first encounter with a new, otherworldly universe."

Schnittke's fellow Russian Alexander Glazunov technically never completed his ninth and lived for another twenty-six years (dying in 1936), presumably escaping his fate.

On the other hand, Ralph Vaughan Williams composed his ninth symphony at the age of eighty-five and died about six months later. This is not too surprising, given his advanced age. However, he died in the early hours of the morning of August 26, the very day that he was supposed to attend a recording session for his ninth symphony. It may just be a coincidence, but then again . . .

The yellow clarinet

Theatrical lore abounds with unlucky colors, but these are less common in music. There is one curious exception: a yellow clarinet must not be allowed in the orchestra pit if the music is for a play. If such an instrument is present, things will invariably go wrong for the orchestra and the actors. The origin of this belief is obscure, but yellow is often considered an unlucky color in the theater.

Certain shades of yellow were once thought to attract evil spirits. Further, in medieval times yellow and green were often associated with the devil in morality plays, an early form of drama intended to instruct the illiterate masses by scaring the hell out of them. These open-air plays were frequently accompanied by music, a practice that was an early precursor to bands and orchestras accompanying plays in more recent times.

The clarinet itself is a much later invention (eighteenth century), but somewhere along the line the idea of using a yellow one was accepted as a bad omen. Why the clarinet? Why not a violin, or a xylophone, or a nose flute? Well, the color was apparently a popular one for the instrument in the nineteenth and early twentieth centuries, and this probably collided with existing theatrical superstitions about yellow, so it was banned from theater orchestras. No one knows just what might happen if such a clarinet is used during a play, but it's probably best not to tempt fate.

Unlucky Friday—or at least a noisy one

Everyone knows about the fear of Friday the 13th, the origin of which is often attributed to the story of Jesus being crucified on a Friday (confusingly called "Good Friday") and having been betrayed by Judas, the thirteenth member of the group. At least that's one theory. Fridays in general have gotten a bad rap ever since, despite being the most longed-for day of the typical work week. One old English folk song even warned, "Never be born on a Friday, choose some other day if you can." Unfortunately, the tune offered no advice on how to go about this.

There is an odd nineteenth-century superstition that says if a man goes courting his lady on a Friday and gets found out by the townspeople, he will suffer a strange fate indeed: he will be followed home by a group of musicians making all kinds of noises on pan lids with tongs, pokers, and other implements—kind of a Victorian version of Stomp.

This warning to young would-be Romeos goes beyond the ringing ears and headache that may result from the cacophony made by rowdy pan-bangers. It's trying to call attention to the lusty young lad and reveal that he is up to no good, a kind of public shaming. Indeed, the historical basis for this odd practice is easy to locate. There was a medieval French tradition called *charivari* that spread to other countries and lasted well beyond the Middle Ages. It involved people going out into the streets wearing grotesque masks and making loud, obnoxious music on rustic instruments, often in connection to newlyweds or an upcoming wedding. The noise was made to express disapproval of certain types of marriages—like those who were remarrying or had "inappropriate" spouses—as well as of adultery, unwed mothers, wife beaters, and a host of other offenses. It was a way of expressing community disapproval and even belittling or humiliating anyone who deviated from society's norms.

A crowd of these revelers makes an appearance in the *Roman de Fauvel*, as we saw earlier, but rather than shaming Fauvel on his wedding day, their purpose is to cheer him on and encourage him to do the deed. Since Fauvel and his followers were an inversion of all things good and right, it makes sense that these noisemakers were doing the opposite of what they were supposed to do. The manuscript represents them in grotesque costumes and masks, flashing their butts and singing their dirty little ditties. Imagine what the Victorians would have thought!

Morning singing brings tears

"If you sing before seven, you will cry before eleven." So goes the old saying, an odd warning indeed. Why, if you were happy or inspired enough to sing at such an early hour, would you regret it before noon?

Does that mean that monks who sang those early services were perpetually unhappy? Maybe.

There are a few possible origins for this idea. The most likely harkens back to the old Protestant work ethic—ah, so forget about the monks—that basically states that you have to earn your happiness each day. Singing before you've earned the right to do so is most assuredly a way to bring bad luck on yourself.

I have my own theory about this: imagine some eighteenth-century opera tenor in Venice, full of himself and riding on a wave of popularity, bounding out of bed early one morning to launch, full-voiced, into his showcase aria. The upstairs neighbor isn't quite so fond of his joyous expressions of virtuosity and sends down one of his servants to give said male diva a smacking with a cane or just a good old fist. Chastened and black-eyed, the tenor learns the hard way that not everyone appreciates genius.

Actually, the idea that any musician would be up at 7:00 a.m. is universally laughable. A musician who is up then probably never went to bed the night before, or hasn't yet realized that the alcoholic haze from the previous evening's festivities hasn't yet worn off, and the hangover from hell will descend on his unsuspecting head by 11:00, bringing tears—hence the proverb.

Circus band superstitions

There weren't too many touring orchestras in the United States in the nineteenth century. The expense, hassle, and time it would take (via slow trains) rendered the whole thing mostly impractical. If you lived in some little town in the middle of nowhere, your best chance of hearing live music played well would come from a traveling circus. These productions brought wind bands with them for all of their musical needs. If people heard European classical music at all, it wasn't so much from string orchestras but from these smaller groups who introduced the works of contemporary nineteenth-century composers to American audiences.

Consisting mainly of brass and percussion (and perhaps a woodwind or two), these groups were very versatile. They could provide music for the big top circus, a local theatrical production, a town function, a wedding—you name it. They were jacks-of-all-trades, and if not the most skilled, they were certainly spirited. John Philip Sousa had a famous touring circus band, as did circuses like the Ringling Brothers and Barnum & Bailey.

As traveling bands, they endured a lot of hardships and saw many things. It was only natural that over time, some superstitions would arise about how to make things go more smoothly. George Brinton Beal, an American lecturer, writer, and critic, wrote about two songs that acquired superstitious associations in his 1938 book *Through the Back Door of the Circus with George Brinton Beal.*

It was believed that playing a piece called "Suppe's Light Cavalry March" on the circus lot invited disaster, even death. It is rumored that soon after the song was played in Oklahoma, there was a train wreck that killed sixteen people. Another time its performance resulted in a fierce wind that killed thirty-eight people unlucky enough to be in its path. A third tragedy ensued when, immediately after playing the piece, one musician dropped dead on the spot—so, no more march. It was apparently not even wise to carry around the sheet music for this tune. Beal never specified exactly when these incidents were supposed to have occurred, but he stressed that they were taken very seriously: "You may not believe this but most circus folks do, at least those who know the facts."

A second song, entitled "Home Sweet Home," could never be played except during the last concert of the season. If it were played sooner, it would mean the closing of the show and probably the end of the tour.

These beliefs must have had some basis in a story or urban legend that got repeated and passed around enough for them to take hold. Maybe something bad really did happen once, and that was enough to inspire these warnings. In any case, circus bands were integral to the spread of music in those frontier days, and not even irrational fears could stop them.

Sexist superstition at the first American musical

It's always been difficult to be a woman in the Old Boys' Club of the music world (or anywhere, for that matter), and having some stupid superstitions attached to your gender doesn't help matters. This one is particularly odious:

In the year 1866, the first American musical was about to premiere in New York at a venue called Niblo's Garden. The show was called *The Black Crook*. It was over five hours long—good lord, what were they thinking?! It wasn't even a real effort to create a new American musical art form, but rather just a strange mixture of elements including music, dance, and a Faustian story about an evil German noble, Count Wolfenstein (great name!), who wants to marry a village woman against her wishes. His attempts to have her fiancé sacrificed to the devil fail, and true love wins the day. The whole thing was pieced together like Frankenstein's monster in an attempt to draw a crowd and make some money. It was a bit of a mess, but they had to start somewhere; it included the all-important element of prototype showgirls, which are still a mainstay in musicals today, for better or worse. Mark Twain wrote favorably about the production and its spectacular dazzle.

On opening night, the manager, William Wheatley, stood by the doors as the crowds waited to enter the theater. Apparently, people were intrigued enough to come and see the show. Noticing that the first customer in line was a woman, he emphatically refused to let her be the first one into the building, insisting that it would ruin any chance of success the show might have. She was probably shocked and more than a little offended, but Wheatley stood firm and a man entered first. Was this just a dumb superstition residing in the mind of a Victorian-era misogynist? Most likely.

For the record, the show ran for 474 performances and was a massive hit. Imitators sprang up almost immediately, and the American musical was born. Wheatley was triumphant and smug, and even claimed later that while he was not superstitious, the show's success was due in part to his refusal to let a woman be the first patron into the theater. What would have happened to the show had he not been such an insistent jerk? Would the American musical have taken off anyway? I'd say it's very likely.

Schoenberg and the number thirteen

Arnold Schoenberg, the inventor of the twelve-tone system and champion of all things numerical in music, was also obsessed with numbers and numerology in the non-musical parts of his life. He had a morbid fear of the number thirteen, known in psychological lingo as triskaidekaphobia. For instance, he called his opera *Moses und Aron*—changing the spelling from the more traditional "Aaron" because it made his title twelve letters rather than thirteen. Why he had such an extreme fear is not known, but having been born on September 13, he saw this number as a bad omen, hanging like a dark cloud over his whole life. For him, it symbolized the forces of death and destruction. He worked hard to ensure that it could not dominate him by avoiding the number as much as possible.

He believed that if he stopped work on a composition for any amount of time, whether due to writer's block or any other reason, he would return to find that the measure where he had left off was most often a multiple of thirteen. To him, this pattern proved that the number was working against him. In order to avoid giving in, he would sometimes number his measures as 12, then 12A, then 14. He would defend his obsession by saying that it was not superstition, but rather belief. It was central to his outlook, and so he saw nothing silly about it.

He conducted his whole life according to various rituals and numerological practices that he thought would bring him good luck and help him to avoid bad luck. When naming his children from his second marriage, for example, he chose the names Ronald and Roland, both anagrams of his own name. When he discovered that "Roland" contained some unlucky numerological potentialities, he changed it to Lawrence Adam so as not to inadvertently curse him with an unlucky name. Whenever possible he also avoided addresses with the number thirteen, as well as the thirteenth floor of buildings.

He was so fearful of the power of thirteen that he felt certain he would die in a year when his age was a multiple of the number. He was terrified of his sixty-fifth birthday, for example. He asked astrologer and fellow composer Dane Rudhyar to cast his horoscope for that fateful year. Rudhyar informed him that while it was a time of danger, it wouldn't necessarily kill him. He was right; Schoenberg escaped and with great relief lived to celebrate his sixty-sixth birthday. He wouldn't have to worry about it again until he was seventy-eight, if he survived that long.

However, something unexpected came up: his seventy-sixth birthday. In that year—1951—an astrologer named Oscar Adler (who was also a musician) wrote to Schoenberg, warning him about the dangers the year would bring due to the numbers of his age: seven plus six equals thirteen. Schoenberg was horrified. Apparently, even with his devotion to numerology, it had never occurred to him to add together the digits of his age. He told friends that if he could only make it through the year, he would be safe again, at least for a while.

As (bad) luck would have it, in July of that year there was a Friday the 13th, the last thing that he wanted to face. Schoenberg had stayed in bed all day, sick with worry and anxiety. At about a quarter to midnight, his wife tried to comfort him, telling him that since the day was over and he'd made it through, he didn't have to worry after all. Apparently, he looked at her and died on the spot. The superstitious would love to say that it happened at thirteen minutes to midnight. It seems that he literally scared himself to death.

Speaking of superstitious composers . . .

Rossini, the great nineteenth-century opera composer, was also deeply superstitious and believed strongly in evil spirits and omens. Once, he received a fine gold watch from King Louis Philippe of France. When Rossini proudly showed it off to his friends, one of them noticed an engraving in Arabic on its face; none of them could decipher it, so no one could tell him what it said. Rossini took this as a bad omen and put the watch in a desk, never showing it to anyone again. He was also wary of the evil eye and its potential for harm. He always feared Friday the 13th, and sure enough, he died on November 13, 1868, a Friday.

Once accused of dabbling in magic as a boy, Mozart was said to be superstitious and afraid of the dark, evil spirits, and ghosts. As we have seen, he may have believed that the commission for his Requiem came from the Angel of Death himself, so he was very reluctant to finish it, believing he would die when it was completed. It is rumored that an audience in Naples claimed he was wearing a magic ring and only played so well due to its supernatural power. He proved them wrong by removing the ring and playing the harpsichord with equal skill.

When conducting an orchestra as a young man, Tchaikovsky was said to hold on to his chin because of a pathological fear of his head falling off while at the podium. If true, this habit was more likely due to nerves and stage fright than anything else—but the man was a hypochondriac and suffered from many ills, both real and imagined, so why not spontaneous decapitation among them? Actually, this story may have come from a critic mocking the way the composer conducted. Tchaikovsky did take long walks for creative inspiration, fearing that if he cut them short, even by a little, disaster might ensue. In his last days, Tchaikovsky refused a treatment involving immersion in a hot bath, probably since his mother had died of cholera while undergoing a similar procedure. This seems to strengthen the argument that he died of cholera, since he may have feared he would meet the same fate as his mother.

The great conductor Leonard Bernstein always wore the same pair of cufflinks for every concert. They were a gift from fellow conductor and composer Serge Koussevitzky, and Bernstein would not perform without them. He and friends would kiss them for good luck before he went out on stage to conduct.

The Spanish composer Manuel De Falla was a hypochondriac who tried to avoid seeing guests when there was a full moon or during the months of the equinoxes (i.e., March and September) because he believed that these times were bad for his health. He also feared drafts, and could spend five hours a day or more cleaning himself and preparing for the day, not eating breakfast until the afternoon.

The English composer Gustav Holst had an interest in astrology and learned to cast horoscopes, which he did as a hobby for his friends, though it never became any kind of obsession for him. Instead, he was quiet about it, even a bit embarrassed. However, he did base his most famous work, *The Planets*, on the astrological qualities of seven planets—Mercury, Venus, Mars, Jupiter, Saturn, Uranus, and Neptune—rather than astronomical. This often surprises people who assume that this work, a precursor and inspiration for so many science fiction movie soundtracks, must have been a musical interpretation of the actual planets of our solar system: their colors, sizes, orbits, and other physical features.

So what should we make of all this? It could be said that if even the brightest, most talented, and most gifted can succumb to these eccentricities and flights of irrational fancy, what hope is there for the rest of us? On the other hand, it's the very nature of the creative mind to seek out new connections and relations that others don't see or imagine. In view of scientific ideas such as chaos theory and the butterfly effect, who can say just what the exact relationship between two given things really is? The mind that fears the Angel of Death at the door or a conspiracy of numbers is also the mind capable of producing artistic masterpieces.

8

Some Final Musical Oddities

And so we end with a few final stories that don't quite fit into the other chapters: a potpourri of the peculiar, an inventory of invective, a miscellany of the musically odd, a grab bag of the grotesque. Learn how harsh weather may have helped make beautiful string music—or not; where the world's most famous ringtone came from, which composers hated their own work, how Mozart's skull may have been retrieved from his grave—or not; and why some pieces of Beethoven's skull ended up in California—or not.

The mystery of the world's greatest violins

Renowned Italian violinmaker Antonio Stradivari (1644–1737, a very long-lived fellow!) is famed for creating some of the greatest violins, violas, and cellos ever built. Stradivarius is world famous, an early brand name known even to casual classical music audiences and non-fans. The almost-mythic quality of these instruments has made them sought after by the greatest musicians in the world for more than three centuries. The level of craftsmanship and the limited availability have also made them insanely expensive, sorry to say to anyone who would like to own one as a conversation piece.

Scholars, instrument makers, and fans alike have long puzzled over what it is that makes Stradivari's creations so exceptional. While theories abound, some of the more interesting ideas have emerged in recent years. One seems like an elegant explanation on the surface: in the early 2000s, a tree-ring scientist and a climatologist proposed that the wood used in Stradivari's instruments may have been affected by the unusually harsh climate of the time. The second half of the seventeenth century in Northern Europe was the time of the Maunder Minimum, a particularly cold point in the Little Ice Age that began in the later Middle Ages and may have helped to make that miserable era known as the fourteenth century quite a bit more miserable. Said Ice Age reached its peak in the seventeenth century, and as a result, trees grew more slowly and regularly all year round in response to the harsh climate. This slow, consistent growth can affect the quality of wood for the better, making it more resonant and better able to handle the stresses of being a part of a complex musical instrument.

So, did such climate change inadvertently affect Stradivari's violins and other creations, unintentionally making them masterpieces? Possibly, but quality of wood is only one factor in the construction of any instrument. Intriguing though it was, this study was doubted by many. A counter-theory suggests that it was the unique combination of chemicals in the mix used to treat the wood (which one recent study revealed included borax, iron salts, fluoride, and chromium, among others), probably to help preserve it before it was shaped and carved into various instruments.

Interestingly and amusingly, researchers conducted a double-blind experiment at the Eighth International Violin Competition of Indianapolis in 2010. Three historical and classic violins, including a Stradivarius, were placed with three modern, though excellently made, counterparts. The testing panel asked a selection of twenty-one violinists to compare them for sound quality and playability. The musicians would have no idea which instrument they were playing at any given time. Care was taken to conceal the instruments' identities by having the musicians play in dim light, and perfume was used to mask any individual wood aromas, among other controls. The result? Almost every time the Stradivarius failed to be the preferred instrument, either for sound quality or playability, losing in 80 percent of the evaluations when it went head-to-head with another violin. When the musicians were asked about their overall preference, the Strad also lost out, and a modern violin was the clear favorite.

Now, this is by no means the last word on the subject, but it does present fascinating evidence that reputation, tradition, and hype can all play a role in establishing something as being great or otherwise. Strads are clearly wonderful instruments, but are they really in a class by themselves? Or is this legendary honor just the result of centuries of praise and even clever marketing on the part of Tony and his apprentices? Perhaps only the struggling trees in those Italian winter forests know for sure.

The ringtone heard round the world

It's one of the most famous little tunes in the world. Everyone in the cell phone age knows it, and most people probably have had it on their phone at one time or another. We are talking, of course, about the Nokia ringtone. At the height of its use, it was estimated to be heard around the world about twenty thousand times per second; just imagine if royalties could be collected on it! What is the origin of this little piece, and how did it end up being the most-heard tune of all time?

The simple melody is actually from a longer piece by the Spanish composer Francisco Tárrega (1852–1909), a guitarist of great skill who helped popularize the instrument for solo recitals. Tárrega's childhood was actually quite troubled, or rather, he seemed to be quite the maker of trouble. Born in Villarreal on Spain's central east coast, he showed an early talent for guitar but ran away from home more than once. When studying in Barcelona, he decided to try making a living as a guitarist in the city's cafés and restaurants; he was all of ten years old. Hey, dream big. A few years later, he ran off to Valencia with a group of Roma ("gypsies"). His father found him, but once again he ran off; this habit was getting ridiculous. At some point his youthful wanderlust subsided, and he attended the Madrid conservatory beginning in 1874. His bad decisions about hasty departures seem to have ended, and he became a successful guitarist and performer over the next forty years.

The tune in question comes from a section in Tárrega's piece *Gran Vals*, written toward the end of his life in 1902; there was some speculation that this little melody was originally composed by Chopin, but the argument is not very convincing. This small snippet of music in an otherwise mostly unknown piece would seem an odd candidate to be the tune heard round the world. So what happened? Well, it had to do with lawyers and the need for a composer to be dead. Musician Thomas Dolby explained to the BBC:

> One night, a marketing guy stuck his head around the door of the engineering department and thought he heard somebody playing tunes with a phone. And in fact, the engineer said, "no, no, I'm just trying to tune it to get the most annoying frequency."
>
> And the marketing guy said, "well, could you make it play some tunes?" so he knocked up half a dozen and they said, "these sound great, let's ship it." But it turned out that the lawyers then stepped in and said, "well, you can't ship just a pop tune; there's royalties to pay, there's clearances to get—unless the composer has been dead for seventy-five years or more."
>
> And they said, "are any of these by dead composers?" Well, that one that has now become famous as the Nokia theme was actually composed over 150 [*sic*] years ago by an obscure waltz composer, and so that was the one they went with and it became the most successful jingle in history.

The early 1990s was still the stone age of cell phones (the silicon age?). Two of Nokia's executives decided, on the basis that Tárrega was conveniently quite dead, that the piece had merit as a ringtone and selected four bars of music that had the right feel. These measures contained the now-famous melody, and the ringtone debuted in 1994. It has been tinkered with and modified over the years, but the tune remains and is famous in a way that its composer never could have imagined when he was a boy fantasizing about wowing crowds in Barcelona coffee shops.

Composers who hated their own works

It seems like a constant curse of the artist to feel somehow compelled to create, but then, after laboring over a new work for days, weeks, months, and more, to be unsatisfied or even hostile to the final product. Some composers have shown the particularly bad habit of never-ending tinkering with their work that makes things like dating said pieces or assigning opus numbers more than a bit difficult. Chopin notoriously liked to make small changes to his pieces, for example. It's damned inconsiderate to biographers and admirers.

Many composers suppress or discard their "juvenilia," that is, the works that they wrote when they were young and still new to the whole composition business. George Butterworth destroyed many of his works before going off to World War I, not wanting them to be discovered in case he didn't return. Holst referred to his youthful compositions as his "early horrors." Vaughan Williams lamented that he was still making money off music written as a young man, calling these payments the "ill-gotten gains of such sins of my youth as 'Linden Lea' [a song from 1902] which becomes every year more horribly popular."

The idea of not being satisfied with one's work is often actually a good one; it shows that the person is willing to improve. However, this attitude can be self-defeating and destructive if taken too far. So if you sometimes feel that your best isn't good enough, or that you are receiving recognition you don't deserve (the dreaded "imposter syndrome"), here is a small sampling of composers who have shared your views. They're pretty good company to be in.

Wagner's early opera *Rienzi* was written before he had fully developed his mature style. Set in medieval Italy, it tells the story of a populist outlaw who stands against wealthy oppressors. It also has the dubious distinction of being one of many inspirations for Hitler, who later in his life possessed the original manuscript. Despite the success and acclaim that it brought him, Wagner himself found the work "repugnant."

Tchaikovsky's *1812 Overture* is one of his most famous works, commemorating the victory of Russia against the armies of Napoleon. It was written as a commission, and Tchaikovsky declared that it was "very loud and noisy and completely without artistic merit, obviously written without warmth or love." He hated the piece and the fact that it became popular. As we saw earlier, he disliked many of his works but did feel that he finally had produced something of value in his *Pathétique* Symphony only shortly before he died.

Edward Elgar's *Pomp and Circumstance* March No. 1 contains the quintessential theme of higher education, played for graduation ceremonies and in film or television scenes set at a university. It was a major hit for Elgar, but its popularity meant that his other works were overlooked, and this would later annoy him. He had actually succeeded in rubbing academia the wrong way in 1905 when he delivered a series of talks, the Peyton lectures, at the University of Birmingham, where he had recently taken the position of Chair of Music. Unfortunately, these talks were a rambling mess of ideas and an artistic manifesto that opposed many other English musical movements of the time. The establishment reaction to his lectures was so hostile that he withdrew from academia and returned to concentrating on composition. He saw increasing criticism of his music as time went on.

Elgar's younger contemporary, Gustav Holst, experienced a similar problem with *The Planets*. The inspiration for endless science fiction movie soundtracks, this work is by far the most famous thing he ever composed. Even most classical music fans are hard-pressed to name another of his pieces. This proved to be a problem for him throughout the 1920s. It had been a huge success so everyone expected him to compose *The Planets Part II*, but he wanted to move on and write other things, a perfectly reasonable position to take. Critics and audiences were not very understanding of this wish, and his popularity faded as the decade progressed. This didn't really bother him, however, and he went on composing what he wanted. He was philosophical about it, once saying, "It's a great thing to be a failure. If nobody likes your work, you have to go on just for the sake of the work. And you're in no danger of letting the public make you repeat yourself."

In between whippings and other eccentric behavior, Percy Grainger was, as we saw, a brilliant concert pianist. One piece always bothered him, however—a setting of a Morris dance called "Country Gardens." Made as a birthday present for his strange and controlling mother, it sold absurd amounts as sheet music (something like twenty-seven thousand copies a year by the mid-1920s!) and became a concert favorite. Every audience that saw him perform demanded it as the obligatory encore, and if he tried to exit the stage without playing it, he would essentially be prevented from doing so; the crowds simply would not leave. He eventually loathed this fairly insipid tune, a jaunty little number that brought him enormous amounts of money over the years but came to define him in ways that he hated.

Ravel's *Boléro* is another world-famous piece, and that is part of its problem. Although it is hardly the best thing that he ever wrote, its popularity has overshadowed many of his other works. Its endless repetition came in for some harsh criticism when it was first performed in 1928, but for whatever reasons, there was enough demand for it that it came to be associated with him more than his other, better pieces. This surprised him; he didn't like it much and always wondered why orchestras wanted to play it and audiences wanted to hear it. Several decades after his death, the popularity of the movie *10* only made things worse.

In contrast, Beethoven was willing to defend his work even when he knew it was subpar. He composed *Wellington's Victory*—or *The Battle of Vitoria*—in collaboration with Johann Nepomuk Maelzel, the inventor of the metronome. Beethoven never liked this piece, and he understood the criticism it received in its own time. However, while agreeing that it was a poor work, he still defended his own ability against loud-mouthed and opinionated critics, declaring that what he sh** was better than anything they could have created; how many artists of all kinds have wanted to say that to critics over the centuries! Not surprisingly, he had a falling-out with Maelzel, who later apparently died from alcohol poisoning, but that's another whole story.

Mozart's skull

Mozart's Skull could just as easily have been the title of this book; its possible after-death adventures are certainly odd enough to merit a book title. Beethoven is just a little more famous, however, so his skull wins out. It's the same reason that the book is not called *Haydn's Head*, though that is, admittedly, pretty catchy.

In 1902 the Mozarteum Foundation in Salzburg acquired a skull that was missing its lower jaw, a skull that may have come from a very important person. It was said that a gravedigger, one Joseph Rothmayer, dug up Mozart's body from its shared grave in 1801 (another account says 1799). Contrary to popular belief, these graves usually only held a small number of bodies, which was a good thing for Rothmayer, as he had plans for Mozart's remains. Providing skulls to the right buyers could be very lucrative. There was a period when such things were venerated almost like relics, particularly those of very famous individuals. Having the skull of a famous artist, philosopher, or composer would be quite the conversation piece, ethics and respect be damned.

Rothmayer marked the skull with a wire and noted the body's position when he initially buried it so that he could identify it later. Why he waited several years to retrieve it is unknown and immediately makes the legend suspicious, but such graves were commonly opened up some years later and reused, so maybe he took advantage of this practice to hide the fact that he was essentially grave robbing. Some accounts say that Rothmayer held on to the skull for decades, which seems odd and casts further doubt on the whole story.

In any case, the story goes that the skull passed to various owners in the nineteenth century; in 1892 an article in the *Neue Freie Presse* newspaper proclaimed that Mozart's skull had been identified based on observations made some decades earlier by physician and poet Ludwig August Frankl, who received it from an anatomist named Joseph Hyrtl. It had previously belonged to Joseph's brother, Jacob. He had acquired it from a gravedigger, who presumably had familial or professional ties going back to Rothmayer. Jacob apparently was unsettled about possessing it and once even contemplated throwing it into the Danube.

Of course, this announcement caused quite a stir and produced more than a few skeptics. After the Mozarteum Foundation took possession of the skull, they placed it on display in the home of Mozart's birth before eventually transferring it to the Mozarteum Library in 1940, as the chaos of war threatened far more than just the arts. During that time, a few strange stories circulated: some staff reported being frightened by the object, claiming that music or even screams were heard coming from the cabinet that contained it. Was the ghost of the great man unhappy with his situation?

In 1987, Gottfried Tichy, a paleontologist at Salzburg University, examined the skull and declared it to be genuine, noting that it belonged to a small man between the ages of twenty and forty. Mozart was said to have toothaches, and there was evidence of rickets and tooth problems. It also showed signs of having taken a hard hit, such as a fall, and Mozart was known to have suffered from headaches in his last year or so. Such damage could be evidence of a fall or a similar injury that might have caused his pain. This was not the last word on the subject, however: in 2006 mitochondrial DNA tests were conducted, matching the skull against genetic information from Mozart's maternal grandmother, Euphrosina Pertl (what a magnificent name!) and from that of his niece, Jeanette.

The results showed that the skull was not related to the bones of these female relatives, which should have been the end of the story, but there was a slight problem: the results for the two female samples proved that they were not related *to each other*! And yet, their bone samples had been taken from the Mozart family vault. So, either the skull is Mozart's and the women are not genuine family members, or it's not his and one of the women *is* a Mozart, but the other is not, or maybe none of them are.

It's a deliciously inconclusive and frustrating result that only deepens the mystery. The skull is no longer on display, incidentally, but visitors can make arrangements in advance to see it at the Mozarteum Library, if they so wish. Bruckner certainly would have.

And while we're on the topic of mysterious skulls . . .

Beethoven's skull

Poor Beethoven could not get a break in life or death. A mere day after he died, what passed for forensic scientists in the early 1800s proceeded to cut open his skull. Was this some perverse attempt to find out what made the man tick? Actually, they were quite genuinely trying to discover the source of his deafness, and given that sawing open his skull hadn't been an option a few days earlier, now they had a chance to examine the ear bones. Beethoven, in fact, had requested that his doctor try to find the source of his hearing loss and make it available to the public, so they were simply following his wishes—but we still don't have a diagnosis.

There was a great interest at the time in the pseudoscience of phrenology, and some believed that the size of the brain could tell much about someone's nature, since different mental faculties were thought to reside in different regions. The skull, as the casing for the brain, could be measured to determine the size of various portions of a brain and thus reveal how "developed" one was in those given areas.

Sometime before the 1888 exhumation of Beethoven's body (when Bruckner so lovingly cradled the great man's head and had to be thrown out), some skull fragments—presumably from that initial cutting—were believed to have come into the possession of one Romeo Seligmann, professor of the history of medicine at the University of Vienna. There had been a previous exhumation in 1863 for medical purposes, so Seligmann might have acquired them around then. These small fragments were passed down through Seligmann's family, and by 1985 they resided with one of his descendants in northern California.

Two doctors from Vienna conducted tests that year and, believing that they had a DNA match with some of the composer's hair, declared with confidence that these small pieces were indeed from Beethoven's skull. It seemed to be a splendid confirmation of the claims that a small, if grotesque, piece of the world's greatest composer had come to the New World, passed on as a kind of odd family heirloom. The fragments were presented on loan to the Ira F. Brilliant Center for Beethoven Studies at San Jose State University.

This claim went unchallenged for many years; however, more recent testing has cast serious doubt on the findings. These newer tests confirmed that the main fragment showed no evidence of having been cut through, which would have had to be the case during that first postmortem operation when it was cut with a handsaw. Further, a few small bone fragments that some believed to have come from Beethoven's ear bones were tested and also found not to have been his. Instead, they were merely parts of the larger fragments that had failed the test. In the end, it seems that none of these bits and pieces once belonged to Beethoven. Between being hacked up, pillaged of its ear bones (which must have been lost after the autopsy), cradled by a determined admirer, and allegedly brought in pieces to the New World, Beethoven's skull endured about as much trauma as the man himself. If any fragments did come from that first autopsy, they're probably now lost to history.

Last Words

Congratulations! You have bravely wandered through some of the dark alleyways, creepy forest paths, and abandoned mansions of music history, and learned more than you probably ever wanted to know. It's fascinating to realize just how much great art can come from times of trouble and despair, and that's what we should take away from this journey. Regardless of, or perhaps due to, the misfortunes they encountered, the musicians and composers of our classical tradition have enriched the world immeasurably with their splendid works. We have more than a thousand years of amazing music to enjoy, and in the end, where it came from is not nearly as important as where it takes us.

I will leave you with this inspirational quote from George Bizet, composer of the famed and tragic opera *Carmen*: "As a musician I tell you that if you were to suppress adultery, fanaticism, crime, evil, the supernatural, there would no longer be the means for writing one note."

Okay . . . that was kind of depressing. How about this one instead, from George Bernard Shaw: "Music is the brandy of the damned."

Well, that's no good either.

Actually, a favorite quote of mine comes from Friedrich Nietzsche, and serves as a great way to wrap up: "Without music, life would be a mistake."

On that, I think we can all agree.

Suggestions for Further Reading

With luck, your interest is now piqued, you can't get enough, and you want to know more about music history, but where to start? It's a topic that can seem completely overwhelming, so here are some suggestions for delving a little deeper.

Online Resources

The granddaddy of music research tools is *Grove's Dictionary of Music and Musicians*. This multi-volume encyclopedia first appeared in the late nineteenth century and has been a mainstay of music studies ever since. College and university libraries will almost certainly have it, and many good public libraries might, too. Just about anything you can imagine related to classical music and more is in these volumes, and the work is a great way to expand your knowledge by dipping in wherever you like. For those so inclined, it is also online and available by subscription at: www.oxfordmusiconline.com.

It's all well and good to talk about classical music, but listening to it is vital, and here, you might feel completely lost. An excellent online resource is the *Naxos Music Library*, the largest digital collection of classical music recordings in the world. Naxos has licensing deals with hundreds of record labels to bring their catalogs online. It requires a somewhat pricey membership, but considering that you get access to well over

120,000 recordings (at the time of this writing) with all of their artwork and notes, it's a ridiculously good bargain. Type in the name of any composer and dozens, if not hundreds, of recordings will come up. Click away and listen at your leisure. It's literally more than you can listen to in a lifetime. Find it at: www.naxosmusiclibrary.com.

Many labels and artists also have YouTube pages, which can be a more economical way of beginning your listening journey. Try typing in composers or genres and see what comes up.

What about Wikipedia? This resource is much maligned, sometimes with justification, sometimes not. If you bear in mind that anyone can edit the content, and that sometimes the information is outdated or incorrect, it can be a useful starting point. Almost all of the composers in this book have their own pages, for example, and the entries seem pretty accurate. If the information is sourced properly and/or there is a useful bibliography, go ahead and have a look. You just might want to verify what you read in other sources.

Books

For those who prefer individual books, here are some goodies to keep you busy:

David Barber, *Bach, Beethoven and the Boys* (Sound and Vision, 1986, reprinted 1996 and 2011). A good introduction for younger readers, this is a humorous look at various aspects of classical music over the centuries.

Rick Beyer, *The Greatest Music Stories Never Told: 100 Tales from Music History to Astonish, Bewilder, and Stupefy* (New York: HarperCollins, 2011). This covers different kinds of music—including rock, jazz, country, hip-hop, and classical—for unusual stories and anecdotes.

Brian Levison and Frances Farrar, *Classical Music's Strangest Concerts and Characters* (London: Robson Books, 2007). This book focuses mostly on accounts from the last few centuries (and a few from earlier times) of composers' and musicians' daily lives and performances, and the strange things that happened therein.

Elizabeth Lunday and Mario Zucca, *Secret Lives of Great Composers* (Philadelphia: Quirk Books, 2009). This looks mainly at the biographies of composers from the eighteenth to the twentieth centuries, with plenty of bits about scandals and darker things.

Nicolas Slonimsky, *Lexicon of Musical Invective* (New York: W. W. Norton, reprinted 2000). Very funny and informative, this classic work covers bad reviews of both composers and concerts from the eighteenth to the twentieth centuries.

Nicolas Slonimsky, *Slonimsky's Book of Musical Anecdotes* (New York and London: Routledge, 2002). More fun from Slonimsky, this includes wonderful tales and anecdotes about the great composers that you won't get in school or concert programs.

More from Tim Rayborn

I would be remiss if I didn't shamelessly promote some of my other offerings, in this case two books, two recordings, and two websites:

A New English Music (Jefferson, NC: McFarland, 2016). This book looks at the revival of classical music in England from the later nineteenth century and into the twentieth. It includes detailed biographies of several key composers, including Percy Grainger, Peter Warlock, George Butterworth, Gustav Holst, and Ralph Vaughan Williams. Their lives were fascinating, and they left us some magnificent music.

Against the Friars (McFarland, 2014). A study of the medieval friars (the Franciscan and Dominican orders), and those who thought they were not such a great idea. Includes a lot more information on the *Roman de Fauvel*, the goliards, and other French musicians and poets who mercilessly mocked and attacked them.

Cançonièr – *The Black Dragon: Music from the Time of Vlad Dracula*. With a title like that, how can you resist? This early music group (co-directed by Tim) brings to life music from the infamous Impaler's time. We likely wouldn't have lasted long in his presence (he probably didn't even like music), but we hope you will think favorably of this recording. Available at Amazon, iTunes, and CD Baby, among others.

Honey from the Thorn: Music of Medieval England. Music from the twelfth to the fourteenth centuries. Not much medieval English music survives (there is much more French and Spanish repertoire from the same time), but these are some of the nicest pieces, in my humble opinion. Available at Amazon, iTunes, and CD Baby—basically all the usual outlets.

For musical things of all kinds, visit: www.timrayborn.com

For writing things of certain kinds, visit: www.inkhornwriting.com

Acknowledgments

Even though most writers dream of having a Walden-like place to retreat to where they can craft their masterpieces, books aren't written in total isolation. We always need others to read through our drafts, look for the inevitable mistakes, and tell us that we're wonderful—or not. Several people deserve my thanks as I put this work together and finished it, after tinkering with it on and off for a long time.

Thanks to Skyhorse for finding the subject matter intriguing enough that they wanted to get the book out there to the innocent and unsuspecting masses, and to Olga Greco for her meticulous and thoughtful edits, which have made this a better book than it was. Many thanks also to my agent, Maryann Karinch, who believed in the project as soon as she read about it, and has encouraged me with her enthusiasm. A number of people read chapter drafts as the book was nearing completion, and offered helpful feedback and comments, so lots of thanks to: Allan J. Cronin, Nawal Doucette, Trisna Fraser, Joshua Lapan, Kimberly Mackoy, Gilbert Martinez, Emily O'Brien, William Osser, Alina Rotaru, Keith Spears, Annie Valdes, and Matt Washburn.

Finally, thanks and love to Abby and to our adorable, and occasionally exasperating, feline toddlers.

About the Author

Tim Rayborn is an internationally acclaimed musician who plays dozens of unusual instruments that quite a few people have never heard of and frequently can't pronounce. These include medieval instrument reconstructions and folk instruments from Northern Europe, the Balkans, and the Middle East. He has appeared on over forty recordings to date, and his musical wanderings and tours have taken him across the United States, all over Europe, to Canada and Australia, and to such romantic locations as Marrakech, Istanbul, Renaissance chateaux, medieval churches, and high school gymnasiums.

Tim lived in England (a country he adores) for nearly seven years and has a PhD from the University of Leeds, which he likes to pretend means that he knows what he's talking about. He has written a number of books and magazine articles about music and history, and undoubtedly will write more. He currently resides in Northern California amid many books, instruments, and cats, and is at least somewhat obsessed with cooking excellent food.